FROMMER'S

COMPREHENSIVE TRAVEL GUIDE
SYDNEY '91-'92

by John Godwin

Y0-CZO-527

PRENTICE
HALL
PRESS

NEW YORK • LONDON • TORONTO • SYDNEY • TOKYO • SINGAPORE

FROMMER BOOKS

Published by Prentice Hall Press
A division of Simon & Schuster Inc.
15 Columbus Circle
New York, NY 10023

ISBN 0-13-326935-3
ISSN 0899-2770

Manufactured in the United States of America

CONTENTS

MAPS

Dollars Down Under

The Australian currency is also called the dollar, in this case the **Australian dollar** (A$), and is equivalent to about 75¢ U.S., give or take a few fluctuating points each day. This means that U.S. $1 will get you roughly A$1.25. Keep this favorable exchange rate in mind when comparing prices. The following table is meant only as a guide to help when you are calculating costs.

Note: All prices cited in this guide are in Australian dollars, unless otherwise indicated.

A$	U.S.$	A$	U.S.$
.05	.03	20.00	15.00
.10	.07	25.00	18.75
.25	.15	50.00	37.50
.50	.35	75.00	56.25
1.00	.75	100.00	75.00
2.00	1.50	150.00	112.50
3.00	2.25	200.00	150.00
4.00	3.00	250.00	187.50
5.00	3.75	300.00	225.00
10.00	7.50	400.00	300.00
15.00	11.25	500.00	375.00

Inflation Alert

It is hardly a secret that inflation continues to batter the countries of the world. The author of this book has spent laborious hours attempting to ensure the accuracy of prices appearing in this guide. As we go to press, we believe we have obtained the most reliable data possible. Nonetheless, in the lifetime of this edition—particularly its second year (1992)—the wise traveler will add 15% to 20% to the prices quoted throughout these pages.

PAST IMPERFECT

Travelers have the habit of comparing each place with another place, yet nothing annoys Sydneysiders more than being told that their city resembles San Francisco. Which, superficially, it does . . . except for being five times as big, twice as hot, and half as hilly. But the locals consider San Francisco a charming provincial backwater and their own town the metropolis and queen of the Pacific region, and find the comparison very faint praise indeed.

Apart from being the largest, oldest, and liveliest city of the Australian continent, Sydney is the only Australian city boasting an internationally recognized landmark: the pearly scallop shells of the Opera House, now nearly as familiar a symbol as the Statue of Liberty, the Eiffel Tower, or the Coliseum. Today the major effort of Sydney's people is aimed at showing the world that there is considerably more here than this celebrated piece of architectural confectionary.

Sydney is astonishingly beautiful, made so by a harbor setting for which the only term is "breathtaking." The immense harbor expanse divides the city in half, creating a foreshore of 150 miles, splintering the coastline into hundreds of inlets, coves, and bays and putting a large portion of the city within sight and walking distance of the ocean. Since Sydney is hilly, the harbor gesticulates at you from the most unexpected angles, offering an endless kaleidoscope of views. With hundreds of colored sails dotting the water, with green foliage marking the shoreline, with ruffles of breakers fringing golden beaches, with white ocean liners docked at the very tip of the high-rise business district, the overall effect is magical.

That wondrous ocean setting has resisted all assaults on the city's beauty by greedy developers and mediocre urban planners. They linked the north and south shores with one of the ugliest bridges extant, a clumsy slab of steel and mortar nicknamed "the Coathanger," turning most of the downtown area into a chaotic, log-jammed mess. They spread an endless rash of drab red-roofed suburbs inland, with patches in between that look like mass graveyards for secondhand cars. But no matter what they perpetrated, Sydney remained a gem among cities, embraced by the Pacific like a lover, protected against all the ravages that myopia and a fast-buck mentality could inflict.

Having recently celebrated its 200th birthday, Sydney is a matron by New World, but a debutante by Old World, standards. It is the capital of the state of New South Wales, but not of Australia (that honor belongs to Canberra). With some 3.5 million inhabitants sprawling over 670 square miles, Sydney today is one of the largest urban areas on the globe—something you had better keep in mind when you start sightseeing. And if Sydney is a surprise package for tourists, it would positively stupefy the founding fathers, who held about as much hope for it as you would for a basket case.

THE COMING OF THE CONVICTS

The ocean inlet called Botany Bay was first explored by Capt. James Cook, perhaps the greatest navigator of all times, in 1770. He proclaimed the land a British possession, noted some curious animals "like deer with the heads of mice, which hop" and then sailed on. Nothing much else might have happened for quite a while if it hadn't been for the American Revolution.

Until then, America had been used as a convenient dumping ground that kept Britain's jam-packed prisons from bursting at the seams. After the breakaway of the American colonies, it was no longer possible to unload convicts on them. King George's government considered alternatives and came up with a perfect one: the immense empty island-continent "down under," lying 14,000 miles away—outer space by 18th-century measurements.

And so it came that on January 26, 1788, a fleet of 11 badly battered transports dropped anchor at what is now Sydney Cove. They carried a small military escort and 736 male and female convicts. There were no major criminals among them—those were still publicly hanged—but poachers, pickpockets, prostitutes, Irish rebels, and cardsharps. They were rowed ashore and given their first task: to build their own prison.

Their real prison, however, was the gigantic wilderness that surrounded them and their total ignorance about it. Nothing was known about the continent, not even its shape. Nobody was even sure the place was an island. It was a place where the seasons were turned upside down, where the seeds brought from England wouldn't grow, where animals carried their young in pouches, and where the black, unclothes natives spoke languages unrelated to any other on earth. Several convicts attempted to escape by *walking* to China which, they believed, lay over the next mountain range.

These were the first of more than 100,000 convicts transported over from Britain and clustered in a series of hell-holes along the Australian coast, where only the toughest survived the early years. Rum was the universal solace for a time the only currency, flogging post and gallows the prime labor incentives. When Captain Bligh (of *Mutiny on the Bounty* fame) became governor of New South Wales and tried to suppress the illicit rum trade, his own officers rebelled against him and ignominiously shipped him home.

The convict heritage, which today has a certain prestige, left a lasting imprint on Sydney. It contributed to the fierce egalitarianism of Australians, their distrust of authority, the ribald iconoclasm of their humor, and their political obstreperousness. The antipodean colonies weren't exactly pleasant places to rule, as the English satirist Hilaire Belloc indicated when he wrote:

We had intended you to be
The next Prime Minister but three,
The stocks were sold; the Press was squared,
The Middle Class was quite prepared,
But as it is! . . . My language fails!
Go out and govern New South Wales!

COLONIES TO COMMONWEALTH

Gradually conditions Down Under improved. Convict transportations ceased in the 1840s and the chained "Gentlemen of the Broad Arrows" were replaced by successive waves of free immigrants. Most of them came in search of gold, but stayed on to prosper from other sources. Not all, by any means. One of the worst gangs of goldfield thugs, the notorious "Sydney Ducks," moved on to California to continue their trade and were duly hanged en masse by San Francisco vigilantes.

By the turn of the century the erstwhile penal settlements had become thriving colonies, growing increasingly rich on wool, wheat, meat, and coal exports—and with it, increasingly independent. The time had clearly come for political emancipation.

In 1901 the six colonies of the continent transformed themselves into the six states of the self-governing Commonwealth of Australia. By then Sydney had grown into a large and rather rowdy city of nearly half a million. And because it was perpetually battling Melbourne for national supremacy, a brand-new capital, Canberra, was built halfway between them.

Sydney's ethnic and cultural image then was completely different from what it is today. It was untouched by even a breath of cosmopolitanism. Its population was almost solidly Anglo-Irish, except for a few thousand Chinese who had come over during the goldrushes and now ran restaurants, market gardens, and small shops. The enormous influx of European and Asian immigrants, which shaped the city's present face, did not begin until after World War II.

A DIVIDED SOUL

Sydney suffers (or benefits) by having a curiously split personality that goes much deeper than what casual visitors can see. A local journalist summed it up when he said, "We drive on the left with American road signs." On the one hand there is a certain sentimental attachment to the Crown and the British stepmother across the sea. This is visibly symbolized by the umpteen "royal" parks, buildings, and monuments around the city, and invisibly by the tens of thousands of local sons who sailed from Circular Quay to fight and die at Britain's call in three wars.

On the other hand, Sydney has an aggressively republican, antiestablishment facet to its character. You only have to drop in on some of the "off-Broadway" stage performances to get a sulfurous whiff of these sentiments. Coupled with a lifestyle that is much closer to that of California than to any other model, these conflicting tugs on its heart strings have made Sydney a quite contrary—and therefore very interesting—place. Where else in the world would you find families eating traditional English Christmas dinners on a beach in 90° Fahrenheit heat? And if you look at the Australian flag flying from the buildings, you will note that it still bears Britain's Union Jack in the upper-left corner above the six stars of the Southern Cross.

There is also another kind of conflict dividing the soul of Australia in general and Sydney in particular—an ongoing struggle between hedonism and wowserism. "Wowser" is Aussie for a puritan bluenose, and has been defined as a person living in dread that someone, somewhere, might be having a good time. Wowserism has always been a strong element in Australian history, and at certain periods its disciples more or less ruled the country. From circa 1918 to about 1960 they kept the Commonwealth locked in a kind of moral and culinary kindergarten by means of legislation that made 19th-century Boston seem wildly liberal.

They saddled the nation with liquor laws that made civilized dining a near-impossibility, civilized drinking a total one. They imposed a censorship that banned virtually all adult books, plays, and films, and tore gaping holes into those they allowed in. They prohibited Sunday movie and stage performances, curtailed Sunday train excursions, and in some states went so far as to lock up children's playground swings on the Sabbath. They would have locked up the beaches if that had been technically possible, but they did manage to bar bikinis long after these had become accepted swimwear everywhere else.

When the reaction to Mother Grundy's reign set in, it was understandably drastic. Today all Sydney beaches are topless, the language in vogue on local stages turns the air blue, the town boasts a nightlife district that matches that of Marseilles, and the ads appearing in the periodicals would curl an American's hair. Not so long ago the word "homosexual" wasn't permitted in print. But to quote author Robert Hughes, "When urban Australia came out of the closet, as it did in the seventies, it almost ripped the doors off their hinges."

At this point in time the wowsers are in full retreat. Only in the liquor department do you get reminders of their existence, as you'll see in the restaurant chapter. How long this retreat will last is anybody's guess. For puritanism is as much inherent in the Australian character as in the American—simply the reverse side of the same coin.

II

FAST FACTS ABOUT SYDNEY

This chapter is designed to forestall the annoyance connected with not knowing how, where, when, and for how much certain essential items can be obtained. It can't cover every eventuality, but lists all those I could think of and that readers of my previous books have indicated as important.

AIRLINE OFFICES: The headquarters of **Qantas,** Australia's international airline, is at the corner of George and Jamison streets (tel. 02/436-6111).

There are two major internal airlines: the government-owned **Australian Airlines,** 70 Hunter St. (tel. 02/693-3333); and the privately operated **Ansett,** at the corner of Oxford and Riley streets (tel. 02/268-1555). In addition, **Air New South Wales,** (tel. 02/268-1111), has flights to many of the smaller towns within the state.

AIRPORT: Sydney's **Kingsford Smith International Airport,** the main gateway to Australia, is located in Mascot, about five miles from the city center. *Newsweek* magazine once described it as being run "with Aussie-friendly efficiency," but alas, t'aint no more. With more daily flights than Paris's Charles de Gaulle Airport and an annual 24% increase in tourist arrivals, the friendliness lingers but most of the efficiency has faded. In other words, Kingsford Smith suffers from the same ailments as most other international airports these days. There are long overlapping lines at reservations counters and Customs checks, wild scrambles for long-delayed baggage, invisible luggage carts, and absentee porters. As a dessert, so to speak, the government charges you a $10 departure tax when you leave. On the plus side, it must be stated that the airport has all the necessary facilities, from currency exchange and showers to around-the-clock cafeterias and car-rental counters. A major effort is under way to upgrade Kingsford Smith back to the pleasant facility it once was.

The excellent **airport bus** service delivers you to your hotel and costs $3.50. **Cab** fare is around $14.

AMERICAN EXPRESS: The local office is at A. E. Tower, 388 George St. (tel. 02/239-0666).

AUTOMOBILE ASSOCIATION: Members of U.S. motoring

associations enjoy reciprocal rights to all services of the **National Roads and Motorists Association (NRMA),** with head office at 151 Clarence St. (tel. 02/260-9222).

BABY-SITTING AND CHILD CARE: Your hotel can probably come up with a baby-sitter for you. Or you might try . . .
   The **Hyde Park Family Centre,** at the corner of Park and Elizabeth streets, provides facilities for mothers of infants and small children to change and breast-feed them, heat bottles, etc.

BANKING HOURS: Most banks are open from 9am to 4pm Monday through Thursday and 9am to 5pm on Friday.

BUS TERMINALS: Long-distance **interstate buses** leave from the Pioneer Terminal, at the corner of Riley and Oxford streets (tel. 02/268-1331).
   Suburban buses leave from Circular Quay for the eastern suburbs and beaches, from Carrington and York streets at Wynyard Park for the northern suburbs and beaches.

CABS: Much used and even more in demand. Sydneysiders take taxis like New Yorkers, usually hailing a cruising cab. Rates are $1.10 at flagfall and 65¢ per kilometer thereafter. The major taxi companies are **Taxis Combined** (tel. 02/332-8888), **Legion** (tel. 02/20-918) and **RSL** (tel. 02/699-0144).

CAR RENTALS: See Chapter III, "Getting to Know Sydney."

CLIMATE: Sydney's seasons are the reverse of those in North America and Europe, though not as contrasting. September to November is spring, December to February is summer, March to May is fall, and June to August, winter. The variations involved resemble southern California. While winter can get fairly frosty, it doesn't entail snow. Summer is hot, humid, and subtropical, alleviated by cooling squalls of wind known as "southerly busters." During spring and fall you are liable to get a mixture of the above, plus heavy rain. In general it's an outdoor climate, and the locals make full use of it.

CLOTHING: What to take depends largely on when you come, but in any case include at least one warm sweater or jacket. Generally Sydney dresses informally, but on certain occasions a bit of polish is considered de rigueur. Some of the posher restaurants won't allow male customers in without a tie, and a few even insist on coats. Women tend to wear more skirts and fewer pants than their American sisters, but that's entirely optional. The most widespread summer wear for men consists of walking shorts, knee-high socks, and short-sleeved shirt with or minus a tie. It looks rather smart, faintly military, and is acceptable office garb. Women frequently wear tropical whites, men *never*. (See Appendix II for clothing size conversions.)

CONSULATES AND EMBASSIES: All embassies are in the capital city of Canberra, but should you lose your passport or face some other similar problem, there are consulates for many countries in Sydney. The **U.S. Consulate-General** is at the corner of Elizabeth and Park streets (tel. 02/261-9200); the **Canadian Consulate-General** is at 50 Bridge St. (tel. 02/231-6522); and the **Consulate-General of the U.K.,** at 1 Alfred St., Sydney Cove (tel. 02/27-7521).

CRIME: Less prevalent than in large American cities, but enough to warrant some caution. There are fewer muggings, robberies, and rapes, but a lot of purse-snatchings, car thefts, hotel burglaries, and pickpocketing. Much of it is drug-related, as is the norm now in most urban areas. On the other hand, you hardly ever get short-changed in shops or by cab drivers.

CURRENCY: Australia, you'll be glad to hear, deals in **dollars** and **cents.** Paper money, however, is called "notes," not "bills." Coins come in 1¢ and 2¢ copper pieces; 5¢, 10¢, 20¢, and 50¢ in silver; and $1 and $2 in brass. Notes are $5, $10, $20, $50, and $100.

The Australian dollar is equivalent to about 75¢ U.S., give or take a few fluctuating points each day. This means that $1 U.S. will get you roughly $1.25 Australian. Keep this exchange rate in mind when comparing prices.

Reminder: All prices cited in this guide are in Australian dollars, unless otherwise indicated.

CURRENCY EXCHANGE: You'll get better exchange rates for your American dollars or dollar-denominated traveler's checks at banks than you will at your hotel. The **Thomas Cook Currency Exchange Centre,** under the Hyatt Kingsgate Hotel, Kings Cross (tel. 02/356-2211), is open seven days a week.

DENTAL EMERGENCY: For emergency dental services after hours, phone 02/692-0598; on Sunday and public holidays, call 02/692-0333.

DOCUMENTS: North American visitors need a valid passport and an Australian visa to get into the country. U.S., British, and Canadian drivers' licenses are accepted for driving during the length of your stay.

DRUGSTORES: In the "chemist shops" you can get almost, but not quite, the same range of items as in the U.S. In tourist areas they're heavy on souvenirs, mostly hideous and made in Taiwan. There are all-night chemist shops at 197 Oxford St., Darlinghurst, and 28 Darlinghurst Rd., Kings Cross. For a recorded list of 24-hour pharmacies by area, call 02/438-3333.

DRY CLEANERS: There are hundreds of them all over town. Some of the most centrally located are **P-Jays,** 79 Pitt St. (tel. 02/232-7440), **Maurice,** Centrepoint Block, Castlereagh St. (tel. 02/233-2987), **Florida,** 55 Elizabeth St. (tel. 02/231-1309).

ELECTRICITY: It's 230–240 volts, A.C., and plugs are flat three-pin types. The more expensive hotels feature wall sockets ("power points") that fit U.S. plugs; the cheaper ones don't. You'll need an adapter/converter to make your electrical gadgets work. But check with your hotel before you plug in any small appliances you have brought with you.

EMERGENCIES: To call the **police, ambulance, or fire brigade,** dial 000 from any telephone—no coins needed. For the **Poison Information Centre,** phone 02/519-0466. (See also "Dental Emergency," above, and "Medical Emergency," below.)

EYEGLASSES: For optical repairs or prescription work, see the **OPSM** branches at 183 Macquarie St. (tel. 02/217-1948), or 73 King St. (tel. 02/217-1885).

GAS: It's called petrol here (gas is only what you cook with). It sells for about 60¢ per liter, which is about $2.25 a gallon.

HAIRDRESSERS: As good as, as numerous as, and cheaper than in the U.S., though they keep shorter hours. Prices vary, but average around $13 for men's, $25 for ladies' cuts, around $20 for a shampoo and set.

HANDICAPPED INDIVIDUALS: Such persons can profit from **Consumer Information for the Disabled,** at 58 Oxford St., Darlinghurst (tel. 02/331-2606).

HOLIDAYS: Public holidays batten down Sydney's hatches fairly tight, except for Kings Cross, which generally ignores them. They are New Year's Day (January 1), Australia Day (last Monday in January), Good Friday, Easter Monday, Anzac Day (April 25), Queen's Birthday (second Monday in June), Labour Day (first Monday in October), and Christmas and Boxing Day (December 25 and 26).

HOSPITALS: I hope you don't need them, but just in case, here are some of Sydney's major public hospitals: **Sydney Hospital,** Macquarie St. (tel. 02/230-0111); the **Royal Prince Alfred,** Missenden Rd., Camperdown (tel. 02/516-6111); and the **Prince of Wales,** High St., Randwick (tel. 02/399-0111).

MAIL: Decidedly the weakest link in the Australian service chain. The **General Post Office (GPO),** the main post office in Sydney, is on Martin Place between Pitt and George streets. There's a section here dealing with telegrams, international telephone calls, and stamp sales that's open 24 hours a day, seven days a week (tel. 02/230-7014).

Post offices are open from 9am to 5pm Monday through Friday. Mail delivery comes once a day on those days—that is, when the staff isn't on strike (pardon me, "industrial action," which covers everything from a full-scale stoppage to a whimsical snail's pace called a "slowdown"). When not indulging in such upheavals, postal workers are extremely pleasant and helpful, but that doesn't speed the mail any.

Standard letters within Australia cost 36¢; overseas aerogrammes, 60¢; airletters to the U.S., $1.10.

MEDICAL EMERGENCY: For an **ambulance,** dial 000 from any telephone—no coins needed. Major hospitals are Sydney Hospital (tel. 02/230-0111), Prince of Wales Hospital (tel. 02/399-0111), Royal North Shore Hospital (tel. 02/438-0111), and St. Vincents Hospital (tel. 02/339-1111).

MELBOURNE: The capital of Victoria, the second-largest city in Australia, Melbourne is Sydney's particular bête noire. The sentiments are reciprocal. Sydney's shops stock derogatory postcards about the rival metropolis in the south. The latest bumper sticker I saw read, "Come to Sunny Melbourne. Two Billion Flies Can't Be Wrong."

NEWSPAPERS: Sydney has two daily morning papers, the *Sydney Morning Herald* and the *Daily Telegraph,* and two daily afternoon papers, the *Sun* and the *Daily Mirror.* In the morning there's also the *Australian,* which isn't local but a national daily and has the heaviest coverage of overseas news. The Sunday papers closely resemble their U.S. counterparts, consisting chiefly of columnists, sports pages, comic strips, and similar Sabbath fare, interspersed with horoscopes and whatever news items didn't make the dailies. The *Herald* and the *Australian* are full-size, quality papers and the rest are popular tabloids. The *Herald* has the most comprehensive local entertainment section.

PHOTOGRAPHY: Nearly all chemist shops (drugstores) sell and process film. For camera equipment as well as repairs go to **Paxton's,** 285 George St., or **Fletchers,** 317 Pitt St.

PUB HOURS: Theoretically, they run from 10am to 10pm, but in practice they vary according to the establishment. Kings Cross drinking spots keep their own hours, serving drinks as long as they have customers. Elsewhere it depends on whether a pub puts on live entertainers or recorded music, or poetry readings or turkey raffles or any combination of the above. It's impossible to figure out by slide rule, but offers gratifying field research.

PUBLIC TOILETS: Mostly situated in parks, though department stores, hotels, and bars will let you use their facilities. The **Hyde**

Park Family Centre, on the corner of Park and Elizabeth streets, provides facilities for mothers of infants and small children to change and breast-feed them, heat bottles, etc.

SAFETY: Whenever you're traveling in an unfamiliar city or country, stay alert. Be aware of your immediate surroundings. Wear a moneybelt and don't sling your camera or purse over your shoulder; wear the strap diagonally across your body. This will minimize the possibility of your becoming a victim of crime. Every society has it criminals. It's your responsibility to be aware and be alert even in the most heavily touristed areas. See specific chapters for more information.

RADIO STATIONS: Also known in the British version as wireless, Sydney's radio networks depend heavily on pop music and call-in chatter of the intellectually undemanding kind. But you also get classical music on 2BL, current affairs on Radio National (576 FM), and continual broadcasts of parliamentary debates on 2PB 630.

SHOE REPAIRS: As fast as in the U.S. and about as expensive. Some of the midtown repairers are **Brice's,** P60 Imperial Arcade, Pitt St., and **Well Heeled Shoes,** 19 York St.

SHOPPING HOURS: General shopping hours for most stores are 9am to 5:30pm Monday through Friday and until noon on Saturday. Many stores, however, stay open until 9pm on Thursday. Again, though, Kings Cross is an exception to the rule. There, a lot of shops stay open seven days a week, often till midnight. This includes book, souvenir, and clothing retailers, as well as tobacconists, delis, and pharmacies.

TELEGRAMS: You can send them from any post office or through your hotel switchboard, or by dialing 015.
The General Post Office (GPO), Martin Place between Pitt and George streets, has a section dealing with telegrams, international telephone calls, and stamp sales that's open 24 hours a day, seven days a week (tel. 02/230-7014).

TELEPHONES: Public phones are numerous; those in actual working order, less so. Telephone books frequently look as if an army of soldier ants had marched through the pages. The red or gold phones found in shops, bars, and hotel lobbies are better bets. A call costs 30¢ on either type. Most telephones let you make STD (long-distance) and ISD (international) calls directly. Charges vary according to distance; the maximum charge on weekdays for three minutes is $2. Local calls from hotel rooms usually cost around 50¢. The General Post Office (GPO), Martin Place between Pitt and George streets, has a section dealing with telegrams, international telephone calls, and stamp sales that's open 24 hours a day, seven days a week (tel. 02/230-7014).
To call Sydney from the U.S., you should know that the country code for Australia is 61 and the **city code for Sydney** is 02.

TELEVISION: Sydney has television stations broadcasting four major networks: the government-run Australian Broadcasting Company (ABC), which shows no commercials, and the private stations ATN7, TCN9, and TEN10, which show a great many. ATN7 also runs a continuous program of news from the U.S. from midnight to dawn Monday through Friday. A fifth channel, SBS, presents multicultural programs in various languages and excellent foreign-language movies with English subtitles. You'll find Australian video fare very similar to American, with the ABC taking the place of PBS, except that the humor is more risqué and the commentaries more bland.

TELEX: If your hotel doesn't have the facilities, you can Telex messages from the General Post Office, on Martin Place between Pitt and George streets. Call 02/232-6071 for information.

TIME: Because of the International Date Line, Sydney is a day ahead of North America. In addition, because the seasons are reversed, when North America is on Standard Time, Sydney is on Daylight Saving Time, and vice versa. Thus from roughly early March to late October, when it's noon (Standard Time) on Tuesday in Sydney, it's 10pm (Eastern Daylight Time) on Monday in New York and 7pm (Pacific Daylight Time) in California. And from late October to early March, when it's noon (Daylight Saving Time) on Tuesday in Sydney, it's 8pm (EST) on Monday in New York and 5pm (PST) in California.

TIPPING: The outstretched palm is not symbolic of Australia, and there is less tipping here than in most countries (which makes the Aussies such lousy tippers when abroad). Neither hotels nor restaurants add service charges to their bills. However, it is customary to tip 10% to 15% in the plusher restaurants, to give about $1 to hotel porters for carrying luggage, and to let cab drivers keep small change from the fare.

TOURIST INFORMATION: See Chapter III, "Getting to Know Sydney."

TRAIN STATION: Long-distance **interstate trains** leave from the Central Railway Station, on Eddy Avenue where George and Elizabeth streets converge. For information, call 02/954-4422.

TRAVELER'S CHECKS: U.S. traveler's checks are accepted virtually everywhere, but banks are the best places to cash them. Banks charge a small fee per transaction (not per check), and usually ask to see your passport.

WATER: Absolutely safe, and better-tasting—because it has fewer chemicals—than in most cities in the U.S.

WEATHER: You can phone 1196 for a forecast, which is every inch as accurate as the one you get at home. Weather forecasters share a trait with psychic prophets: they're brilliant at predicting what the weather was like yesterday, less good at saying what it's going to be tomorrow. Temperature figures are given in degrees Celsius, quite different from the Fahrenheit degrees you're accustomed to. For a conversion table, see "Metric Conversions" in Appendix I.

Sydney's winter temperatures rarely drop below 8°C (44°F), but in summer you can get several days in a row climbing to the 34.7°C (a scorching 100°F) mark.

III

GETTING TO KNOW SYDNEY

1. ORIENTATION
2. GETTING AROUND
3. USEFUL INFORMATION
4. A SMATTERING OF STRINE

Sydney is like a giant people-eater and now contains about two-thirds of the population of New South Wales. The metropolitan area stretches inland from the Pacific Ocean to the foot of the Blue Mountains, from Broken Bay in the north to Port Hacking in the south. Luckily we only need concern ourselves with relatively small patches of this vast expanse, but even those are big enough to make a little geographical know-how important.

1. Orientation

The area is bisected by **Sydney Harbour** (actually Port Jackson, but nobody calls it that) dividing it into Sydney proper and the **North Shore.** Spanning the water at the narrowest point is the unlovely but essential Harbour Bridge, choked with traffic at most hours, but offering magnificent views when you don't have to drive. The vast majority of tourist attractions and accommodations are clustered south of the bridge, a point that absolutely delights the elitist North Shore set. But then, so are the most luxurious mansions and the poshest suburbs.

The harbor is a wonderful jigsaw of hundreds of islands, peninsulas, coves, and inlets, many with their own miniature beaches. The famous surfing beaches, of course, are not inside the harbor but on the open seafront.

The focal point and the center of the city is **Martin Place,** a large pedestrian plaza fringed by outdoor cafés and bustling with office workers taking their lunch break in the sun. On weekdays there is usually a rock, jazz, folk, or dance ensemble performing in the sunken stage area. If you stand with your back to the pillars of the General Post Office (GPO), you're facing due north. That is the direction of the **Harbour Bridge,** of **Circular Quay** (terminal for all ferry services), and at the tip of Bennelong Point, the **Opera House.** Northeast and east stretch the **Royal Botanic Gardens** and their southward extension, the **Domain.** Southeast of you lies **Hyde Park,** from which point William Street runs straight and rather steeply uphill to **Kings Cross,** which is a kind of adjunct to the center city.

South of you, at the grubby end of Pitt Street, stands **Central Station,** the country and interstate rail terminal. Also **Chinatown,** crammed with Chinese eateries. Due west extends **Darling Harbour,** Australia's most ambitious urban-development project. Two streets away to the northwest is **Wynyard Station,** the terminal for the city's train and bus transportation. And going either through or by Martin Place are all of the city's main shopping streets: George Street, Pitt Street, Castlereagh Street, and Elizabeth Street.

If you look at a map you'll see that the GPO is located on a peninsula, as is much of Sydney, which accounts for the congestion of its central sections and the endless sprawl of suburbs reaching farther and farther inland. The actual city area is minute compared with the horizon-filling vastness of those suburbs.

Sydney has no ghetto districts in the American sense. Its ethnic minorities are scattered throughout the metropolis, though you do get certain concentrations. The Italians are in Leichhardt, the Vietnamese in Cabramatta; a neglected and impoverished Aboriginal enclave lies in Redfern, near Central Station. Sydney does have poor, disintegrating neighborhoods. These tend to shift under the impact of "gentrification." Not long ago, for instance, Surry Hills and the well-nigh unspellable dockside region of Woolloomooloo were such areas. Since then the narrow-chested terrace rows have been transformed into chic little town houses, driving the rents up and most of the original inhabitants out.

In fact, the Sydney equivalent of the American Victorian brownstone is the formerly working-class terrace house, preferably with the proletarian frontage intact, but with the interior upgraded to art nouveau and a BMW parked outside. The curlicued wrought-iron balcony railings known as "Sydney lace," once believed worthless and sold for scrap, now fetch antique prices. And if you can get a couple of brass coach lanterns, polish them to a high shine, and stick them over the entrance, you've got it made, mate.

It so happens that Sydney is also Australia's largest industrial center, making almost everything you can think of, including nuclear reactor equipment. But the factories are concentrated in pockets kept well away from the high-class residential and recreation areas. Tourists can spend weeks here without running across a manufacturing plant.

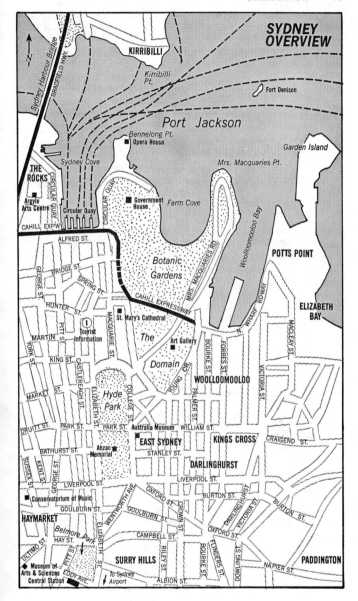

There is no actual "wrong or right" side of the tracks, but certain suburbs count decidedly as top-grade, as distinct from merely "trendy." They lie strung along the shorelines of the lower reaches of Sydney Harbour, along the eastern oceanside from **Double Bay**

to **Palm Beach,** and **Vaucluse,** and in the leafy, tucked-away regions of the North Shore, where residents have fought bitter battles against the introduction of such vulgarities as hotels, hamburger stands, and movie theaters.

---

2. Getting Around

Sydney's public transportation system is like the proverbial curate's egg—excellent in parts. Fortunately it is excellent in just those parts that concern you. The system uses buses, electric trains, and ferries, and you can get **transport information** about all of them by calling Metro Trips (tel. 02/954-4422) daily from 7am to 10pm.

BY TRAIN

The fastest, and dullest, way to get around is by train. The carriages are comfortable double-deckers only slightly disfigured by graffiti. The routes are partly above, partly below ground, and they operate on seven major lines. Study the route maps displayed in all stati ns for destinations and connections. Trains run from 4:30am till midnight. Travel is by sections, starting with a short ride for $1. Children under 4 travel free on the entire system, and those between 4 and 16 at half fare.

BY BUS

There are also two free bus routes. Route 777 takes you through the city center and Route 666 runs from Hunter Street, at Wynyard, to the Art Gallery of New South Wales. You can save quite a bit of money by purchasing a **Day Rover** that lets you travel on all trains, buses, and ferries in and around Sydney for one day. They cost $7 and are available at train stations and bus depots.

BY FERRY

The terminal for all ferry services is **Circular Quay,** which isn't (and never was) circular. Ferries connect the city with the North Shore and traverse the harbor from 6am to 11:30pm. The craft in use range from racing hydrofoils to wallowing little tubs, and make delightful traveling, particularly on sunny days. Destinations are clearly marked on the individual piers and the main services run to Manly, Neutral Bay, Taronga Park Zoo, Kirribilli, Balmain, Cockatoo Island, and Hunters Hill. Fares depend on distance. A single trip on the inner harbor costs $1.10 for adults, half price for children.

BY CAR

Before getting behind the wheel, *please* make a point of studying the rules set out below. I prefer my readers alive.

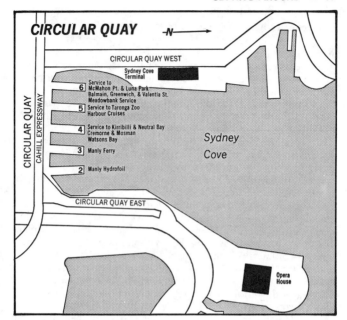

Rules of the Road

Sydney traffic is not quite as maniacal as that of, say, Paris or Buenos Aires. But it's heavy, fast, and at some points very badly regulated. Two glaring danger spots are the intersection where William Street runs into Kings Cross and the junction of George Street and Broadway at Central Station. Motorists are generally law-abiding (the fines are too heavy to ignore) but they have some pervasive bad habits. They insist on right of way, regardless of circumstances. They're very cavalier about giving signals, and count among the world's worst tailgaters, virtually crawling up your exhaust in order to make you move faster.

Traffic drives on the left-hand side of the road and cars therefore have right-hand steering. At crossings you look right-left-right. The other important points to remember are to give way to all cars at "T" intersections if you're approaching on the stem of the "T," and to give way to cars coming from the right at intersections, unless they have traffic lights or "stop" signs. Wearing seatbelts is *compulsory*, and failure to do so can earn you a stiff fine.

You very quickly get accustomed to right-hand steering wheels, although you'll find yourself groping for the handbrake on the wrong side. The most enduring nuisance for overseas motorists is that they continually turn on the windshield wipers when they mean to flick the indicators.

If you belong to a motoring association at home you are entitled to all services offered by the **National Roads and Motorists Association (NRMA),** 151 Clarence St. (tel. 02/260-9222).

They'll provide you with maps, brochures on road rules, and the best general advice on Aussie automobiling you'll get anywhere.

Rental Cars

Sydney has masses of them, but for reliability you'd better choose one of the Big Three. All have reservation counters at Kingsford Smith Airport as well as downtown: **Thrifty,** 85 William St., Kings Cross (tel. 02/357-5399); **Avis,** 24 William St. (tel. 02/922-8161); **Hertz,** at Kent and Coward streets, Mascot (tel. 02/669-0066).

While overseas driving licenses are valid for up to one year in Australia, overseas insurance coverage is *not.* Compulsory third-party insurance is automatically added to all car-rental contracts; more comprehensive coverage is optional. To rent a car you must be 21 or over, and if you're under 25 you may be asked for a special reference. Rates of all companies are in a wild state of competitive flux. Whatever figures I put down will probably be passé by the time you read this. All companies offer special deals to attract customers, but these change just as often. For example, Thrifty rents medium-size, air-conditioned vehicles at $54 a day, or $44 a day for four or more days. The company also offers special weekend discounts. If you pick up a car anytime on Friday and return it at the same time on Monday, using it for three days, you only get charged for two.

One point needs adding here. Don't hesitate to ask for directions. Sydneysiders look busy, but they'll go out of their way to put you on the right track, frequently attaching some scraps of local lore to their instructions. The only catch is that if you get lost in a tourist area, chances are that whoever you approach will turn out to be another, equally lost, tourist. Spotting a native around Circular Quay, for instance, can be quite a task.

BY WATER TAXI

You'll find other ways of getting to know and getting around Sydney in the chapter on sight-seeing. Here I just want to mention the city's water cab service. **Harbour Taxis** (tel. 02/555-1299) will take you anywhere around the harbor, either to specific points or on general observations tours. The rates vary according to distance. A trip from, say, Circular Quay to Watsons Bay costs around $30.

3. Useful Information

The **Travel Centre of New South Wales,** at the corner of Pitt and Spring streets (tel. 02/231-4444), spreads out the welcome mat on behalf of the state government. Very handy, very helpful, and tremendously busy, their office provides maps, brochures, and information booklets, plus an avalanche of leaflets advertising anything from antique shops to Zanzibarian restaurants. Office hours are 9:30am to 5pm Monday through Friday.

The privately run **Sydney Convention and Visitors' Bureau** operates a small kiosk in Martin Place between Castlereagh and

Elizabeth streets (tel. 02/235-2424), open Monday through Friday from 9am to 5pm. This is also the outlet for **Halftix,** selling half-price tickets for all major theaters, including the Opera House. But don't expect *good* seats for the price.

. . . AND USELESS TRIVIA

Koala bears are not bears but marsupials. Because of their diet of eucalyptus leaves they smell like cough drops, and if you hold one long enough so will you.

Australia is the only country in the world that had a prime minister disappear—without a trace—while swimming (Harold Holt in 1967).

One square yard of Sydney legally belongs to France. It's at the site of the monument to French explorer Comte de la Perouse on Anzac Parade, La Perouse.

The Aussie nickname for God is Hughie, and "Send her down, Hughie," is the outback exhortation for rain.

Sydney's **Incinerator Restaurant,** 2 Small St., Willoughby (tel. 02/958-1700), is actually built inside an old incinerator.

There is an open-air **school for jugglers** in Centennial Park, holding regular midweek classes. Students start on light clubs and graduate when they can juggle burning torches.

Australians use the term "wanker" in both a derogatory and a complimentary form. In politics and business it means being an un-principled hypocrite. But among surfers a "wind wanker" is a highly skilled sailboarder.

The most original sight-seeing ventures in town are **Pat's Uninteresting Tours** (tel. 02/552-2289). The field trips are designed to show you the dullest attractions available, such as a sewage works, the world's largest stop sign, and the most uninspiring display window. They cost $22.50 and are heavily booked.

The term "Aborigines" simply means natives (of anywhere), making the original Australians the only people on earth without a name. They now call themselves **Koories,** but the word is hardly known among the white population.

Balmain bugs are not a species of cockroach but a uniquely Australian—and delicious—type of miniature lobster.

Eating or selling kangaroo meat is illegal in New South Wales.

The Sydney police force employs "booze buses" to give motorists random breath tests. A positive reading on the breathalyzer can earn you a $1,000 fine.

---

4. A Smattering of Strine

Winston Churchill once called Britain and America "two nations divided by a common language," and the same could be said about the U.S. and Australia. While most Sydneysiders are fairly bi-lingual in Aussie-American, it isn't so the other way around. Hence this special and rather important section.

Volumes could be (and have been) written about Down

Underese, which the locals regard as the purest form of English spoken anywhere on earth. Leader in the field is undoubtedly Afferbeck Lauder's *Let Stalk Strine,* the title being the phonetic translation of how a native would enunciate "Let Us Talk Australian." (The author's nom de plume is "Strine" for "In Alphabetical Order.")

Australians deliver words in a flat, nasal drawl, moving their lips as little as possible in the process. Thus Sydney becomes "Sinny" and the capital of Victoria "Melbrn." They shorten words of more than two syllables, then stick a vowel at the end of it. In this manner "compensation" turns into "compo" and a garbage collector is a "garbo." They also employ diminutives whenever possible, making surfers "surfies," mosquitoes "mozzies," and vegetables "veggies."

They call their country Oz (as in *The Wizard of . . .*), but nobody these days calls anyone "cobber" anymore. Even "fair dinkum Aussie" has a distinctly sarcastic flavor. The most commonly used term in this vein is *ocker*—and it's not meant as a compliment. An ocker denotes a rural or urban redneck.

Whether or not you understand this terminology doesn't matter much. What matters are those statements you *think* you understand, but actually don't. Australian phraseology can differ quite drastically from American. If, for instance, a waitress or shop assistant inquires "Are you all right?" and you respond with "Yes, I'm fine," it means you won't get served. The question doesn't concern the state of your health but whether you need attention.

The effect can be just as unfortunate vice versa. I once watched a young Sydneysider conduct a very promising flirtation with a lass from Los Angeles. He got so far as to make a date with her for the following day. "Righto," he said, "so I'll knock you up tomorrow morning." "You will *not,*" she snapped, turned on her heel, and strode off, leaving behind a sorely bewildered Aussie. She didn't know that in Strine "knock up" means to call on.

All this, however, is still not actual Australian slang, which has a vocabulary all its own. It would require the rest of this book to enlighten you on the mysteries of such expressions as "come the raw prawn" or "flat out like a lizard drinking." They're not likely to be used on you, but you will hear and wonder over expressions such as *back o'Bourke* for the bush or outback, *sheila* for girl, *chook* for chicken, *poofter* for homosexual, *daks* for pants, *pom* for an English person, *tucker* for food, *dinkum* for honest or real, and the ubiquitous adjective *crook,* which means bad for anything from the state of the economy to the quality of a sandwich.

I have compiled a short list of terms you *will* encounter regularly and which may mystify you even after you've learned that "she's beaut" represents the ultimate peak of verbal praise.

The list below has the Aussie expression on the left, the American equivalent on the right:

arvo	afternoon
bloke	guy
boot [in a car]	trunk
brolly	umbrella

bonnet [on a car]	hood
bullet, getting the	being fired
bumpers [on a car]	fenders
bludger	loafer
cockies	farmers
duco	car paint
dollybird	young girl
earbashing	talking (too much)
entree	appetizer (*not* the main course)
footpath	sidewalk
full as a boot	drunk
fireplug	hydrant
flake [on a menu]	shark
flog	sell
gee-gees	horses
good on yer	term of approval (sometimes ironic)
good oil	the truth
grog	liquor
knock	criticize
lay-by	buying on deposit
lollies	candy
mate	buddy
mean	stingy
middy	small glass of beer
mole	hooker
plonk	cheap wine
power point	electric socket
push	gang
queue	to line up—for anything
ratbag	any kind of villain
schooner	large glass of beer
serviette	napkin
skiting	boasting
shout	to treat (buy for) someone
sport	man, as in "Listen, man"
spuds	potatoes
smoke-o	coffee or tea break
squatter	ranch owner
station	large ranch
stubby	small beer bottle
sweets	dessert
ta	thanks
ta-ta	good-bye
taxi rank	cab stand
tea	dinner
wogs	bugs, flies

A few more points to facilitate communication. Strine has a curious predilection for the feminine gender—nearly everything is a *she,* including the weather, the city, one's job, or the fare on the cab meter. Australians also consistently pronounce "a" as "i," turning "paper" into "piper," and "late" into "lite." The standard greeting formula "Good day, mate," comes out "G'di, mite." They will use the term *bastard* without any human connotation whatever, referring, for instance, to a stretch of road as "She's a bastard," to mean lousy.

Finally, a difference in spelling and counting that has wreaked havoc with addresses and telephone numbers. Australians say "double" whenever a letter or number occurs twice in succession. They will spell out Paddington "p-a-double-dee-" etc., and 4466 as "double-four double-six." If they hear you repeat letters they'll quietly assume that you stutter.

AND NOW FOR A COMMERCIAL . . .

For a budget-oriented trip all around the Down Under continent, I'd suggest you take along my *Australia on $40 a Day*. One of the series of Frommer Guides, it documents hundreds of economy accommodations and restaurants—the most difficult types of establishments to find on your own. You get full descriptions—not mere listings—plus particulars about transportation, attractions, sights, sports, shopping, nightlife, and culture.

The book covers all the major cities and regions of Australia. And the coverage is done by an insider; someone who knows where and how to get the maximum value for your dollar.

IV

WHERE TO STAY

1. DELUXE HOTELS

2. MODERATELY PRICED HOTELS

3. APARTMENT HOTELS

4. BUDGET HOTELS

5. HOMESTAYS AND FARMSTAYS

As Australia's main port of entry and premier tourist center, Sydney boasts an immense array of accommodations in every conceivable price and comfort category. But there is a degree of desperate confusion about the nomenclature applied to them. This stems from the bluenose laws slammed down during the continent's "wowser" period for the sole purpose of restricting the sale of liquor.

These laws stipulated that in order to qualify for a liquor license a "public house" had to be a hotel as well—that is, it had to accept overnight guests. For most hotels, however, only the bar trade was profitable; lodgers were a dead loss. In consequence many establishments followed a system that complied with the letter of the law while letting the spirit go hang. They maintained a few guest rooms, preferably empty and purely for show. If some benighted wayfarer actually requested a bed, the rooms were always taken, usually by the proprietor's aunts or cousins. They got away with this by means of political pull and judicious palm-greasing. And the result is that even today a fair portion of "hotels" listed in the yellow pages aren't hotels at all, but simply taverns.

There is still no clear distinction between the genuine hotels and those that merely act as liquor dispensaries. To make matters worse, the Aussies call both varieties "pubs." And to confuse matters a mite more, there are the so-called private hotels, actually guesthouses, which have no liquor license, may or may not serve food, and exist *solely* for accommodation.

Australian hotel terminology takes a bit of translating as well. "Lift," for instance, means elevator, "private facilities" denotes private bathrooms and toilets, and "tray service" stands for room service. Some Sydney establishments include breakfast in their tariff; most do not (you will find this clearly indicated in the following hotel descriptions). In any case, "Continental" indicates breakfast consisting of a cereal, juice, toast, and tea or coffee (bearing no resemblance to any European repast), while a "full" or "cooked" breakfast means the works, including eggs (even a mushroom omelet), bacon, or sausages.

Virtually all Aussie hostelries provide tea/coffee-making facilities in their rooms, a feature other countries should copy. This custom is so universal that I haven't listed it in individual descriptions—you can take it for granted. The only distinction is that some establishments also supply gratis cookies (biscuits). Some of the larger places provide free matches, but these are a minority. Soap supplies are usually generous and are at least as good as the American quality. On the other hand, very few hotels will give you a washcloth, so it's wise to carry your own.

Bathrooms, as a whole, are excellent, with unlimited hot water and fair supplies of towels. But even in some upper-bracket hotels bathrooms come equipped with showers only. If you must have a tub, you should make this clear before moving in.

The best part about Sydney hotel bills is the absence of government taxes or service charges. A good many hotels, however, impose surcharges for certain holiday periods. This is left entirely to the discretion of the management and can apply to just a couple of days over Christmas or to the entire length of school vacations. Since these extra charges seem to change from one season to the next it's a good idea to inquire about them first. And while we're discussing good ideas, if you're paying in U.S.-currency traveler's checks, cash them at a bank. I have found that the exchange rate given by hotels always lingers a few points below the bank rate.

---

1. Deluxe Hotels

If you rate a hotel by the number of movie scenes and video commercials that have been shot in, around, and from it, then the **Regent,** 199 George St., Sydney 2000 (tel. 02/238-0000), ranks as Numero Uno. Opened in 1983 and located about a minute's stroll from Circular Quay, the Regent offers panoramic vistas quite irresistible to folks with cameras in search of grandeur.

A Note on Prices
All prices cited in this guide are in Australian dollars. As we go to press, $1 Australian = approximately 75¢ U.S., which means that a hotel room listed at $100 a night actually costs only about $75 in U.S. dollars.

Behind a sloping beige stone frontage rises a fluted 36-story tower (actually 35, because there's no 13th floor) housing 620 rooms and suites. The foyer is vast and quietly magnificent, constructed of polished granite, with a central atrium warmed by diffused sunshine from a skylight above. There are green shrubs, small trees, and fresh flowers wherever you look, scarlet armchairs and settees to enfold you, and a famous English afternoon tea ceremony: tea served from silver samovars, accompanied by watercress sandwiches and little cakes, costing around $15 per sipper.

The Regent has two restaurants, including the illustrious Kables, two cocktail bars, and one of the finest jazz-dedicated supper clubs in Australia, Don Burrows. The guest rooms follow the theme of cool, understated elegance that distinguishes the lobby. Most of them have superb harbor or city views, and all come with three telephones, bedside controls for TV, radio, and lights, and executive desks. The marble bathrooms are heaped with free first-class toiletries, and every guest gets a snowy toweling robe. Few decorations, but luxurious comfort at every turn. You pay between $255 and $550 for singles or doubles (depending on the views), and from $650 upward for suites.

Although even younger than the Regent, the **Inter-Continental,** 117 Macquarie St., Sydney 2000 (tel. 02/230-0200), presents a wonderfully mellow Victorian face to the world. This modern hotel hides discreetly behind the shell of the old State Treasury (built in 1851), whose venerable sandstone walls now enclose the lobby —possibly the handsomest in the Southern Hemisphere—a marble-floored central Cortile surrounded by three levels of vaulted arcades, sprinkled with palms, flowers, and wicker chairs, illuminated by torchères in the evening.

The Inter-Continental houses five restaurants, cafés, and taverns, an indoor rooftop swimming pool, and a fitness center with every conceivable massage, stretching, pulling, and running device. Also an arcade of shops, salons, and boutiques, and a lavishly equipped Business Centre offering computers, telexes, copying machines, and secretaries on call. Between them the staff speaks 15 languages, including Cantonese, Japanese, Malay, and Vietnamese. There are beauty salons for women and men, a house doctor on 24-hour call, and full room service around the clock.

The 531 rooms and suites all have commanding views, pastel décor with Australian themes, large built-in wardrobes, and a range of free giveaways that include bathrobes and little baskets brimming with bath accessories. All come with three telephones, in-house TV movie channels, electric hairdryers, music and radio systems, minibars, refrigerators, and superbly sprung beds. They cost from $285 to $390 for singles or doubles, with suites starting at $430.

Compared to the two hotel giants above, the **Sebel Town House,** 23 Elizabeth Bay Rd., Elizabeth Bay 2011 (tel. 02/358-3244), is an intimate little retreat—but only in comparison. A gleaming white structure, the Sebel stands on the borderline of Kings Cross and acts as a magnet for every visiting movie, stage, video, and concert star from around the globe. Their often gaudy attire adds a certain casual flavor to the otherwise conservative foyer. The adjacent cocktail bar is festooned with the signed portraits of media celebrities who have graced the bar stools, and frequently the floor as well.

Sebel's has a classic Edwardian restaurant, the Encore, famous 24-hour room service, and a welcoming board in the lobby that is eagerly scanned by reporters, autograph hounds, and groupies alike. The roofdeck has a heated swimming pool and Finnish sauna (but minus birch rods) and downstairs is an opulently splendid Function Centre for weddings, banquets, and other such insurrections.

The 164 guest rooms and suites are spacious, sleekly luxurious, and equipped with timber-paneled walls, telephones, remote-control TV sets, bathroom scales, hairdryers, baskets of toilet articles, and cleverly sited lighting fixtures. Color schemes are kept in soothing brown and salmon hues and the bathroom mirrors are large enough to reflect a harem. Single rooms start at $265, doubles at $280, and the Marina suites at $500.

The **Boulevard,** 90 William St., Sydney 2000 (tel. 02/357-2277), is a massive gray stone edifice in which the keynote is bigness. Everything is large: the lobby, the social facilities, the rooms, even the elevators. The foyer, in fact, resembles a royal reception hall and could easily engulf a guard of honor. The hotel lacks a swimming pool, but has every other imaginable convenience: an intimate bistro and a panoramic restaurant, the 25th Floor; one of Sydney's plushest nightspots, Williams; an adjoining shopping center; plus Telexes, secretarial services, steambath, massage salon, and multilingual staff.

The 273 guest rooms and suites range from large to huge—no chance of anyone getting claustrophobic here. Furnished with subdued stylishness, they welcome you with enough "nibbles," soft drinks, and liquor to stock a grocery. In-house movies for the TV set, terrycloth bathrobes, minibars, refrigerators, shampoos, bath salts, shoeshine equipment, and a heap of other comfort creators come as standard items. So do ironing boards, a rare touch other hotels should copy. Room service operates around the clock, the carpeting is sinfully rich, and the illumination can be adjusted according to need or mood. Singles or doubles cost the same: $268 per night.

The **Sydney Hilton,** 259 Pitt St., Sydney 2000 (tel. 02/266-0610), is so fused with the chic Royal Arcade that you can hardly tell where one stops and the other begins—the smart shops just continue. Towering over the city, the Hilton has everything you expect from that international luxury chain, plus a few unique local touches—for instance, the Marble Bar in the basement. This wonderful ornately curlicued piece of Victoriana was marked for demolition when the hotel was put up. But the powerful Builders' Laborers Federation refused to destroy it, and the management wisely left the bar intact and built the Hilton over it. Today this extravaganza is a municipal landmark and a goldmine for the owners.

The Hilton has four other bars at various levels, two restaurants, a café, and a swank disco called Juliana's. It also offers one of the best-equipped business centers in town, a super-size swimming pool, and computerized door locks coded for each individual guest. The guest rooms are furnished in the now traditional Hilton style: soothing color schemes, huge wardrobes, blissful beds, and finger-tip convenience—carefully planned—for every gadget around. Singles or doubles run from $270 to $340, while suites range from $450 to $750 per night.

The Old Sydney Parkroyal, 55 George St., The Rocks 2000 (tel. 02/252-0524), is actually an infant, having opened in 1984. But it stands rooted in history. This is the cradle of Sydney, site of the original settlement, and the hotel actually incorporates the brick walls of warehouses built in the 1830s. Tradition is big here. Every morning and evening, at 8am and 6pm sharp, a detachment of the regular army dressed in 18th-century uniforms marches up to raise and lower the flag over the building.

The Parkroyal has an immense central atrium the size of a ca-thedral, overlooked by eight gallery floors containing the guest rooms. The arrangement achieves a wonderful sense of spaciousness coupled with old-world elegance and quite disguises the thoroughly modern fixtures of the hotel. These include a rooftop pool, sauna, and health spa, two cocktail bars, two restaurants, telex machines and secretarial services, and 24-hour room service.

The 172 rooms are not large, but excellently furnished, some overlooking the ocean liners berthed at Circular Quay, just across the road. All rooms have telephone trios, hairdryers, minibars, and ironing boards. There are special rooms for the disabled, fitted with wider doorways and lower toilets. Singles or doubles pay the same rate here: $255 per night.

The **Southern Cross,** at the corner of Elizabeth and Goulburn streets, Sydney 2000 (tel. 02/20-987). A converted apartment block, the Southern Cross greets you with a small, smart lobby, its ceiling studded with little lights, and an adjoining cocktail bar that looks like an elite private club. The hotel also has a multistar restau-rant, a rooftop garden setting with pool, plus secretarial/telex services, 24-hour dry cleaning, baby-sitters, and a sauna.

The 184 rooms and suites are of medium size, in russet and beige color schemes, and feature extra-large beds and dressing areas in front of the bathrooms. Wardrobes are not only spacious but equipped with the quietest sliding doors I've ever handled. A lot of other items come with the room: shoeshines and morning papers, plush bathrobes and regular executive desks, free in-house movies, radio, digital alarm clock, refrigerator, and individual climate con-trol. The hotel stands a block away from Hyde Park, which places a jogging track at your doorstep. Singles or doubles range from $255 to $295; suites start at $385.

---

2. Moderately Priced Hotels

Nearly all the establishments listed here offer private bath-rooms; the few that don't are clearly indicated. Some of these hotels could pass as deluxe, others border on the budget bracket, but the majority sit squarely in the middle.

DOWNTOWN

In a superb location between the green expanse of Hyde Park and the business district stands the **Koala Park Regis,** at the corner of Park and Castlereagh streets, Sydney 2000 (tel. 02/267-6511). Surrounded by duty-free shops, the hotel occupies ten floors in a soaring high-rise that also contains five floors of parking garages. The small lobby is on the ground floor; the actual hotel starts on the sixth. There is a rooftop swimming pool, a restaurant on the premises, fax and telex facilities, and the airport bus service. The 120 rooms and suites are medium-size, newly and cheerfully furnished in light woods, and offer views of either the park or the thronged streets. All have color TVs, dial telephones, pleasant rustic prints on the walls, refrigerators, and bathrooms with showers. There are bedside and fluorescent mirror lights, but none on the ceiling. The wardrobes appear a little cramped for two persons. The hotel is well carpeted and has efficient elevator service. Singles cost $95; doubles, $105.

Smaller, more intimate, but equally well situated is the **Hyde Park Inn,** 271 Elizabeth St., Sydney 2000 (tel. 02/264-6001). Also facing the park, the inn has a handy wall map of Sydney on which landmarks light up when you push a button. The inn does not take convention groups and only favors small tours, offers air conditioning in all rooms, smart little snack kitchenettes in most. The 85 rooms are spacious, very tastefully furnished, lavishly endowed with wardrobe space and lighting fixtures. All come with color TVs and dial telephones, but the bathrooms have showers only. Rates here include a light breakfast and start at $105 for singles, $120 for doubles.

Central Plaza Hotel, corner of George and Quay streets, Sydney 2000 (tel. 02/212-2544). A big ivory-colored block rising opposite Central Station in midtown, the Plaza features four huge clocks above the entrance showing the time in Sydney, London, Tokyo, and New York. Although tagged as a "resort hotel," this is very much a business establishment, equipped with every modern aid for international conventions and conferences. The lobby is vast, plush, and smoothly efficient, there's a rooftop sauna and swimming pool, a fast-service coffee shop, and a richly ornate restaurant with cocktail bar. Room service functions around the clock and the hotel offers currency exchange, dry cleaning, laundry, and theater and tour booking services. The 116 bedrooms and suites show an intriguing contrast between the streamlined furnishings and the rustic brick-wall setting. All come with baths *and* showers, direct-dial phones, air conditioning, refrigerators, and minibars. Rates range from $165 to $175 for doubles or singles, with suites beginning at $260, a lavish buffet breakfast included.

The **Cambridge Inn,** 212 Riley St., Sydney 2010 (tel. 02/212-1111). Located just off the central business district, this rather velvety establishment boasts small suites as standard rooms. Every one of the 150 units consists of a living room, separate bedroom, and small kitchenette (minus a stove). The décor is kept in ivory and russet tones, furnishings are sumptuous, the bathrooms beautiful, and you get special touches like individual temperature control and 24-hour room service. The Cambridge houses a gourmet restaurant and two cocktail bars for pleasure and a telex machine for business. Rates are $155 for singles, $155 to $175 for doubles.

OXFORD STREET

This area is a kind of in-between that stitches the inner suburb of Darlinghurst to the center city. The two melt into each other with no definable borderline. Oxford Street is an endlessly long thoroughfare, heavy with traffic and crammed with shops, restaurants, and pubs. It is known as a gay hangout, but not obtrusively so, and makes up in zest and variety what it lacks in chic.

Greetings Oxford Koala, at the corner of Oxford and Pelican streets, Sydney 2000 (tel. 02/269-0645), despite its faintly ludicrous name, is one of the handiest accommodation spots in town. A huge reddish-brown structure looming at Oxford Square, it shares a shopping arcade block with the terminal of Pioneer and Greyhound bus lines. Tour groups stream in and out constantly, but the hotel staff manages crowds with remarkable ease and smoothness. The Koala caters to the business world as much as to tourists, offering secretarial services, telex, fax, photocopying, and desktop publishing facilities. It also has an oversize, heated rooftop pool. The 343 rooms and suites are of fair size, furbished in a very practical style and equipped with refrigerators, color TVs, dial telephone/alarm clocks at bedside, individual temperature controls, and modern bathrooms. You pay $109 for singles, $119 for doubles; executive and family apartments start at $161. The hotel restaurant serves fast breakfast, buffet style, then switches to more leisurely table service for lunch and dinner.

Waratah House, 108 Oxford St., Darlinghurst 2010 (tel. 02/332-4118), is a surprise package with all the goodies hidden under plain wrapping. This is a small private hotel with a rather cluttered little lobby, 12 rooms, and no elevator. But the rooms are charming, the facilities extensive, and the rates astonishingly low. The Waratah has a stylish little coffee lounge on the ground floor, serving breakfast (included in the tariff), plus air conditioning in all bedrooms, as well as color TV, telephone, bath and shower, and in some, private balconies. The furnishings are modern, bright, cheerful, and very comfortable, the carpeting excellent, the wardrobe space ample. Rates are kept to painless levels: $75 for singles, $85 for doubles, from $95 for twin-bedded suites.

KINGS CROSS

Sydney's version of Montmartre, Soho, Greenwich Village, or North Beach is different by also being the town's major hotel region. While undeniably a red-light district, the Cross also offers some of the finest accommodations in Australia, and more of it than any other place. Don't be confused by the various district names in this section—Kings Cross is actually a border area between three inner divisions. If a hotel is listed here, it's in the Cross region.

Right where the Cross crosses, at possibly the busiest junction in Sydney, rises the **Crest Hotel,** 111 Darlinghurst Rd., Kings Cross 2011 (tel. 02/358-2755). Resembling an immense slab of white and dark chocolate, it adjoins the Kings Cross railway station and is surrounded by a cluster of bars, cafés, shops, and boutiques.

Equally convenient for large tour groups and business travelers, the Crest handles huge numbers of both with ease, aided by what may be the smoothest elevator service on the continent. The hotel has excellent business facilities, a sheltered swimming pool, a sun-swept restaurant, and a pleasantly subdued bar (as distinct from the more boisterous watering holes downstairs). The 232 bedrooms are furnished in smart beige and ivory hues, air-conditioned, spacious, and virtually soundproof. All have color TVs, dial phones, radios, refrigerators, large wardrobes, excellent lighting, and impressive city or harbor views. From way above you can watch the electric trains running to and from downtown like so many miniature toys. Rates are a standard $135 to $155 for singles or doubles.

The **Hampton Court,** 9 Bayswater Rd., Kings Cross 2011 (tel. 02/357-2711), conveys an impression of Edwardian stateliness by means of a foyer decorated with stained-glass windows and a staff dressed in Tudor costumes. Although the hotel has three nightclubs on the premises, this is mainly a family establishment. Club action is kept well separated from the living quarters. The 126 units are spacious, air-conditioned, and equipped with kitchenettes. Some of the rooms tend to be dark, but the furnishings are new, wardrobe space is ample, and all units come with color TV and telephone. Accommodations range from singles to family suites holding four or six people. Singles go for $80, doubles run $88, and triples are $96.

There is nothing even remotely Edwardian about the **Plainsman,** 40 Bayswater Rd., Kings Cross 2011 (tel. 02/356-3511). A dazzling white ultramodern structure, this motor inn shows a scarlet awning to visitors and features large viewing windows at street level. A small establishment with only 38 units, the Plainsman offers the advantages of intimacy and every up-to-the-minute convenience except a swimming pool. The lobby has a luxury ranch-style air, aided by flowering shrubs and russet carpeting. The bedrooms are of fair size and fitted with separate kitchenettes. No restaurant on the premises, but half a dozen are within strolling distance. Bedroom furnishings are stylish, with large mirrors, good armchairs, and bright color schemes. All bathrooms have tubs as well as showers, and every unit contains color TVs, dial telephones, and individually controlled air conditioning. Singles or doubles cost $92, an extra person $10.

The **Gazebo,** 2 Elizabeth Bay Rd., Elizabeth Bay 2011 (tel. 02/358-1999), is one of the most beautiful hotels in town and edges into the deluxe bracket, except that its tariff scale is somewhat lower. An eye-catching structure, consisting of an ivory-colored 17-story tower with a more conventional square addition, the hotel produces a grandiose overall effect. The lobby follows the circular shape of the tower and manages to be both vast and svelte in equal proportions, in shades of blue and ivory and sprinkled with delightfully welcoming armchairs. On the reception desk stands a huge bowl of apples, a gesture aimed at Japanese visitors who regard apples as luxury fruit.

The Gazebo has a heated rooftop pool with sauna, two restaurants (one of them a glassed-in affair that *looks* like outdoors but isn't), a chic cocktail bar, and 400 bedrooms. Some of the rooms come with balconies and panoramic views, plus electronic combination lockers for valuables. All of them feature air conditioning, free in-house movies, and refrigerators, plus exceptionally handsome furnishings, vast beds, vast wardrobes, hairdryers in the bathrooms, baskets of free toiletries, telephones, radios, and cunningly paired twin lamps at desks and bedsides. Singles or twins are priced at the same rates, depending on whether you choose the deluxe or executive type, start at $185 and $197 respectively.

The **Manhattan,** 8 Greenknowe Ave., Potts Point 2011 (tel. 02/358-1288). A massive five-story block, this establishment caters to large tour groups and has a tremendously busy lobby, equipped with leather settees and enough space to swallow up the passenger list of a jumbo jet. Located on a quiet side street, the Manhattan offers "superior" and "standard" rooms, the latter with shared bathrooms. Furnishings and fittings are comfortable in both. The hotel has a stylish restaurant and cocktail bar and 161 bedrooms, recently renovated. Bathrooms have tubs and showers, and all rooms are furnished with color TV, telephone, and refrigerator. Rooms with private baths cost $82 for singles, $98 for doubles; with shared facilities, $52 and $74 respectively. Children under 2 stay free in their parents' room.

Also tucked away in a quiet corner is the **Clairmont Inn,** 5 Ward Ave., Kings Cross 2011 (tel. 02/358-2044). Although the frontage offers a face of modern functionalism, the interior has a surprisingly cozy air, a happy combination of streamlining and plushness. The foyer sets the tone: black tile floors and a network of ceiling lights pleasantly softened by the abundance of greenery and flowers arranged on the low center table. On the small side—with only 71 rooms—the Clairmont nevertheless boasts an indoor pool with sauna and spa, a fine restaurant, and very pleasant cocktail bar, as well as a guest laundry. The rooms strike the same nicely balanced mixture of charm and utility. Extra handbasins outside the bathrooms enable two people to get cleaned up simultaneously. Telephones, radio clocks, electric hairdryers, refrigerators, air conditioning, color TVs, and good light fixtures add to the utility. All are combined with matching color themes and the kind of furniture that could just as well stand in a good suburban living room. The corridors here are rather plain, but it's what's *behind* the walls that counts. Rates are a standard $105 for all rooms, single or double.

Finally we come to two hotels standing within a few doors of each other on tree-lined Macleay Street, which has an elegant air but also a lot of traffic and late-night activity.

Château Sydney, 14 Macleay St., Potts Point 2011 (tel. 02/358-2500), is designed along classical French lines, the entire frontage of the green-and-white seven-story building taken up by gracefully curved little balconies. While not exactly a château, the hotel preserves touches of plush intimacy that give it an ambience all its own. Nothing mass-produced about this establishment, from the small, chic walnut-colored lobby with mirror panels along the walls to the exquisite little restaurant and the Latin-style cocktail bar with vaulted archways and lantern illumination. Although small, with only 94 rooms, the Château also has a swimming pool, a guest laundry with ironing facilities, telex machine, and round-the-clock room service. Bedrooms are tastefully decorated, air-conditioned, and equipped with minibars, color TVs, bedside panel controls, and, on the higher floors, wondrous city and harbor views. Bathrooms come with showers only. Tariffs depend on what kind (if any) of view you want, ranging from $154 for viewless to $176 for harbor views. These rates apply for both singles and doubles.

The **Sheraton Motor Inn**, 40 Macleay St., Potts Point 2011 (tel. 02/358-1955), offers an unusual standby rate at which you can get any room that happens to be vacant for $75. Blessed with a particularly attentive staff, the Sheraton features a coffee lounge as well as a Japanese social club. The 60 bedrooms are smartly, though not lavishly, furnished, have built-in TV sets, full-length bedroom mirrors, bedside push-button telephones, and plenty of space all round. Bathrooms have showers only. Rates, again depending on the view you get, run from $128 single to $138 double.

EDGECLIFF

Now we move east to the adjoining district of Edgecliff and the **Metro Motor Inn,** 230 New South Head Rd., Edgecliff 2027 (tel. 02/328-7977). Standing diagonally opposite the Edgecliff rail and bus station, the Metro is a small, glass-fronted building on a very busy road. Modern, convenient, and bland, the hotel has a modest lobby with adjoining breakfast lounge and a great deal of room comfort. All 36 bedrooms are air-conditioned, and have bathrooms with tubs and showers, color TVs, telephones, and clock-radios. Furnishings and décor are good standard motel-style and the hotel conveniences include a guest laundry and video movies screened free each night. There's a rooftop garden deck with panoramic views. The staff will arrange baby-sitters. You pay $88 for singles or doubles.

DOUBLE BAY

Called "Double Pay" by the locals, this is one of Sydney's poshest neighborhoods, awash with Jaguars and Volvos, a region where the delis sell beluga caviar and truffled pâté and the boutiques display no price tags.

The **Savoy,** 41 Knox St., Double Bay 2028 (tel. 02/326-1411), is itself a little boutique of a hotel, though the price tag is middling moderate. A snowy frontage with marine-blue awning set amid the outdoor cafés and chic shops of the area indicates the tone of the place. Definitely not high-tech, the Savoy has no elevator and the reception is up two flights of stairs. But the establishment is utterly charming, the 36 rooms furnished in all light wood and pastel hues, intimate lighting, and avant-garde prints. The Savoy has no restaurant, but a light breakfast, served by your bedside, is included in the tariff. Guest rooms come with comfortable couches, refrigerators, telephone/clock-radios, air conditioning, color TVs, small bathrooms (shower only), and electric hairdryers. The staff is as amiable as the decor. Rooms are divided into "standard" and "deluxe," rates starting at $125 for a standard single or double, climbing to $145 for a deluxe double including Continental breakfast.

On the same street, but built over an exceedingly svelte shopping center, is the **Cosmopolitan,** Knox St., Double Bay 2028 (tel. 02/327-6871). Most of the ground floor is taken up by a sophisticated café-restaurant with a terrace portion that might have been transplanted from the Champs-Elysées, except that the coffee is better here. The sumptuous reception lobby is up on the third floor, decked out with huge leather settees in ivory and scarlet shades and an impressive historical mural depicting Old Sydney Town.

The Cosmopolitan has a beautiful swimming pool and sundeck area, fringed with shrubs and plants, and probably the most multinational clientele of any suburban establishment in Sydney. The facilities include telex, fax, and photocopying machines, the staff are experts at arranging sight-seeing tours, and room service operates till midnight. The 85 guest rooms have individually controlled air conditioning. Of medium size, with state-of-the-art fittings, they feature vast built-in double wardrobes; bedside, mirror, and wall lighting; color TVs; push-button telephones; and bathrooms with tubs and showers. Singles or doubles run $119.50 to $139.50, with a $3.50 surcharge per person for public holidays (of which there are many).

BONDI

Pronounced Bondy, the name conjures up the most famous strip of surf and sand in Australia, and the celebrated beach is there all right, but not everywhere. This means that Bondi is a very large suburb and sprawls way inland. From Bondi Junction it's several bus stops before you catch sight of water. Most of Bondi, in fact, is a rather charmless region of red-roofed brick homes, rendered interesting by an array of multinational shops and restaurants.

Greetings Bondi Junction, 79 Oxford St., Bondi Junction 2022 (tel. 02/389-9466), towers at one of Sydney's major traffic hubs with a train and bus station at the doorstep and the center city an eight-minute ride away. A huge shopping center beckons nearby and the hotel is a model of efficient modern utilitarianism. The restaurant specializes in fresh Aussie food—but prepared by Swedish chefs. Guest rooms come in generous dimensions and pleasant light-blue shadings with silent carpeting, good wardrobe space, and fair lighting, plus streamlined bathrooms, color TVs, dial telephones, air conditioning, radios, and refrigerators. They are classed into "standard" and "balcony" categories, the latter with small private balconies and the views that go with them. Standard tariffs run to $87 for singles, $95 for doubles; balconies cost $92 for singles, $99 for doubles.

A small, modern, green-roofed, red-brick motel that lives up to its name, the **City Beach Motor Inn,** 99 Curlewis St., Bondi Beach 2026 (tel. 02/365-3100), stands within wafting distance of the ocean. There's a swimming pool on the premises, although in this locality you hardly need it. The 25 units, while not lavishly furnished, are well equipped with air conditioning, electric blankets for cool nights, telephones, refrigerators, and color TVs. It also has a laundry in the house and a restaurant directly opposite. Singles pay $84; doubles, $92; triples, $128.

The **Bondi Beachside**, 152 Campbell Parade, Bondi Beach 2026 (tel. 02/30-5311), is the somewhat less velvet-lined sibling of the Double Bay's Cosmopolitan, and correspondingly more economical. Located right on the beachfront, the hotel shares premises with a steak house and a seafood restaurant. You may not need either because all suites here come with fully equipped kitchens. The lobby is small and unpretentious, but the 64 units are of fair size and decorated in appropriate ocean shadings of blue and emerald green. Wardrobes are a bit cramped (and off the floor), but lighting arrangements are excellent and some of the rooms have grand ocean vistas. All come with thermostat temperature control, bathrooms have tubs and showers, and you get color TVs and telephones, plus a cocktail bar on the premises. Each room has a private balcony. Singles or doubles run $66 to $85.

You will find more accommodations in the Bondi region in the apartment hotels and budget brackets. Right now we're off to a considerably more distant and picturesque beach location.

MANLY

Lying seven miles from the center city across the harbor as the seagull flies, Manly is best reached by either the whizzing hydrofoil (13 minutes) or the plowing ferry (35 minutes). This is a real resort with palm-fringed promenade, shopping and entertainment centers, four surfing beaches, and six calm-water harbor beaches.

Fronting the very edge of Manly's finest surfing beach is the **Manly Pacific International**, 55 N. Steyne, Manly 2095 (tel. 02/977-7666). From the outside this establishment looks like merely another block of modern seafront apartments, but the interior reaches international luxury standards, though at lower tariffs. The hotel houses Gilberts, a lavishly handsome restaurant specializing in marine delectables, an equally elegant cocktail bar, a second, more informal restaurant, and Dalleys nightclub, Manly's smartest mingling center. The Pacific has a large swimming pool and relaxation deck (despite the beach at its front door), and public rooms plush enough for society weddings or global conferences. Guest rooms are beautifully furnished, the decor resembling a sunburst of amber and scarlet. Large, air-conditioned, and caressingly carpeted, they have every possible convenience gadget without allowing technology to intrude on the charm. The main lobby and grand staircase are decked in greenery and fresh flowers, and at night the subdued thunder of the surf helps you sleep. Rates are the same for singles or doubles, prices depending on whether your room has an ocean view or faces west (inland). You pay $260 for the former, $220 for the latter.

Periwinkle, 18 E. Esplanade, Manly 2095 (tel. 02/977-4668), was built in 1895 and carefully preserves its 19th-century patina. A very attractive little guesthouse with wrought-iron colonial verandas overlooking an inner courtyard, the place has the high ceilings and spacious bedrooms characteristic of the period, as well as a cozy guest lounge with open fireplace, proud staircases, and some—not all—modern conveniences (bathrooms, for instance, are shared). There's a sunroom with color TV, a guest kitchen, laundromat, plus refrigerators and large ceiling fans. A light breakfast is included in the rates, which come to $60 for singles, $66 for doubles, $72 for a family of three.

3. Apartment Hotels

Apartments are termed "flats" or "units" here, and Sydney has many apartment hotels. Those available are great money-savers, particularly for couples, groups, or families. The difference in expenditure between eating in restaurants and preparing your own meals can be as much as 40%. All the establishments listed below offer full-size kitchens. I haven't included any with so-called kitchenettes, in which nobody can do serious cooking.

The **Florida Motor Inn,** 1 McDonald St., Potts Point 2011 (tel. 02/358-6811). Standing at the bottom of a quiet, tree-lined dead-end street of Kings Cross, the Florida is almost hidden by a curtain of greenery. Sydney's nightlife center lies only blocks away, but none of its din reaches this oasis. The hotel has a beautiful lawn and palm-fringed swimming pool with sauna, hand tennis, table tennis, and barbecue facilities, plus a most obliging staff.

The 91 units range from studios to one- and two-bedroom apartments, the latter comfortably sleeping six people. Some units are air-conditioned and all are spacious, with large built-in wardrobes, wide beds, color TVs, dial telephones, bedside clock-radios, and masses of cushions. The all-electric kitchens come with complete cooking and eating equipment, including wineglasses and egg cups; the bathrooms have tubs and showers, and shampoo. The studios rent at $119 for singles, $127 for doubles. One-bedroom units range from $142 for one person to $158 for four.

The **Medina,** 70 Roslyn Gardens, Elizabeth Bay 2011 (tel. 02/356-7400), a converted apartment block on an attractive residential street, is a handsome white building fronted by balconies and a rock garden with miniature waterfall. Guests use a private entrance that avoids the lobby, which strengthens the homey atmosphere of the place. The apartments are of fair size, tastefully furnished, air-conditioned, and fitted with luxurious deep-pile carpets, large wardrobes with mirror-faced sliding doors, and (in some) balconies offering delightful views.

All units have color TVs, push-button telephones, streamlined kitchens with all culinary utensils, and modern bathrooms (some with showers only) with ventilators that operate simultaneously with the lights. Apartments range from single to standard and deluxe, the tariffs starting at $60 per day for one person in a single to $84 for two people in a deluxe.

Medina Executive Apartments, 63 St. Marks Rd., Randwick

2031 (tel. 02/399-5144), the posher companion establishment of the above, is set in a beautifully landscaped park area of an inner suburb, close to Sydney's Showground and racecourse. This Medina consists of 60 luxurious two-bedroom units, widely spaced for elbow room. The dining areas are smart enough to entertain business contacts in, and all apartments have terraces, color TVs, and air conditioning. A pool, sauna, health spa, and gym are on the premises, along with telex facilities, laundry, and barbecues.

Peace and quiet reign supreme (except for bird calls) and the interiors are decorator designed, the kitchens equipped for gourmet cooking. You pay $160 per night single or double, $980 per week. Serviced once a week.

The Northside Medina, 167 Willoughby Rd., Crows Nest 2065 (tel. 02/430-1400). The third link in this apartment chain is located just across the Harbour Bridge, near St. Leonards rail station. A modern four-story building enclosing a tropical green garden courtyard with a thatched-roof gazebo, good-sized swimming pool, deck chairs, and barbecue facilities. The decor of the self-contained apartments is kept in delicate shades of antique white and burgundy; the furnishings include couches and settees that are simultaneously elegant and comfortable, the wall-to-wall carpeting is new and springy, and the mirrored doors of the built-in wardrobes slide in blissful silence. Other amenities include direct-dial telephones, color TV, spacious kitchens with microwave ovens, electric ranges and refrigerators, and deft little touches like daily newspaper and milk deliveries to your door. Apartments are individually air-conditioned.

You pay $100 for a studio here, $120 for a single or double one-bedroom unit. (Guests who arrive with a copy of this book get a 10% discount.)

The **Hyde Park Plaza,** 38 College St., Sydney 2000 (tel. 02/331-6933), is a fashionable white block facing the green expanse of the park. Some of the greenery seems to have crept into the foyer, which has subdued lighting, silently sliding glass doors, and enough plants and shrubs to fill a small garden. The Plaza offers more than just apartments. There is a very stylish restaurant at ground level with an adjoining cocktail bar, a rooftop recreation area with swimming pool, spa, and sauna, a Laundromat, valet service, plus fax and telex facilities.

The 180 units vary from studios to two-bedroom and family suites. All are air-conditioned, with full-size electric kitchens, color TVs, telephones, linen, and utensils. Some (not all) also have private terraces. Room decor is light and charming, with elegant rattan furniture, occasional tables, and excellent modern wall decorations. The specialty here are flexi-suites that can be rapidly converted to fit different groupings. Tariff depends on size: you pay $165 for a single regular, then up through half a dozen categories to $370 for a three-bedroom flexi-suite. A light breakfast (room service) is included in the price.

Beehive Apartments, 132 Sussex St. (at the corner of King St.), Sydney 2000 (tel. 02/290-9200). Located at the harbor end of King Street, this shiny new accommodation complex offers just that

—accommodation, with no other facilities except excellent security. The 36 units are split-level (the bedroom is upstairs) and completely self-contained. The rooms are not large, but are furnished in bright ultramodern style and equipped with every appliance, from color TVs to private laundries. There is ample wardrobe and kitchen space, every kitchen has a dishwasher, and the apartments can sleep up to four people. Rates are a standard $140 for singles or doubles; additional guests pay $10 each.

The **Merlin Plaza,** 2 Springfield Ave., Potts Point 2011 (tel. 02/356-3255). Although in the very heart of Kings Cross, the Merlin stands on a quiet little piazza with trees and a patch of lawn, well isolated from the traffic and revelry. A pleasantly contemporary building, fronted by balconies, the hotel has a very swank lobby, a Japanese restaurant on the premises, and a swimming pool and spa, as well as a roof garden with barbecue facilities.

The 120 suites are large, bright, and air-conditioned, with tasteful decor in pastel shades; some have panoramic city views. The kitchens are compact, fitted with dishwashers, and each apartment comes with a washing machine and dryer, plus the customary color TV and telephone. Furnishings appear brand-new, the wide beds invite indolence, and all bathrooms feature tubs and showers. A one-bedroom single or double costs $150. The two-bedroom units start at $170.

The **Roslyn Gardens Motor Inn,** 4 Roslyn Gardens, Kings Cross 2011 (tel. 02/358-1944), an economy establishment of surprising quality, contains 29 units in an attractive yellow-brick building fronted by balconies and waving palms. The lobby is unassuming, but the units have everything required for independent comfort: fully equipped all-electric kitchens of fair size, air conditioning, private balconies, color TVs, bathrooms with tubs and showers, and ample wardrobe space. The rooms are rather small, and the color schemes tend to be heavy on dark-brown hues. Lighting is somewhat deficient, but the beds are excellent and you get clock-radios as well. Singles cost $59; doubles, $69. Additional guests pay $15 each.

Victoria Towers, 145 Victoria St., Potts Point 2011 (tel. 02/357-3400). A modern nine-story structure with an unusual wavy stone awning over the entrance, the Victoria stands in a mellow tree-lined street of old terrace houses and an ambience reminiscent of Paris. On the premises are a restaurant, swimming pool with grand city views, a garden terrace, and telex and photocopying machines. The 48 units are equally divided between studios and one-bedrooms. All have their own balconies, lovely views, well-equipped kitchens, and streamlined bathrooms. The rooms also come with writing desks, intercoms, color TVs, telephones, and refrigerators. A lot of good taste has gone into decor and furnishings: couches and armchairs in elegant gray and beige, lighting fixtures wherever you need them. Studios start at $105 for singles; one-bedroom apartments, at $125.

The Stanford, 1 Hollywood Ave., Bondi Junction 2022 (tel. 02/389-8700). Located just off the center of Bondi Junction's shopping and transportion focus, this massive modern block has 48 new, self-contained apartments, but none below two-bedroom size. The building also houses a pool, spa and sauna, and fax, telex, and message services. The units are extremely well equipped with comfort creators and labor savers: kitchens come with dishwashers and trash disposals; individual laundry facilities within the apartments feature washing machines and dryers. Every suite has a half-enclosed terrace balcony for al fresco meals and soul-nurturing ocean views. Also color TV, radio, dial telephone, and front-door intercom. You choose between two- or three-bedroom apartments or family-size penthouses. Daily rates for two-bedrooms are $180; three-bedrooms, $205. Penthouses run $280 to $350.

Greetings Bondi Beach, 136 Curlewis St., Bondi Beach 2026 (tel. 02/365-0155). Standing within sight and sound of the ocean, this beige-brick building has a dentist's office on the premises, a small, smart reception lobby (with a brass bar-style footrail around the desk), and 56 newly renovated bargain apartments. The units are surprisingly spacious, nicely furnished in superior motel style (very superior beds), and feature color TVs, dial telephones, sufficient cooking and eating equipment, and extra-large refrigerators. Rates are simple: $88 singles or doubles.

---

4. Budget Hotels

Sydney boasts a formidable number of places in this category, so the list below is merely a sample slice. Missing, for instance, are the 20 or so hostels sprinkled all over the city. Or the cluster of cheap hotels at Kings Cross that will rent rooms by the hour. The features to remember about this list are that most of the rentals do not include private bathrooms, most of the buildings are somewhat elderly, and some of them lack lifts—pardon me, elevators.

The **YWCA,** 5-11 Wentworth Ave., Sydney 2000 (tel. 02/264-2451), looks like an office building, and three of its eight floors are in fact given over to offices. The others comprise the Y, which takes women, couples, families, and groups—but no single men. There's good elevator service, a large and low-cost cafeteria, TV lounges, laundry facilities, and absolutely sparkling bathrooms. Bedrooms are of fair size and functional, and have nice carpeting, mirrors, spacious wardrobes, and flourescent ceiling lights. Some (not all) are equipped with hot- and cold-water handbasins. Rates depend on whether or not you want a private bathroom, and start at $33 for a bathless single, $55 for a double.

Hotel Bondi, 178 Campbell Parade, Bondi Beach 2026 (tel. 02/30-3271). Built in what might be described as "seaside architecture," this place is a landmark and social center, rising white and vast on Sydney's most celebrated surfing beach promenade. There's *lots* of action, with appropriate sound effects, in four bars, a beer garden, bistro, and billiard room, all running hot every weekend. The bistro meals are both excellent and cheap, and the downtown bus stops at the front door. Bedroom furnishings are not elegant, but sufficient, and every room has TV, refrigerator, telephone, and bedside lamps. Rates run $50 to $70 for singles, $60 to $150 for doubles.

Thelellen Lodge, 11A Consett Ave., Bondi Beach 2026 (tel. 02/30-1521). Also within spray distance of the beach, but in complete contrast to the above, the Thelellen is a quiet little place with a front lawn and only 14 guest rooms. Homey and comfortably furnished, the rooms have electric fans, hot- and cold-water basins, color TVs, radios, refrigerators, and tea/coffeemaking facilities. Light breakfast (an extra) is served at your bedside. Rates start at $15 per person.

The Great Southern, 717 George St., Sydney 2000 (tel. 02/211-4311), is a large, refurbished old timer from the days of the great railroad hotels. Located downtown at the Central Station end of the city, it has a stylish and slightly rustic-looking lobby, a restaurant on the premises, and 110 guest rooms. Very busy bar trade here, but the living quarters are kept in almost soundproof seclusion. Bedrooms are compact without being cramped, furnishings simple but adequate. The rooms feature hot- and cold-water basins and share 20 good bathrooms between them. Laundry facilities for guests. The rates are $36 for singles, $50 for doubles.

Kirketon Hotel, 229 Darlinghurst Rd., Kings Cross 2010 (tel. 02/360-4333). An exceptionally well equipped and well run budget house, behind a rather plain exterior. The lobby looks drab, but the 64 bedrooms are excellently maintained and equipped with telephones, radios, TVs, refrigerators, and smoke alarms. You have the choice of rooms with private bathrooms and those with hot- and cold-water basins and shared bathrooms. Breakfast (included in the rates) is served in the Thai restaurant on the premises. Rates run from $38.50 to $58 for singles or doubles. For those on truly tight budgets there are also two bunkrooms (accommodating four persons each) costing $22 per sleeper.

SUPER-BUDGET ACCOMMODATIONS
The following places are in Kings Cross, but very well managed and impenetrable to even a glimmer of the region's red lights.

The **Macquarie Hotel,** at the corner of Hughes and Tusculum streets, Kings Cross 2011 (tel. 02/358-4133), is an attractive white building on a quiet corner directly opposite the Wayside Chapel. It has four stories, but no elevator. Also 60 guest rooms, ranging from smallish singles to self-contained family apartments housing three people comfortably. Half the rooms have private bathrooms and the others share communal bathrooms on each floor. There's no lounge area, but there is a restaurant on the premises. The rooms are nicely furnished and well carpeted, each with hot- and cold-water handbasin, color TV, ceiling fan, dial telephone, and built-in wardrobe with full-length mirror. The front door is kept locked; guests use their own keys. Rates start at $45 for singles, $50 for doubles.

Springfield Lodge, 9 Springfield Ave., Kings Cross 2011 (tel. 02/358-3222), is a pillared white building resembling a southern plantation mansion, fronted by a charming terrace with wrought-iron tables and chairs. The street is a fairly sedate plazalike affair, although just off throbbing Darlinghurst Road. Bedrooms are functionally furnished, some with private facilities, and the hallways are excellently maintained. You get ample lighting and wardrobe space, and pay according to whether or not you want a private bathroom. Singles rent at $24 and doubles go for $28; with private facilities it's $10 more.

---

5. Homestays and Farmstays

This is a program that enables overseas visitors to stay as paying guests in Australian homes, either in urban or country areas. The choices run all the way from inner Sydney suburbs to sheep and cattle ranches in the far west, the settings from mildly luxurious to modest and simple. As a general rule Homestay rates include only bed and breakfast; Farmstays offer full board with meals of farming proportions.

All the homes in question have been inspected and classified as "superior," "quality," or "economy," and priced accordingly. In the Homestays rates run from around $40 for an economy single to $50 for superior accommodations. Farmstays cost from a bottom $88 to $105 and upward on one of the great rural properties. The listings give you some idea of the surroundings to expect, plus the interests of your hosts. A couple of samples for quality Homestays in the Sydney area:

"Outgoing family living in town house with panoramic views over famous Bondi Beach. Many and varied restaurants nearby. Two minutes to city bus. Hosts interested in horse-racing, education."

"Newly decorated guest area in spacious home in prestigious suburb. Host retired, pioneer of early aviation, hostess in theatre. Homely atmosphere. Animal lovers."

For listings and application forms, contact **Bed & Breakfast Australia,** P.O. Box 408, Gordon, N.S.W. 2072 (tel. 02/498-5344).

V

EATING AND DRINKING

1. THE TOP CHOICES
2. MODERATELY PRICED RESTAURANTS
3. BUDGET RESTAURANTS
4. OLD STANDBYS, CAFÉS, AND PUBS

Sydney today is one of the world's great centers of gastronomy, but its eating facilities were created in a unique and rather tragic fashion. Every war and political upheaval around the globe generated a flood of refugees into Australia. They brought their culinary skills with them, and frequently that was all they brought. Thus immediately after World War II there was a mushrooming of Polish, Czech, Yugoslavian, German, and Rumanian establishments. A little later came the Hungarians. Then the Vietnamese and Cambodians and Koreans. At present Sydney is awash with Thai eateries. A sprinkling of Italian, Greek, and Chinese restaurants had always existed. Taken together they add up to a culinary spectrum that ranges from Argentinian to Yemenite, covering every international nuance in between.

Some 40 or so years ago the gastronomic scene was frankly dismal. Australia's national diet was standard Anglo-Irish, only slightly alleviated by the high quality of the meat and vegetables. Australians rarely drank either wine or coffee, but habitually drank tea *with* their meals. Cheese resembled flexible soap and bread was a crustless white square with the flavor of blotting paper.

Regulations enforced by the reigning wowser faction were partly to blame. They made al fresco dining almost impossible and the harmonizing of edibles and potables as difficult as humanly practicable. On one historic occasion the minions of the law actually arrested the proprietor of a top-ranking restaurant for serving genuine sherry trifle dessert (he had no liquor license).

It was in the realm of alcohol legislation that the bluenose brigade outdid itself. They used a wartime emergency act, dating back to the *First* World War, to close hotel bars at 6pm and keep them shut all day on Sunday. Since most workers got off at 5pm, the last legal drinking hour became a lunatic stampede in which you needed a shoehorn and a hand grenade to get near the bar. Restaurant drinking was restricted by constantly reducing the number of liquor licenses available for the purpose. These laws were kept in force by a strange alliance between the wowser lobby and the liquor barons. Publicans were keenly aware of the delightful advantages of the "five o'clock swill." They could sell as much grog during one frenzied hour as they would in an entire evening of leisurely sipping. The fact that they did so in conditions resembling a cattleyard didn't concern them in the slightest. So what if their bars looked like green-tiled toilets? They were saving fortunes on staff wages, light bills, furniture, and everything else they would have had to spend in order to make their establishments attractive. The fact that the blue laws virtually eliminated any meaningful competition between them suited the publicans dandy.

Only during the 1950s, after several state referendums, the influx of Europeans, and an enormous amount of media pressure, were the laws gradually relaxed. Among the incidental and wonderful by-products of this process was the flowering of Sydney's beer and wine gardens, pavement cafés, and outdoor restaurants that blend perfectly with the climate.

One hangover from the wowser epoch, oddly enough, works out in favor of the dining public. This is the institution called BYO, which stands for "Bring Your Own" (bottle, that is). Since liquor licenses are still expensive, many of the less pricey establishments operate without them. You buy your own potations (there is always a bottle shop in the vicinity) and the restaurant supplies the glasses. The advantage? Well, a passable bottle of riesling costs around $7 over the counter. Served by a waiter it would be $10.

A GASTRONOMIC PRIMER

The plethora of new restaurants has made Sydneysiders rather faddish eaters: certain foods are "in" at one moment, out the next. Currently the rage is something called nouvelle cuisine, which consists of tasty half-rations sold for double prices. Brought into vogue by figure-conscious women, who rave about it, it doesn't go over nearly as well with their hungry male escorts.

Local Specialties

Actually there is no such thing as an Australian cuisine, but there are a number of outstanding national dishes. They don't include kangaroo-tail soup, which is difficult to obtain and mostly canned for export to the Far East. There is, however, roast spring lamb in mint sauce and carpetbagger steak (beef tenderloin stuffed with oysters). And that earthy but wonderful local combination, steak and eggs: a plate-size steak with two fried eggs on top, which some rural families still eat for breakfast. Also a selection of seafood that ranks among the world's finest: the small sweet Sydney rock oysters prepared Kilpatrick, with a slice of fried bacon; Queensland snapper, coral trout, and the tender and subtle-tasting barramundi (not obtainable anywhere outside Australia); Moreton Bay bugs, an outrageously misnamed species of miniature crustacean; Tasmanian scallops and lightly grilled John Dory, another fish found only in Australian waters; and Victorian yabbies (a small type of lobster) and their larger relative, the crayfish.

Here I must mention two Oz specialties which might be mercifully forgotten, but loom so large that they can't be ignored. One is the meat pie. This Down Under equivalent of the hot dog and hamburger consists of an outer crust of soggy pastry filled with anonymous meat, the whole concoction drenched in tomato sauce before consumption. It tastes nearly as gruesome as it sounds, and the inhabitants of Oz put away astronomic quantities of it. Everybody eats them, from members of Parliament to construction workers, often two or three at one sitting or standing. A Melbourne football crowd gobbled up 40,000 of them on a single memorable Saturday afternoon. Together with chips (french fries) these pies could be said to form the basic diet of a large segment of the population. Since no one has ever quite fathomed the mystery of their meat contents, I would advise visitors to treat them with caution.

The other great Aussie addiction is to a dark and odorous yeast spread called Vegemite. "Addiction" is the right term, because many Australians seem unable to survive when deprived of it. They drag jars of the stuff along with them wherever they go, including Antarctic surveys. When residing in foreign parts they spend vast amounts of time scouring the shops for it, loudly bemoaning that none of the substitutes they find tastes like the real thing. Vegemite is not an acquired taste—you have to be reared on it from childhood. Spread *thinly* on toast, the flavor is pleasant in a salty way. But you'll never become a real aficionado unless you've had it for breakfast since you were six.

A handful of specialties aside, Sydney's gastronomic excellence is based on foreign cooking—though not necessarily cooked by foreigners. Imported—that is non–Anglo-Irish—establishments outnumber the native variety by at least five to one. The restaurant scene is dominated by hundreds of small, family-run, and modestly priced eateries dishing up Greek moussaka, Indian curries, Hungarian goulash, Yugoslav raznici, Chinese dim sum, Austrian schnitzel, Italian lasagne, Mideastern felafel, Polish dumplings, German sauerbraten, and so on—usually cooked by mom and served by pop and daughter.

The same variegated influence pervades the delicatessen stores, which are among the best, cheapest, and most cosmopolitan found anywhere. Not even the famed New York delis can match the quality of the rollmops, salami, mortadella, Camembert, brie, liptauer, pickled cucumbers, potato salad, and ham sold here—and with the exception of certain deluxe dispensaries, at far lower prices. One reason for this is that a Sydney sandwich is just that, not a triple-layer vegetable pile as in America.

Bush Tucker

Ironically, the latest Oz food fashion is actually the oldest. These are the delicacies of the original Australians, the Aborigines, hitherto ignored or despised by the white usurpers of the continent. But a television series on bush tucker, aired for the 1988 bicentennial, evoked a tremendous public response and produced a wave of recipe books and at least one commercial enterprise that grows and packages this line of edibles, which is traditionally gathered only by nomadic tribesmen.

Now you can actually get a taste of such culinary curiosities as roasted witchety grubs (the flavor resembles shrimp), hairy litchi, wild ginger, burrawang nuts, green ants, and sautéed mangrove worms, alongside a portion of grilled python or crocodile steak, or goanna tail (which tastes like chicken) preceded by bunya nut soup and concluded with a sorbet made from wattle seeds.

A few of these items appear on the menus of some deluxe Sydney restaurants—at prices that would make an Aboriginal hunter's head spin. You can also mail order them from the **Bush Tucker Supply Company,** P.O. Box B103, Boronia Park, N.S.W. 2111.

Local Brews

Although in recent decades Australians have learned to appreciate their wines, beer remains the national drink, the native nectar. Statistically, Aussies down 30 gallons of beer per throat annually, a figure that becomes even more impressive when you remember that this national consumption total counts children and teetotalers. This puts them slightly below the Belgians and Bavarians—but only slightly. On the other hand, Oz beer is so much stronger than either the continental or American brews that their intake should count about 20 points more. This seems an opportune place to warn you that you can get loaded on Australian beer very quickly, unless you make a point of asking for the "light" varieties.

Every Australian state has its own brands of beer, and the quality is universally high, though New South Wales doesn't quite come up to the standard of the Tasmanian, Victorian, and Western Australian products. Beer sells in small "middies" or large "schooners," with a middy costing from $1.40 to $1.80, depending on where and in what manner of pub you order it. If you're drinking in a group, custom demands that you "shout" in turn, meaning that every member of the group pays for a round in sequence. But *never* out of sequence—Australians take a dim view of anyone ramming largesse down their throats, unless that person has just backed a winner at the races.

The Australian wine industry is almost exactly as old (or young) as the Californian, and in some respects strikingly similar. After generations of indifference, Australians have finally taken to their grape products with such enthusiasm that the growers can't keep pace with the demand. The most illustrious wine region in the country is South Australia's Barossa Valley. But New South Wales has its own wine country, the Hunter Region, which we'll visit for a little sampling. As a whole, Australia is great on light table wines, not so good in the heavy varieties, fair in the champagne range. The vermouth, dry or sweet, is outstanding, as are riesling and chardonnay. Claret, moselle, chablis, and sauterne are a joy to drink — and cheap to boot, as long as you buy them over the counter. Once a restaurant markup goes on top, it's a different story.

If you wish to delve deeper into this fascinating study, you can get highly knowledgeable and erudite brochures by writing to the **Australian Wine and Brandy Corporation,** Box 3649, GPO, Sydney 2001.

Another drink, coffee, enjoyed an even more remarkable rise in popular favor. Just 20 years ago Australians were as devoted to tea as the English, but the present generation has switched to coffee. Chief reason for this was the introduction of the espresso machine, which changed the process of coffee making. Today these miracle contraptions have proliferated, and when you order coffee you almost automatically get cappuccino. If you don't like the froth or the chocolate shavings, order a "flat white" (unless you want it black). In Sydney the product is generally excellent, but in the smaller towns it's still safer to stick to tea. Coffee, again depending on location, ranges from $1 to $2.20 per cup.

An Introduction to Sydney's Restaurants

Let me start by saying that restaurants fill about 1,600 column inches in the Sydney telephone books, so what you get here is necessarily a mere sampling. Some of my Sydney friends will fume over the omissions, but that can't be helped. Even in the top price bracket, the smallest, it is quite impossible to list anywhere near the total number of establishments. You must assume that there are many more where these chosen few came from.

It is likewise impossible to enforce strict separation between independent, hotel, and pub restaurants. Some of the best eateries are located in elderly pubs and several of the elite establishments in hotels (as well as some of the worst). What you'll find, therefore, is a mixture of all three. At the end we'll conduct a pub crawl, a fast-paced trot around the hostelries in which the food is as highly rated as the liquor. Geographically most of the places described are in central locations, with only a few excursions to the outer suburbs.

1. The Top Choices

These are *some* (nowhere near all) of Sydney's deluxe restaurants. On the international price scale they rank slightly below equivalent establishments in New York, Paris, or London, but not very much. Your check depends largely on what manner of potables you order—you can double it by imbibing certain vintage wines. In all places in this price bracket advance reservations are advisable; in several they are essential.

A Note on Prices
 All prices cited in this guide are in Australian dollars. As we go to press, $1 Australian = approximately 75¢ U.S., which means that a restaurant meal listed at $40 actually costs only about $30 in U.S. dollars.

 Bilson's, International Passenger Terminal, Circular Quay West (tel. 02/251-5600). An amazing establishment that still carries the name of an illustrious chef (Tony Bilson) who left years ago to found a restaurant of his own (Fine Bouche). But no matter—Bilson's fame as a premier gourmet restaurant remains as firmly fixed as the splendor of its location. Set on the upper level of Sydney's main ocean-liner dock, the place features wraparound glass walls offering a permanent vista of the Opera House, the bridge, and most of the magnificent harbor. And the clientele could pass for a who's who of visiting overseas celebrities and the stars of Australia's entertainment, sports, and political firmament.

 The fare is in keeping with the patronage. The menu changes monthly, but a characteristic selection would be smoked water buffalo salad, venison pie, roasted hare with sauce poivrade, a classic escalope of salmon les frères Troisgros, braised ham in red wine sauce, veal sweetbreads champignons, and—if you can manage a conclusion—a superlative lemon soufflé. The wine cellar is among the half dozen best (some say *the* best) on the continent. And in the guest book your signature might stand beside those of Mick Jagger, Paul Hogan, Wendy Hughes, or—possibly—Prime Minister Hawke. A three-course dinner here would come to over $100. Open six days a week, till 10:30pm; closed Sunday. The lunch menu, Monday though Friday, is more limited but also less costly.

 Prunier's, 65 Ocean St., Woollahra (tel. 02/32-1974), is a hallowed dining haven of the upper crust located on one of the finest residential streets, bristling with flag-flying mansions housing foreign consulates. The cuisine is French, the setting ultra-plush, the service ambassadorial. The prices . . . well, appropriate.

 Prunier's lies sheltered behind a beautiful floodlit garden, bordered by a patio. You can dine in this half-open flower-decked vestibule or in the actual dining room adjoining it. The decor is understated and restful, with an air of exclusivity that only certain international establishments can conjure up. The menu is unchanging, though every evening has its own "specials," recited verbally by the waiter. As an entrée you might select the cold crayfish soup, made of chilled fresh tomatoes with floating morsels of lobster meat, or the Queensland crab with sliced avocado. (Crayfish, by the way, is the usual Australian term for lobster.) Main courses, while mostly French, are downright Teutonic in proportion. This is one of the few top-notch hostelries where they actually heap your plate.

 As a main course you might select one of the beef or poultry creations. The beef is magnificent and comes grilled exactly as ordered. I had my filet marinated in ginger and brandy, served with a green apple salad. The ginger flavor comes through slight and subtle, just enough to impart an iota of fiery sweetness to the meat. The wine list offers you the choice of either ordering the brands listed or making a special request for aged wines. If you choose the latter, the bottles, not another list, are brought to your table. The bill for three courses (not including wine) will be around $60. Prunier's is open Monday through Saturday till 10pm.

Bayswater Brasserie, 32 Bayswater Rd., Kings Cross (tel. 02/357-2749). Considered by many the best of its breed in town, this French-Italian gourmet spot has the distinction of also serving light snacks apart from regular repasts, as well as breakfast on Saturday and Sunday. The clientele is top-heavy with wealthy business executives and the atmosphere is one of gilt-edged activity. Seating arrangements include a charming and almost secluded courtyard and a secluded back room that's downright idyllic. The setting is part pub, part bistro—you choose one or the other according to mood. During the day the light streams in through glasshouse windows, but at night the place becomes darkly romantic, filled with promises not written on contract forms.

There's nothing standard about the Bayswater's bill of fare. The menu is almost adventurous in its variety. Appetizers, for instance, include a plate of freshly made goose sausages served with sweet potato, thick peasant-style lima bean soup, and chickpea puree. Main courses follow the same pattern, or rather the absence of a pattern: there is a veal tongue that melts in your mouth accompanied by avocado, a rare choice between pan-fried octopus and barbecued calamari, rolled stuffed loin of lamb with sweet okra, plus a vast array of pasta dishes, from meat to marine, that you won't usually find in the plusher restaurants. But this is precisely the special charm of the BB (as its legions of fans call it) as it can suit very nearly every palate—though not quite every purse. For dessert the BB offers possibly the richest hazelnut torte south of the equator. A three-course meal will hover somewhere between $25 and $38. Open every day till 11:15 pm. Reservations a *must.*

Barrenjoey House, 1108 Barrenjoey Rd., Palm Beach (tel. 02/919-4001), is another contender for the Parsley crown. A great many highly knowledgeable locals swear that this is Sydney's finest hostelry, but their judgment may have been influenced by the superb surroundings. The Barrenjoey is quite a ways out of town, nestling secretively in a corner of Palm Beach. You can reach it by taking the Palm Beach bus, departing every 30 minutes from Wynyard Station, but it's a lengthy ride. In case you don't feel up to the homeward haul the same evening, the establishment also offers overnight accommodation ($75 including breakfast).

Although the place has ample indoor seating, you come here for al fresco meals, framed by some of the most glorious beach vistas this town can offer. The outdoor dining area is a canvas-covered courtyard, cool on even the hottest days, with the air of a tropical patio. The garden grows wildly luxuriant all around and the ocean

Revolving Restaurants

Sydney has three revolving restaurants, which are more frequently confused than any other attraction. The reason is that two of them happen to be located in the same tower and run by the same company. At the **Sydney Tower Restaurant,** Centrepoint, at the corner of Pitt and Market streets (tel. 02/233-3722), we are concerned only with level 1, the International Restaurant (level 2 is a moderately priced self-service eatery).

The catch with revolving restaurants the world over is that all the emphasis rests on the panoramic viewing, with little left for the food. This is definitely not the case here. True, the vista below is enthralling, but so is most of the menu. A warning note here: Your vantage position is 1,000 feet up, so if heights interfere with your appetite, you'd better dine somewhere else. For most patrons the slowly unfolding city and harbor panorama is sheer joy, and the management guarantees you a ringside seat, though not necessarily by the window. The revolving mechanism works silently and smoothly, as does the service. Menu and wine list are somewhat shorter than you would expect in a svelte establishment, but that's the only concession made to the special nature of this aerie.

Lunch and dinner menus are the same here, but the luncheon fare comes considerably cheaper. For dinner, all appetizers cost a standard $10; all main courses, $20. Only the dessert prices vary. Among appetizers are fresh avocado pear with creamy fish mousse, and a wonderfully tangy seafood terrine with mango-yogurt sauce. Turning to the main courses, there is an unusually good smoked loin of pork in cutlet form, served with red cabbage in a delicately pungent caraway sauce, or a classic rack of lamb, floating in a red wine and mustard sauce. For dessert you couldn't do much better than to order the mascarpone with amaretto, an Italian specialty allegedly prepared from a "secret" recipe (I have no idea of the ingredients except that they are *dolce*, alcoholic, and ambrosial). This repast (minus wine) costs $45.

If you're interested in Sydney's third revolving restaurant, it's the **Summit,** on the 47th floor of Australia Square Tower, George St. (tel. 02/27-9777). The Summit is slightly more expensive than the Sydney Tower, and somewhat more traditional. It has dancing six nights a week.

All the above establishments are open all week till midnight. Let me add at this point that Australia Square happens to be round, probably for the same reason that Circular Quay is rectangular.

breeze acts like a perfumed caress. The courses keep coming, and it's hard to tear yourself away.

It's equally hard to find a label for the cuisine: "Australian" as far as the freshness of the seafood and vegetables is concerned, but with so many varied and alien touches that you can't press a general stamp on the fare. You might call it "advanced Aussie with a Gallic flair." What's more, the menu changes weekly and so does the subtle shifting of the various culinary influences. Only the splendid wine list remains permanent. For starters you'd do well to choose among the changing pâtés—both the quail and the pork variations are dreamy. Then an oceanic dish, such as the whole broiled lobster in hazelnut-oil dressing. For dessert, try one of the fruit mousses: mango or peach or melon alongside a serving of exotic ice cream such as rhubarb or passion fruit. The place is absolutely packed with Sydney's sophisticated palates and those who wish to pass as such. Three courses will come to around $45, excluding wine, naturally. Open seven days a week till 10:30pm, but the wondrous courtyard is open only in summer.

For more outdoor dining and scenic enchantment, but of a different kind, there is the **Phantom of the Opera,** 17 Circular Quay West, The Rocks (tel. 02/27-2755). This hostelry is associated with the Australian Wine Centre and has the pleasant duty of acting as a sampling room. You get a selection of some 37 wines by the glass and can decide by tasting which one you'd like to drink with your meal. On a mellow evening you might sit on the open deck and find the harbor spectacle so engrossing that you forget about dinner—temporarily, anyway. Even the Old Coathanger of the Harbour Bridge becomes a thing of charm and beauty when viewed in the dimming light. All around you the boats and ferries skim, the lights start twinkling, and you lean back and let the magic enfold you—aided by the sampled wine.

Service at the Phantom is leisurely, but the food is worth waiting for. If you've never tasted seafood kebabs, this is the place to try them. Or the absolutely masterful mushroom entrée, consisting of fresh mushrooms baked with thin strips of bacon and glazed with melted cheese. Or the Madam Butterfly, steamed mussels with shallots in a white wine and cream sauce. Since this is very much a seafood house you should stick to marine edibles for your main course. Perhaps the platter of grilled prawns and baby octopus. For dessert there are light hazelnut concoctions in various forms. The Phantom is undoubtedly a tourist place, but without the usual flaws of such establishments: it doesn't cut corners on the cuisine and it certainly doesn't hurry one set of patrons to make room for the next. A full meal comes to around $30, but this more than doubles in one fell swoop if you order a bottle of one of the magnificent vintage wines you sampled beforehand. Open seven days a week till midnight.

Imperial Peking, 15 Circular Quay West, The Rocks (tel. 02/27-7073). There are actually four Imperial Pekings in Sydney, all in the same gastronomic class. I picked this one because of its spectacular harbor views (ask for a window table when you make your reservations) and intriguing history. This is the dream come true of Alfred Lai, architect by training, restaurateur by inclination. Lai saw his chance when he heard of a decrepit old warehouse standing empty on Circular Quay. He put both his talent and his money to work and transformed it into an absolutely gorgeous eating palace, which today ranks as one of the top trio of Chinese restaurants in Australia. Make no mistake—what you get here is haute cuisine Mandarin style, the only fare in the world that can beat the French for sheer subtlety and variety. In case you haven't tasted it before, it resembles the ordinary Cantonese version about as much as a custom-tailored Savile Row suit resembles a pair of jeans. Chow mein is not on the menu.

Possibly because of its location, the Imperial's fare emphasizes seafood rather more than is usual in Chinese restaurants. And the wine list is vastly more extensive. If you dine here with a local, he'll be able to point out some of the VIPs clicking chopsticks around you—the Imperial draws them like a magnet. Crabs, lobsters, and the delicious little yabbies are kept live in huge glass tanks until the moment you order them. You can also get real bird's-nest soup, not the insipid imitation. Otherwise it's a rather agonizing choice from a menu featuring over 180 dishes (not including an auxiliary listing of daily specials). Have a stab at the abalone in mustard sauce or the salt-and-pepper mudcrab, if your palate craves something fiery. Or switch to dry-land critters, like the delicately spiced Peking shredded beef or the beef in plum sauce. A well-balanced repast here will cost around $35. Open Sunday through Thursday till 10:30pm, Friday and Saturday till midnight.

Oasis Seros, 495 Oxford St., Paddington (tel. 02/33-3377), is a delightfully eccentric place that Sydneysiders have taken to in a *big* way. It's a curiosity in several respects. First, because Oxford Street is generally a site for budget fare, which the Oasis is assuredly not. Second, instead of laying on the old-world chandelier decor, the owners have chosen a streamlined, starkly Scandinavian style of interior in which the most ornamental features are the crisply white table linen and gleaming cutlery. Finally, the cuisine follows no discernible style except the chef's inspiration and imagination. You might call it Franco-Asian with colonial touches thrown in. While this might disturb a culinary purist, it makes eating at the Oasis an adventure and has earned the place a near-fanatical clientele.

The trouble with this kind of inspirational cooking is that whatever table tidbits I quote will probably no longer grace the menu by the time you get to see it. So simply to give you an idea of what to expect: there was a clear lobster soup in which floated wonton stuffed with crabmeat, roast quail with delicately spiced herb stuffing, crisply roasted duck served with Chinese ginger buns and vegetables . . . and so on, right through the equally unorthodox desserts. The wine list is choice, very long, and compiled with the knowing care of an expert—nothing experimental in the nectar department. A glass of French champagne comes on the house. Your meal, excluding drinks, will come to perhaps $70, not surprising in view of the fact that the chef has won several awards for his skill and daring. The Oasis is open five days a week till 10pm; closed Sunday and Monday.

Encore, in the Sebel Town House, 23 Elizabeth Bay Rd., Elizabeth Bay (tel. 02/358-3244), is the restaurant of the Sebel Town House (see my hotel recommendation) and there's nothing even remotely adventurous about *this* hostelry. It's an upper-crust restaurant in the classic tradition: the cuisine, French with a few Australian embellishments; the service, honed to a fine edge; the floral decorations, exactly as they should be. There is an air of cool, refined elegance about the place that extends to the greeting the maître d' bestows on the guests. The crystal glassware and the table silver reflect the high polish of the cedarwood Edwardiana all around. A place for subdued conversation and discreet celebrity spotting, to feast a business client, or to entertain a blasé visitor.

The selection of appetizers is famous here: asparagus tips served with avocados and mangoes in ginger yogurt, or the lamb's brain wrapped in cooked bacon served on an apple glaze. For the main course you might choose a classic filet steak that comes with Café de Paris butter, or the equally classic saddle of lamb. The dessert specialty of the house is dark-chocolate tulips filled with fruit ice creams. You'll pay around $40 for all this. Being a hotel restaurant, the Encore is open for breakfast, lunch, and dinner every day, and serves late suppers after 11pm.

Sir Archibald's, in the Holiday Inn Menzies, 14 Carrington St. (tel. 02/20232, ext. 2744). The Menzies was one of Sydney's staid, traditional top-drawer hotels before being taken over, gilded, and streamlined by the Holiday Inn chain a few years ago. The upstairs dining room, now Archibald's restaurant, underwent a virtual metamorphosis and emerged as an ultra-smart little boutique of epicureanism. A small place, holding only 14 tables, it has a domed ceiling dominated by a majestic crystal chandelier. Far from disturbing the intimacy of the room, the lighting somehow enhances it. Tables made of genuine cedarwood, silk-spanned walls, and chairs upholstered with tapestry complete the impression of romantic salon-size elegance.

The menu is printed not only in French and English but also in Braille, a thoughtful touch that other establishments might do well to follow. The wine list is carefully balanced, prices ranging from a modest $19 to a hefty $145 for a bottle of imported bubbly. In between lie 41 labels of Australian wines, including some famous vintages that would cost you twice as much as your entire meal. The cuisine is French, but the tiered trolley-borne cheese gallery is international. One of the entries is snail dumplings served with mild paprika cream that doesn't overwhelm the delicacy of the snail flavor. For a main course there is a magnificent lobster thermidor, or the lesser-known mixed filets of whiting and shrimp, floating in a champagne-and-orange sauce. The cheese selection is as vast as the dessert array is brief, the most intriguing of the latter being cherries poached in honey and port wine, served with cinnamon ice cream. You won't be surprised to learn that three courses here run around $55 to $60. Open Monday through Saturday till 10pm.

Chez Oz, 23 Craigend St., Darlinghurst (tel. 02/332-4866). The rub with recommending anything "trendy" lies in the fickleness of that attribute. By the time you reach print the trend may have shifted completely. But there's no getting around the Oz. Although currently the trendiest of trendy, it also happens to be one of

Sydney's finest hostelries. But while the public passion lasts, I'd advise you to reserve a table well ahead of time if you wish to avoid a longish wait.

The Oz is located in a deceptively plain and small converted house in a residential section of Kings Cross. You realize how deceptive the façade is the moment you step inside. The flower arrangements are superb, the floors oak, the modern prints on the pale-white walls chosen and hung with a cognoscente's eye for effect. You get ushered to your table with the same courtly amiability as the socialites, movie starlets, foreign diplomats, and native *jeunesse d'orée* around you.

The restaurant offers light nouvelle-style cuisine, slightly California-flavored, but with more generous servings than most nouvelle restaurants. For starters you can order the terrific chicken bouillon, rich with floating ravioli stuffed with goat cheese, or alternatively, the warm scallop mousse in saffron butter sauce. Then perhaps grilled calves' liver surrounded by cooked and peeled pears or the crisped whiting with salad plus the most crunchily delicious french fries you've ever tasted. (Well, yes, it's just fish and chips, but only insofar as both a Yugo and a Jaguar are just *cars*.) The average meal, if you can use the term, comes to $50, excluding the special house cocktails and the wine. Open five days a week till 10pm; closed Sunday and Monday.

2. Moderately Priced Restaurants

The restaurants listed below should actually be classified as "upper-" and "lower-middle" because they span such a wide price spectrum. But I felt that this might make the chapter read like a sociological treatise. Instead I've divided them according to geographical location, which makes more practical sense. A great many of them are BYO, which considerably reduces your drinking expenses. And rest assured, there's always a bottle shop nearby.

IN THE CENTER CITY

Nesting one flight up in the ornately Victorian Strand Arcade is **Claudine's,** 412 George St., Gallery Level, First Floor (tel. 02/233-3473). Not only is there really a Claudine, but she's French-born and the best advertisement her hostelry could possibly get. Hard to say which is the more charming—the restaurant or its owner. Although French and seafood oriented, the menu is fairly international and includes enough veal, beef, and poultry to satisfy those grown tired of marine delectables. You can order a nicely balanced mixture of, say, seafood starters, meat for the middle course, and for dessert—well, dessert. The fare is equally excellent in all categories, and the establishment fully licensed. At lunchtime the swank business crowd predominates; at dinner it becomes a favored rendezvous retreat. You pay around $28 for your meal. Open Monday through Saturday till 11pm.

Dining in a Church

Have you ever dined, wined, and danced in a Presbyterian church? Chances are you haven't. You can catch up on that experience by going to **The Abbey,** 156 Bridge Rd., Glebe (tel. 02/660-1211). Glebe is an inner and not very fashionable suburb adjoining the center city. The church is an edifice built in 1879 by the famous local architect Thomas Rowe. The building was restored in 1980, leaving the exterior intact. The interior now is a stunningly beautiful mixture of church and banquet hall. The high wooden rafters, stained-glass windows, and candle chandeliers blend superbly with the parquet floor and snowy table linen, giving the dining room an air of dignity, supreme comfort, and just a slight touch of austerity.

There is nothing in the least austere about the food, however, among the best served in this town. Or the lengthy and impressive wine list. There is a grand piano, played later in the evening for those who wish to dance. Cost of a meal is around $50. Reservations are essential. Open six days a week till midnight; closed Sunday.

Harpoon Harry's, 42 Wentworth Ave. (tel. 02/264-9089), is a pub restaurant, but of the posh variety. Housed in the Macquarie Hotel, this seafood bistro boasts marble bars, upholstered chairs, and an enormous glass tank alive with lobsters. Harry's is among the top favorites for locals, so advance reservations are recommended. The place serves juicy steaks apart from ocean fare, and a three-course meal costs around $34. They also serve special children's meals at a quarter that price. It's a good place to try some local specialties, Hawkesbury River oysters, for instance, or the John Dory, a fish unique to Australian waters and one of the finest water delicacies on earth. Upstairs on the same premises there is a considerably cheaper snack bar. Open Monday through Saturday till 10pm.

La Normandie, 35 Clarence St. (tel. 02/29-3490), is an established French eating house run by a husband-and-wife team, which seems to attract every French visitor to these shores. French travel agencies and airlines make a point of steering their customers to the Normandie, thus ensuring they won't get complaints on the subject of cuisine. The place also draws a devoted Australian business clientele, mainly executives with educated taste buds. Possibly for their benefit the management has meat pie on the menu—not, to be sure, the standard mystery concoction beloved to football crowds, but a crisply delicious gourmet bread filled with beef bourguignon steak and kidney, or chicken and mushrooms. Otherwise the fare is traditional French: sirloin steak coated in Dijon mustard, roast duckling with herb glaze, and a mouth-melting loin of pork richly brushed with Calvados. The restaurant is fully licensed and has an

Dining with a View

Undoubtedly the most famous address in Australia belongs to **Bennelong,** in the Sydney Opera House, Bennelong Point (tel. 02/250-7578). The Bennelong is the restaurant attached to the Opera House and offers some of the most magnificent views the city can boast. Every table comes with a panorama. It takes a powerful menu to compete with these surroundings, and the Bennelong has it. What's more, the service is tailored for location. The dining process is divided into pre-theater and post-theater meals, served speedily and smoothly at the appropriate times. To further streamline arrangements there are two set-price meals: $26.50 for two courses and coffee or $29.50 for three courses. The place is fully licensed, and drinks, of course, come separately. The breathtaking vista is on the house.

Sitting smack in the center of Sydney's top tourist attraction, the Bennelong tries to please as many global palates as possible, so you get a very mixed fare, all of it well prepared and served with flourish. But this is decidedly a tourist spot, and locals are somewhat scarce. Try some of the more unusual dishes, such as buffalo filets (slightly gamey and very tasty), sugar-cured river trout, and desserts such as the mixture of chocolate terrine and apple caramel. The wines are choice Australians, most reasonably priced. Open Monday through Saturday, with après-opera supper served till 11:30pm.

extensive wine list. Meals add up to $28. Open six days a week till 10pm; closed Sunday.

Capitan Torres, 73 Liverpool St. (tel. 02/264-5574), is as Spanish as the name sounds. Even the wine is Andalusian rather than Aussie. This used to be one of Sydney's prime budget restaurants, but its fame spread and, while still prime, it's budget no longer. The feature that has remained unchanged is the hugeness of the helpings. You'd better bring a healthy appetite if you expect to get through more than one course. The cuisine is spicily Iberian—and this includes Portuguese dishes, like the roast chicken in tomato-and-wine sauce. On the Spanish side you can order a platter of grilled sardines, casseroled quail, barbecued steaks, saffron-hued paella, and the absolutely enormous platter of mixed, grilled seafood. Sangría comes by the carafe, and you need a large one to irrigate this intake of comestibles. It's a happy, noisy, and crowded place, where you can feast for $22. Open daily till 11:30pm.

Italian Village, 7 Circular Quay West, The Rocks (tel. 02/27-8440), is an amazing replica of an Italian village, crammed with artifacts shipped over from various provinces and constructed as one vast three-story restaurant. It's touristy, of course, but simultaneously quite genuine, especially in its offerings of authentic specialties from various Italian regions. On top of this atmosphere you get irresistible views of the opera house and the harbor from all three levels. Try to get an outside table on the Piazza Toscana to experience the full effect of the interior decor and exterior scenery. Each of the three "village" stratas boasts its own bar, so you won't exactly run dry. The fare covers all bases, from basic pizza to a subtly blended dish of octopus marinated in garlic, olive oil, and chili. You can eat well here for $29. Open every day till 10:30pm.

Minar, 2 Albert St., Circular Quay (tel. 02/27-9323). Housed in the Quay Apartment Building—a most prestigious abode—this famed Indian eatery offers an unusually wide selection of vegetarian dishes alongside traditional Indian haute cuisine—as well as harbor views, a distinctly upper-crust clientele, and some of the smoothest, most knowledgeable service in town. The fare is not adventurous but very comprehensive: covering the entire range of palate pleasers from the gentle glow of crushed herbs to the fiery delight of really hot curry selections. The Minar's culinary fame rests on its tandoori dishes (make sure to sample the superb bread) and its outstanding array of desserts and sweetmeats. Equally memorable is the rack of lamb served in yogurt. The Indian dancers who appear on weekend nights seem quite unnecessary; they merely distract from the food. Your check will come to around $25, but only if you ignore the lengthy wine list. Open seven days a week till 11pm.

Machiavelli Ristorante, 123 Clarence St. (tel. 02/29-3748). This is a lunch-only place, operating Monday through Friday from noon to 2:30, but so much an institution that it had to be included. Begun as a side venture of the Toppi family, the Ristorante almost overnight captivated the local luncheon market through its combination of quality food, slick service, and eminently sensible prices. The vaulted white premises have a charmingly rustic air, accentuated by a huge hanging display of bacon, hams, and sausages. The wall is graced by a portrait of cunning namesake Niccolò himself, but all around hang photos of Aussie politicos, past and present. A gentle allusion? Anyway, don't miss the antipasto here, followed, perhaps, by the delicious chicken breasts marsala. The concluding coffee will jolt you through the day. You'll pay around $19.

Diethnes, 336 Pitt St. (tel. 02/267-8956), one of the oldest Greek hostelries in town (established in 1953), has a culinary reputation based on serving everybody's Hellenic favorites. Nothing remotely nouvelle here—the devoted clientele would scream blue murder at innovations. You descend a flight of stairs into a large cellarlike basement, graced with white Athenian pillars and redolent with friendly vibes. Service is fast, efficient, and smiling, and prices are happily reasonable. You order standard and excellent Greek fare (even the Australian John Dory comes with Greek salad). Otherwise it's moussaka, the great cheese-and-spinach pie called spanakopita, dolmades, calamari, and nine various and wonderful lamb dishes. The dessert array is equally solid, mostly drenched in honey and filled with crushed almonds. You could try some of the imported Greek wines to harmonize with the meal. Three courses will come to around $18. Open six days till 10pm; closed Sunday.

The **Lord Nelson Hotel Brasserie,** at the corner of Kent and Argyle streets, The Rocks (tel. 02/251-4044), is one of the few true brasseries, in the exact meaning of the term, in town. It serves the beers actually brewed in the hotel in which it is located. The building is an elderly, white, unpretentious structure, but the upstairs brasserie welcomes you with considerable chic. And it serves a lot of items besides beer—an impressive array of wines, for example, plus an excellent menu that includes lamb brains and Sydney rock oysters Kilpatrick for entrées; grilled spatchcock, and veal Cleopatra (on a bed of steamed rice, drenched in a seafood-and-cream sauce) as main courses; and parfait aux noix (walnut parfait in chocolate sauce) for dessert. This meal would cost about $28, excluding drinks. Open six days a week till 10pm; closed Sunday.

CHINATOWN

Sydney's Chinatown is located in what used to be the grimy end of the city, where the markets sprawled. Some of the markets are still there, but Chinatown has undergone a radical facelift: dry-cleaned, spruced, and gentrified almost beyond recognition. Dixon Street and vicinity seems to consist of restaurants beside and on top of each other. But for customers they depend mainly on the Chinese populace and only secondarily on tourism. For that reason the fare they serve is more authentic than in other parts of town, and some are polite—or condescending enough—to mark certain items "Authentic Chinese Dish" for the benefit of visiting *gweilo.*

The restaurants range from metal-furnished cafeterias reminiscent of army chow lines to ornately silken eating places with superb service, mile-long menus, and appropriate prices. Here I can give you only a very brief rundown of a few of the establishments in the area. Consider each one duplicated at least thrice. Plus a few generalities: The menu term dim sum means something different from what you get in the U.S. In Sydney it denotes a plump little meat dumpling, either boiled or fried, but very tasty in either form. Chinese tea does not usually come as part of your meal—it has to be ordered and paid for separately. And while the vast majority of Chinatown establishments are indeed Chinese, you'll find a few Thai and Vietnamese establishments sprinkled among them.

Dixon Discount, 41 Dixon St. (tel. 02/211-2217), is probably the cheapest eatery in the neighborhood, but of surprising quality (if you discount the decor, of which there isn't any). It's a BYO serving up items like scallops with ginger, crab hotpot with vermicelli, and chicken basted in Chinese wine. You'll pay around $10 for three courses. Open daily till midnight.

New Teahouse of the August Moon, 68 Dixon St. (tel. 02/212-4702). Despite its awful misnomer, this is an excellent noodle restaurant, serving more noodle varieties than I ever knew existed. They come disguised as porridge with various toppings, crispy-dry, soft, in soup, made of wheat flour, or made of rice. You could compose an entire banquet without duplicating a flavor. Three courses cost around $11. Open every day till 1am.

The top-flight establishments are easily recognized corner

buildings festooned with gigantic signs. All are licensed and most offer musical entertainment (of sorts) several times a week.

Emperor's Garden, at the corner of Hay and Dixon streets, Haymarket (tel. 02/211-2135), famous for vegetable rolls and dumplings as well as for its yum cha, is probably the best neighborhood place for Chinese desserts, particularly the custard tart in feathery pastry. Average price for a meal is around $18. Open every day till 2am.

China Sea, 94 Hay St. (tel. 02/211-1698), isn't quite as seafood-oriented as the name implies. You get outstanding steamed chicken dishes (Hakka style) as well as varieties of freshwater fish with aromatic stuffings. Meal prices are around $16. Open daily till 2am.

Choy's Inn, at the corner of Hay and Harbour streets (tel. 02/211-4213), is decked out like a peasant hut, but with a menu no Chinese peasant could afford. It serves delicious lemon chicken, scallops with mangoes, honey-glazed prawns, and other such specialties. Forget about the printed menu and order from the blackboard marked "specials." Meals cost around $20. Open daily till midnight.

Dixon Restaurant, 51 Dixon St. (tel. 02/211-1619). One of the oldest establishments in the area, the Dixon suffers from garish decor but makes up for the defect on the menu. It offers the lengthiest and most poetic explanatory captions I've seen. Some are needed for the unusual choices offered, such as Tibetan lamb hotpot and Kirin rock cod. You get a good balance of familiar standards and exotic tidbits, and large helpings of both. Cost per meal is roughly $18. Open every day till midnight.

AROUND KINGS CROSS

A top-rated establishment that is also BYO, **Macleay Street Bistro,** 73A Macleay St., Potts Point (tel. 02/358-4891), may be your first encounter with such a peculiar breed of hostelry. There are quite a few more in this category, and they help keep your dining expenses down. Not that the bistro is cheap in other respects. While very informal in tone and atmosphere, it's also both chic and trendy, two attributes guaranteed to push up prices. (A perfectly ordinary bread roll to go with your soup costs 80¢!) The decor is light blue on white or vice versa, and kept starkly simple. There are three tables on the sidewalk outside, but these are mostly occupied by waiting customers. The cuisine is "nouvelle Oz" in the best meaning of the term. Courses are light and versatile, enabling you to arrange your own dining pattern that doesn't have to follow the old appetizer/main course/dessert routine, especially since you have to pay extra for the vegetables. Customers rave about the char-grilled lamb kidney and the delicately smoked ocean trout. The lime crème brûlée makes a distinctive and unusual conclusion. Despite a $2 corkage charge (likewise unusual), you can dine here for something between $18 and $26. Reservations are highly recommended. Open six days till 11pm; closed Monday.

Korea House, 171 Victoria St., Kings Cross (tel. 02/358-

6601), is situated above a rather plain pub, but comes as a happy surprise once you mount a flight of stairs. The "house" sparkles a welcome with a beautiful array of tropical fish tanks whose soft bubbling sounds provide background music. There is also a display case in which choice delicacies are laid out like jewelry. The cuisine is authentic, and in case you aren't accustomed to Korean cooking, it's considerably spicier than either Japanese or Vietnamese—some dishes may scorch an unwary palate. As an intro, try the goon man doo, a pan-fried dumpling and bean curd in sauce. Or the skewered chunks of chicken, beef, or fish, highly spiced and stimulating. As a main course you should try the Korean barbecue, which is prepared at your table on a portable electric grill. The barbecue sauces are *hot*, but you can cool your taste buds with the excellent Korean beer. Cost will be around $22. Open daily till 11pm.

Bourbon and Beefsteak, 24 Darlinghurst Rd., Kings Cross (tel. 02/358-1144), is an astonishing multipurpose establishment that only Kings Cross could produce and maintain. The Bourbon is literally all things to all people: breakfast in the morning (and all day), lunch at lunchtime, dinner later, supper still later, live bands and piano music in between. The place is open 24 hours a day, every day, and most of the time it's packed. The interior looks as if the contents of a thrift shop had been spilled over two floors, with bars, tables, and chairs added as an afterthought. But the real surprise is that the food for all meals is excellent, the portions are more than generous, the atmosphere is happily nonchalant, and the clientele is half and half tourists and locals. The menu is downright encyclopedic, ranging from American breakfasts to an array of Mexican dinner specialties. Prices depend on the meal, but a good dinner comes to around $22.

Natalino's, 1 Kellett St., Kings Cross (tel. 02/358-4752). A patriarch of the Kings Cross gastronomy scene, Natalino's has outlasted nearly every establishment in the area by sheer persistent attention to quality. Among locals it's an institution. You have the choice of dining indoors by the fireside or al fresco in the enchanting little garden patio (reserve well ahead for the patio). Service is impeccable, the atmosphere Mediterranean languid, the cuisine standard Italian—but the standard is high. For starters, sample either the various oyster platters, antipasto, or fresh mussels. Main courses are all familiars: veal marsala, tagliatelle marinara, saltimbocca alla romana, rissotto al funghi, etc. The top dessert is undoubtedly the rich zabaglione. The tried-and-true wine list matches the edibles. Your dinner, minus wine, should come to about $30. Open six days till 11pm; closed Sunday.

Edosei, 22 Rockwell Crescent, Potts Point (tel. 02/357-3407), houses the most famous sushi bar in Sydney. You have a choice between breasting the bar or gracing a table in the dining room. There's more privacy in the latter, but you miss seeing the sushi knife-and-cleaver acrobats in action. No matter how often you witness it, it always seems a minor miracle how the chefs remain unscathed and the food emerges delicious. Among the treats here are the Tokyo-style mixed sushi called nigri, and the outstanding grilled squid. The Edosei is one of the very few places that serves Japanese wine (yes, there is such a drink) plus a range of Japanese desserts that may surprise palates more accustomed to the whipped-cream type. A meal would run you between $30 and $35. Open six days till 11pm. Closed Monday.

Dean's Verandah, 13 Kellett St., Kings Cross (tel. 02/358-4177), confuses many patrons because there's another establishment called Dean's Café a few doors up. The Verandah is a stylish dining spot with an air of retrospective chic that aims at a 1930s ambience for a very 1990s clientele. The cuisine is loosely cosmopolitan with Thai overtones—almost impossible to classify, and easy to enjoy. You can order a happy mélange of, say, Thai fishcakes in peanut chili sauce followed by rare roast beef or grilled salmon or ricotta flan. The drinks served here are the work of an inventive cocktail genius and should be treated with respectful caution. Some of the mixtures have delayed effects, as I discovered. Try to get a table on the actual veranda—late-night Kellett Street can double as a floor show. Three courses for around $33. Open Monday through Saturday till 2am, Sunday till midnight.

Some aficionados swear that **Hanaya,** 42 Kellett St., Kings Cross (tel. 02/356-4222), is the finest Japanese restaurant in Sydney; others say it's merely the most crowded. Both may be right, but the Hanaya is certainly stylish and atmospheric, in an air-conditioned way. Waitresses wear rustling kimonos, the background music is plaintively Nipponese, the ornamental pottery exquisite. This is one of the few places that serves Japanese plum wine to accompany your meal. The ingredients used are wonderfully fresh and the menu, supplemented by a sushi list and another list for house specials, is the most detailed and explanatory I've ever perused. One of the specials was a truly memorable entrée of whiting with tofu and chopped onions, tailored inside the skin of an orange. Other outstanding items include nama gaki, oysters covered with sake sauce and garnished with chili, finely minced radishes, and shallots. The sushi dishes are delicately flavored and the teriyaki steak is as aromatic as you'd hope. A meal costs about $30. Open daily till 11pm.

Kings Cross Steak House, 2F Roslyn St., Kings Cross (tel. 02/358-5639). Getting right away from Japanese subtlety, this is a place for robust meat fare. A BYO that keeps *very* extended hours, the steak house is exactly what the label says: a restaurant for beef and kindred vittles. No decor or atmosphere to speak of—you eat off an oilskin table covering under bright illumination. But the fare is hearty, well prepared, and inexpensive, the vibes are cheerful and bustling, and every main course comes accompanied by a salad. The oyster entrées are ocean fresh and the main courses—pasta, steaks, omelets—suit a trencherman's or woman's capacity. A hearty meal costs around $14. Open every day; Sunday through Thursday till 2am, on Friday and Saturday till 4:30am.

Craigend, in the Hyatt Kingsgate, Kings Cross Rd., Kings Cross (tel. 02/356-1234), the neoclassical restaurant of this Hyatt hotel, is named after a mansion that once stood in its place. Its very

tasteful and rather formal decor has white Greek columns matching
the snowy table linen, and waiters gliding rather than marching
hither and yon. This is the antithesis of Kings Cross laissez-faire, an
oasis of courtly splendor, and not as expensive as its appearance
might indicate. Lunch, for instance, is a prix-fixe meal costing $33,
including a bottle of wine. The cuisine is international with an Australian base. To experience the fine balance achieved in the kitchen,
order a meal of, say, eggs Provençal (poached on ratatouille in tomato sauce) then either the beef filet or the delicately poached
Tasmanian trout. The desserts are virtually irresistible, so you have
the agony of deciding between the light Australian strawberry short-
cake with double cream or the heavier and thoroughly French tarte
Tatin with lemon crème Chantilly. Open six days a week till 10pm;
closed Sunday. Reservations recommended.

DARLINGHURST

This district interlocks with Kings Cross, making it quite impossible to say where one ends and the other starts.

Viva Mexico, 217 Oxford St., Darlinghurst (tel. 02/331-
3118), as much an entertainment complex as a restaurant, functions
on no fewer than four levels. The ground floor is occupied by a combination deli and disco, the only such hybrid in town. One flight up
lies the actual restaurant, the next floor is a piano bar, and the top is
the seafood haven **Viva Italia.** With all these functions, the establishment naturally keeps late hours. You can get something to eat here
until 3am during weekends. The dining room fare is good, not too
expensive (except the wine), and not too scorching for gringo palates. The menu includes very fine corn pies filled with beef, eggs,
and olives, plus the customary fajitas, nachos, tacos, rice-bedded
Mexican pork, and empanadas. Surprisingly, the Viva also serves
quite un-Mexican crêpes, which are excellent. Three courses for
around $27, and the place is open every day.

Laurie's Vegetarian, corner of Victoria Road and Burton
Street, Darlinghurst (tel. 02/360-4915). This is an outstanding
success in its culinary class—perhaps because Laurie's is also a BYO
and permits smoking, which a great many local vegetarians do. Spacious, laid back and comfortable, with distinctly leisurely service,
this place has a dedicated clientele that includes folks who normally
won't go near a "veggie joint." The main attractions (apart from
modest prices) are the blackboard specials, which really are *special.*
Watch for the unusual and imaginative tofu dishes—such as bro-
chettes in ginger sauce—the broccoli schnitzel, or the spinach-and-
pine-nut pockets. The fruit and vegetable juices come freshly
squeezed and the desserts are suitably rich. Three courses go for
around $16, so that even the $1 corkage charge won't hurt. Open
daily till 11pm.

Narai Thai, 346 Victoria St., Darlinghurst (tel. 02/331-
1390). One of the multitude of Thai restaurants that have sprung up
in recent years, the Narai has several distinguishing features. One of
them is a lengthy and separate vegetarian menu that comes as a god-

send to the noncarnivores among us. The other is the mildness of the spices used; a blessing for diners lacking asbestos taste buds. The third is the outstanding attentiveness of the service. A small, rather simple hostelry, it offers a very good introduction to Thai cuisine to those unfamiliar with such fare. Meals are both generous and economical, and you can dine well for just $18 to $19, perhaps on one of the satays with pungent peanut sauce, or the vermicelli beef with mushrooms, the rice-paper rolls stuffed with ground pork and chili, or the king prawns with garlic in pepper sauce. The wine list is limited. Open seven days till 10:30pm.

PADDINGTON

Known affectionately as "Paddo," this former working-class, now thoroughly gentrified area, is southeast of Darlinghurst.

The Maestro, 120 Glenmore Rd., Paddington (tel. 02/331-5084). "Stately, velvety, and costly, imbued with oldtime elegance," just about describes this establishment. Guests come here to get pampered, and do—not only by the traditional French-Italian fare, but also by the staff, the impressive wine list, and the luxurious surroundings. You can choose to dine in the intimate courtyard or the plush interior. And rest assured, the owner and host will visit your table to inquire about your well-being, your satisfaction, and whatever special wishes you may harbor. The house specialty is venison, superbly prepared hunter style in madeira, and the roast suckling pig, which appears to have been lifted from a Flemish still-life. For something a trifle lighter there's grilled snapper stuffed with shrimp and oysters, served in white wine. This culinary glory will cost around $30. Open six days till 10:30pm; closed Sunday. Reservations recommended.

Siam, 383 Oxford St., Paddington (tel. 02/331-2669). Located next door to the famous Paddington Market, this BYO dispenses excellent Thai edibles at a brisk pace. Service is exceptionally fast and efficient, though the waitresses will gladly explain any menu mysteries to you. The noise level, however, is way up there. If you've never tasted Thai soup, sample the prawn soup with chili. Then go on to the specials chalked on the blackboard and frequently changed. You'll get acquainted with ocean perch in coconut sauce, the highly spiced Thai fish cakes, and the sweetly tangy chicken wings. For dessert, try the rich and creamy coconut ice. The entire meal will cost around $17. Open seven days till 11pm.

La Galleria, 10 Elizabeth St., Paddington (tel. 02/331-2962), is an airy, bright, and relaxed Italian BYO, where cooks and waiters have faces made famous by their appearances in various Australian TV commercials and daytime soaps. Nothing theatrical about the cuisine, however: it's rich, solid fare, aromatically spiced and served with professional polish. A lengthy list of entrées (try the grilled mushrooms) followed by seven different veal choices or a memorable course of liver prepared in butter and sage. The fresh top-quality ingredients used at the Galleria make even some quite ordinary poultry dishes taste as if you'd never eaten chicken before. A full meal, including dessert, comes to roughly $25. Open Monday through Saturday till midnight.

SURRY HILLS

Paddington's western neighbor, once a seedy, deteriorating neighborhood, now blossoms with smart restaurants, avant-garde theaters, and art deco homes. Symbolic of the rise of the region is **Surry's,** 145 Devonshire St., Surry Hills (tel. 02/698-9681), a cream-colored two-story Victorian, with double doors and leaded-glass windows, converted into an absolutely charming brasserie. You have a choice of dining indoors or on the large open-air deck, but in any case you'll dine very well. Ceilings are high, as befits a period place, potted palms provide indoor greenery, and the manager greets customers as if they were houseguests arriving for a weekend. You read the menu from a blackboard and soon gather that charcoal grills are the house specialty: char-grilled buffalo filet in brandy sauce, char-grilled spatchcock with coconut glaze, char-grilled snapper cutlets with fresh herbs and pine nuts. But you'll also find Thai-style barbecued octopus, chicken-and-veal terrine with onion chutney, and a wicked dessert called "Death by Chocolate." Compared to this concoction, even the cream-rich Pavlova becomes a diet dish. The wine list is quite extensive, though not as innovative as the food. Three courses cost roughly $32. Open every day.

Strelitzia, 26 Buckingham St., Surry Hills (tel. 02/698-3349), was converted from an 80-year-old terrace dwelling into a small, cozy terrace restaurant containing just eight tables. The cuisine, labeled "European," is actually a distinctive mixture of continental and Aussie fare, incorporating the best features of both but true to neither. The huge helpings, however, are most European. You can start with baked squab stuffed with wild rice or the

---

Tennis Anyone?

Located upstairs in the **White City Tennis Club,** 30 Alma St., Paddington (tel. 02/360-6637), is the dining room that used to be the hallowed preserve of members only. After undergoing a face-lift and a culinary metamorphosis it opened its doors to the general public. The fact that table conversation revolves almost exclusively around tennis doesn't prevent this from being a very fine restaurant. A glass wall and open balcony offer a view of the courts below, giving rise to some salty comments from the munching audience. The menu is prix fixe: $19.95 for a three-course meal. And the fare includes some outstanding items like the avocado and mango salad, grilled ocean perch, and rack of lamb. The entertainment provided by the ball lobbers below comes free. The chef's own recreation, by the way, is not tennis but fishing. Open Tuesday through Saturday till 9pm.

country-style pâté with heavy black bread, and then perhaps the gargantuan bowl of fish stew afloat with whole large prawns, or filet of beef in hollandaise. There are also delicious blueberry tartlets to finalize proceedings, but you'll only get to them if you skip a course. Portions are so generous that two rounds are about all most diners can manage. The Strelitzia stands on the edge of the center city and provides a complimentary taxi ride back to your hotel. A meal will cost you around $23, not including wine. Open Tuesday through Saturday till 10pm; closed Sunday and Monday.

Café Elan, 379 Crown St., Surry Hills (tel. 02/332-3858), advertises "Modern Vegetarian Cuisine"—the meaning of which escapes me. But modern or not, this is top class for all noncarnivores. The fare uses a minimum of eggs and dairy products and achieves flavor and variety by the subtle combination of Asian and Middle Eastern ingredients. Licensed as well as BYO, the Elan serves some very unusual herbal wines, tasting much better than they sound. Apart from lunch and dinner, there's a special late supper menu, dished up till 2am and accompanied by musical offerings. Highly recommended are the spicy coconut fritters, mushroom terrine, the baked cashew tofu, and the Lebanese-style lentil bake. For an alternative starter, try the tomato and ginger soup. Desserts change as frequently as the soups, but you won't go wrong with any of the apple, peach, pear, or rhubarb crumbles, which melt on your tongue. A strict no-smoking rule is enforced between 6pm and 9pm. A full meal goes for around $20, not including the potent and aromatic liqueur coffee. Open Wednesday through Saturday. Closed Sunday through Tuesday.

The **Riley Street Bistro,** Forresters Hotel, corner of Riley and Foveaux streets, Surry Hills (tel. 02/211-0627), is yet another revamping job indicative of the area. The Forresters used to be just a corner pub serving characteristic pub grub across the counter. Now you follow elegant black and white tiles to the upstairs bistro, which occupies the entire top floor and consists of four dining quarters, each painted a different pastel hue. Pastel shades in "the Hills" were once a downright anomaly! Servings are still unfashionably large, but now they've acquired sophistication. The menu is short, but the items are long on quality. Try the chicken filets in garlic butter or the Anglo-traditional calves' liver and onions or the distinctly non-Anglo duck breast served in madeira, and afterward the cheese platter or some of the unusual ice cream concoctions. The beer garden in the courtyard is unfortunately too microscopic ever to get a table in. A meal goes for about $22. Open Tuesday through Saturday till 10:30pm.

DOUBLE BAY

Chic, trendy, and expensive, this closest of the so-called Eastern Suburbs never needed revamping of any kind. Typical of the dining spots in this region is the **Hunters Lodge,** 18 Cross St., Double Bay (tel. 02/32-1747), a beautiful, atmospheric establishment with stags' heads, antlers, and hunting arsenals on the walls but, oddly, no game on the menu. The ceilings are laced with heavy black oak beams and hung with baskets of ferns, and there are superb 18th-century sporting prints on the walls, subtle lighting, and a stained-glass window on the stairway beneath a baronial chandelier. The Lodge has won three Golden Plate gourmet awards and deserves another for the decor; the cuisine is European with strong Hungarian accents. For starters there is an aromatic Hungarian fish soup called hatazle, as well as escargot or caviar frappé. As a main course a difficult choice is to be made between entrecôte chasseur with mushrooms in burgundy sauce, kidneys in port wine, or veal medallion with paprika cream sauce. As a finale try the platter of selected cheeses. The total check will be around the $30 mark. Open daily till midnight.

The Cleveland, 63 Bay St., Double Bay (tel. 02/327-6877). One of Sydney's most opulent Chinese restaurants, the Cleveland serves vegetarian meals downstairs, Szechuan cuisine upstairs. Both sections—actually separate restaurants—are lavishly decked out in a distinct Hong Kong style of luxury that revels in mirrors, gilt, and silken drapes. Menus here are regular publications, illustrated with photos of the dishes on offer. The food presented downstairs bears little resemblance to the kind of vegetarian fare you might have eaten before. This is the Buddhist brand, which delights even an inveterate carnivore like myself. I've seldom tasted anything as delicately scrumptious as the white mushrooms with crisp cashew nuts or the coconut milk custard. Upstairs it's heartier and heavier. Try the aromatic duck smoked in camphor tea or the quite un-Gallic, gently gingered frog casserole. Prices are roughly the same in both sections—around $40 for three courses. Open daily till 10:30pm.

ROSE BAY

A few bus stops farther east along the foreshore is Rose Bay. Catch bus 324 or 325 from Circular Quay or Kings Cross.

Dory's, 594 New South Head Rd., Rose Bay (tel. 02/327-4187), is one of those places where you don't know what to admire more: the fare or the view. Sitting right on the bay, overlooking the dazzling expanse of the harbor, framed by one of the city's most scenic suburbs, Dory's is sheer delight. The restaurant is actually built over the water on an old pier and has an open-deck terrace. The place swarms with equal quantities of the local smart set, interstate visitors, and Japanese tourists armed with batteries of cameras. Advance reservations are essential. The fare, of course, is fresh seafood: oysters in every shape and disguise, crayfish (live in tanks and caught on order), crabs, mussels, snapper, and those two wonderful Australian ocean denizens, John Dory and barramundi. Your check will come to around $38. Open seven days a week till 9:30pm.

WATSONS BAY

Perched near the tip of a magnificent Eastern Suburbs peninsula, just below the Gap National Park, Watsons Bay boasts the most famous restaurant duo in Australia: Doyle's. The twin editions of this eating institution are **Doyle's on the Beach,** Marine Parade, Watsons Bay (tel. 02/337-2007), and **Doyle's on the Wharf** (tel. 02/337-1572)—neither place really needs an address. The weekend lines are equally long for both (they take reservations for only a small number of tables). Whether you eat on the beach or on the wharf, you can watch the marine craft bounce by, the windsurfers topple, the bathing beauties parade, and the seagulls thieve. This is Sydney at its absolute best, in permanent holiday garb, and sooner or later every overseas visitor and country relative gets dragged here to enjoy and envy. Among the amenities is a special water-taxi service from Circular Quay right to the wharf (but only till 3pm).

Peter Doyle, the owner, is a celebrity in his own right, and star of countless video exposures. But even without his charismatic touch, the restaurants would be memorable. Their accent, naturally, is on seafood, aided and abetted by a solid and lengthy wine list. A large carafe of excellent house riesling costs $12; a bottle of South Australian cabernet, $14. The seafood selection is enormous, absolutely fresh and not overpriced (but watch out for the $3 surcharge on holidays *and* weekends). Entrées range from baby octopus marinated in olive oil and garlic, to jumbo prawns stuffed with bacon and calamari deep-fried in beer batter. For main courses you could pick the grand-scale platter of mixed seafood, including oysters and roasted tuna; the whole grilled flounder; the pearl perch, a rarity caught only along the eastern coast of Australia; or the sea-farmed pink filets of ocean trout. Dessert selection is limited, and the best item is the homemade brandied chocolate mousse. Meals run from $25 to above $36. For good measure, Doyle's also sells souvenir T-shirts, aprons, and hats. They do *not* take credit cards. Open seven days till 9:30pm.

BONDI

Sydney's most popular beach suburb is chock-a-block with restaurants in every price range.

Lamrock Café, 72 Campbell Parade, Bondi Beach (tel. 02/30-6313), is a versatile place that serves very good breakfast, lunch, dinner, supper, in-between snacks, and some of the wildest cocktails in town (one of them comes in a kind of bucket, with four straws for sharing imbibers). The Lamrock has a beach atmosphere, aided by large glass doors at street level that give you a nice view of the lightly clad parade outside. The fare is supposedly European but really a mélange of Aussie-Asian-Continental dishes that suit virtually all taste buds. You read the changing menu and decide between seafood fettuccine, excellent and solid grills, and such Asian delicacies as ginger-spiced chicken wings. It's a spot to nibble, to sample, or to feast, while listening to Spanish guitar tapes. Your check will range from $11 to $25. Open for three meals and in between, seven days a week till midnight.

Before describing the next place, I must note that it is totally misnamed. The **Gelato Bar,** 140 Campbell Parade, Bondi Beach (tel. 02/30-4033), does sell gelato, but purely as a sideline. It is, above all, one of Sydney's oldest and most respected Hungarian restaurants. Why it retains its deceptive label is a mystery. Better bring a healthy appetite—they don't serve a small dish of anything except butter. Don't expect Central European ambience, as this is a brisk-service place, all bustle and efficiency, with no intimate corners to hide in. People don't come here to romance—they come to *eat*. And the food is terrific. You get all the Magyar and Jewish favorites: chicken or liver-dumpling soup, veal or beef goulash, beef Stroganoff, wienerschnitzel, cucumber salad, and a superlative Hungarian specialty of scrambled eggs with mushrooms and fried sausages. The desserts are downright dreamy, most of them beckoning from glass showcases: Sachertorte and chestnut torte; apple strudel the way it should be, with a feathery-light crust; wondrously rich poppy-seed slices, like black and brown temptations; plus the obligatory Hungarian sweet noodles in melted cheese sprinkled with grated walnuts. The Gelato is BYO and charges 50¢ corkage per bottle. Otherwise your meal will cost around $16. Open six days till, well, "late"; closed Monday.

Bluewater Grill, 168 Ramsgate Ave., Bondi Beach (tel. 02/30-7810), has acquired such renown that it's difficult to grab an outside table (and they won't take reservations). With a cavelike interior, stone floor tiles, a charming outdoor patio, and sweeping views of the day or night ocean scene, the Bluewater is atmospheric as well as chic and exceedingly "in." It's a seafood place, but subtly different from the mainstream. The imprint is partly Asian, partly Californian, which makes for light, flavorful meals served in modest quantities. The interior sound level, however, is distinctly *heavy*. some outstanding specialties here are the grilled swordfish served with a potato-and-garlic purée, fresh eel grilled in honey, and raw ocean trout with tomatoes in walnut oil. Pay attention to the salads, which are as innovative as they are delicious. And you may not have known that stingray (a relative of the shark) makes grand eating when charcoal-grilled in Vietnamese style. Price for three courses, not including drinks, is around $38. Open six days till 10:30pm; closed Tuesday.

Café Neon, 80 Campbell Parade, Bondi Beach (tel. 02/30-8798), is aptly named, insofar as it's bathed in neon light. Occupying the ground floor of a venerable mansion, the place offers huge viewing windows through which to study the passing parade. The interior is gleaming white, with just enough green touches to rest the eyes. There's a smart smallish bar in the background to which couples can retreat when they get tired of viewing and being viewed. The decor is oceanic and many of the patrons affect yachting garb, but the fare is a curious mixture of Mexican and "nouvelle," cuisine with only a few marine specialties sprinkled in. You get tangy nachos, as well as American hamburgers, a surprise dish called chicken Dutcheska, and a grandiose seafood salad rich with fish chunks, crab, prawns, and scallops. Three courses go for under $30. The place keeps flexible hours but is usually going till midnight all week.

Gandhi, 94 Bronte Rd., Bondi Junction (tel. 02/389-6557), is indicative of how the eating scene in Bondi has changed in recent years. Once a solid stronghold of European cookery, the area is now inundated with Asian and Middle Eastern hostelries . . . and the locals flock to them. The Gandhi, dimly lit and simply furnished, is a BYO serving some outstanding clay-oven specialties at modest prices. The dishes not only taste good but are as eye-pleasing and colorful as Japanese fare, though less raw.

There's not much seafood on the menu, but there are several excellent vegetarian dishes like pakoras, a type of fritters served with lentils. The spices used (curry, tamarind, cumin seeds, etc.) are carefully dosed so as not to maul Western taste buds. The prime offering here is undoubtedly the tandoori chicken, served in a sauce that is really hot and tangy. Your meal will come to below $14. Open seven days a week till 10pm.

Little Snail, 96A Curlewis St., Bondi Beach (tel. 02/300-0042), is a real rarity—a BYO that's also French. But the Little Snail has other claims to fame as well. By reputation it's the most romantic restaurant in Sydney, a place where couples retreat not only for dates but for silver anniversaries as well. Romantic without being in the least cloying (the Edith Piaf background warbles aren't exactly schmaltzy), the place is spacious yet somehow intimate, and the service is a model of Gallic smoothness. Despite the name, snails don't loom large on the menu. They come à la bourguignonne and make a superlative appetizer. They may be followed, perhaps, by deliciously fragile quail or roast guinea fowl, or if you crave something heartier, the pork filets poached in milk. Whether you choose from the menu or the specials blackboard, the fare is superb. Corkage comes to $1.50 and meals generally run around $30. Open six days till 10pm; closed Sunday.

GLEBE
An inner suburb and southwestern neighbor of the center city, Glebe was once mainly industrial, but is now making great strides as a restaurant region.

Café Troppo, 175 Glebe Point Rd., Glebe (tel. 02/660-7332), is a café insofar as it serves snacks and lets you sit over them all day and half the night. It's also a fine and inexpensive restaurant. "Troppo" is Strine for nuttiness, and the label may be part of the attraction for the crowds of university students who gather here to debate matters metaphysical and pick up dates. The place is delightfully laid back, thoroughly amiable, and so comfortable that it's hard to get up and walk out. There's seating both indoors and out in a courtyard patio, and the staff is most friendly. It's BYO, so you either bring your own liquor or sip one of the non-alcoholic cocktails on offer. Order the seafood soup as an appetizer, and to follow, either one of the excellent steaks or the heaping seafood basket containing an amazing array of ocean tidbits. The dessert choice is vast, can be inspected behind glass, and has superbly rich chocolate mud cake, among other temptations. The meal will come to around $28, but unless your appetite is roaring you can get by nicely on $14. Open seven days until . . . hard to say; let's make it midnight.

Bogart, 199 Glebe Point Rd., Glebe (tel. 02/692-0936), has nothing to do with Humphrey or trenchcoats, but is a pleasant Italian restaurant that is *both* licensed and BYO (meaning you can order drinks on the premises or bring them along at no extra charge). Bogart has an open fireplace for atmosphere, ceiling fans for coolness, and indoor greenery for ornamentation. While thoroughly Italian, the kitchen goes easy on the pasta dishes, which are kept to a minimum. Instead there's a variety of first-rate veal courses, with the veal slim and tender but not insignificant, as in some hostelries. Unusual and noteworthy are the green prawns, flavored with ginger and served on rice. Three courses cost around $28. Open seven days till 10:30pm.

Rasputin's, 101 Glebe Point Rd., Glebe (tel. 02/660-3906). It's a mystery why such a good restaurant should bear the name of a glutton who had virtually no palate and frequently wolfed down sturgeon and sweetmeats from the same plate. Anyway, *this* Rasputin is run by real gourmets, as evidenced by their preparation and presentation of Russian delicacies. The blini here come with caviar, smoked salmon, and sour cream. The borscht has the true subtle sweet-sour tang so often missing in imitations. You could, in fact, make a sumptuous meal from the appetizers, particularly the Siberian palmein—a wonderful version of meatballs served in sharp sauce. But you'd better leave room for the chicken Kiev or the stuffed cabbage rolls, which often is the chief reason why people go to Russian restaurants. For dessert there's the un-Russian rum baba, which few French restaurants make, for reasons I cannot fathom. Indoors or in the courtyard, you'll eat for something less than $20. Open six days a week till 10pm; closed Sunday.

BALMAIN

This area is another peninsula jutting into the harbor, pleasantly hilly and close to the center city.

Berlin Café, 249 Darling St., Balmain (tel. 02/810-2336). If seeing *Cabaret* left you intrigued with the Berlin scene of the early 1930s, head for here. The atmosphere seems pretty authentic, even to the newspapers, which are free for perusal. Only the political tension is missing. But this is definitely a place in which to linger and to discuss—whatever. The kitchen turns out rich German specialties, from smoked pork sausages served with possibly the finest potato salad in town to meatloaf and beef roulades and kalbsbraten, the particular German version of roast veal. The dessert display is symphonic: apple strudel, rum cakes, superb chocolate domes filled with whipped cream, and the yellow napfkuchen meant to be dunked messily into coffee. The coffee, by the way, is among the finest you'll drink in Sydney. The Berlin is a rare fish in a country where nearly all German establishments are Bavarian or Austrian—a real period piece in an unexpected corner. Meals run around $12. It's strictly BYO, and there's a $1 corkage charge per table. Open seven days till 10pm—which was the time most of the real Berlin cafés used to spring to life.

THE NORTH SHORE

All the establishments mentioned so far are on the south side of Sydney's great water divide. Now we cross the Harbour Bridge to the North Shore, a vast slice of territory with a very lively restaurant scene of its own. Some North Shore patriots are quite fanatical about eating where they live. Whatever their reasons, they certainly have plenty of choice.

Just over the bridge there's a charming oddity of French gastronomy called **Le Petit Savoyard,** 55 Ridge St., North Sydney (tel. 02/923-2336)—charming because the interior is designed like a country auberge with candles on checkered table linen and a tree-shaded courtyard in the rear. It's an oddity because this is a lunch place (closes late afternoon) and serves what I've always thought was a Swiss specialty—fondue. Turns out, I thunk wrong. Fondues are as native to provincial France as to Helvetia, and are connected there with the same customs, to wit: if a man drops his bread into the pot, he has to buy a bottle of wine; if a woman does so, she has to kiss every man at the table, including the waiter if he happens to be standing by. Here the wine bottle would have to be brought—the place is BYO. The fondues are marvelous, come in beef, cheese, or chocolate versions, and may be supplemented by the house pâté. Expect to pay around $18. Open six days a week till 10pm; closed Sunday.

Tony Roma's, 116 Military Rd., Neutral Bay (tel. 02/953-5999). An American rib restaurant is a genuine rarity in this town. The chief reason is that Aussie pork, beef, and lamb ribs don't measure up to their U.S. counterparts in either length or flavor and therefore don't attract as many devotees. Tony's venture may change all that. What you get here is the genuine article—and inexpensive to boot. You also get ice water without having to plead for it, as is customary in Oz eateries. The decor, including paintings of Sinatra and Elvis, may not be what you'd expect in a rib joint, but the ribs are *everything* you'd expect. The pork and beef baby backs are as succulent as any you've tasted in Texas; the lamb less so. The platter comes for $12.50, accompanied by complimentary hot bread and much-needed packs of wet tissues. Other barbecued specialties, such as chicken and prawns as well as charcoal-grilled steaks, are likewise on the menu, and a glass of good house wine costs $2.75. Open all week till 11pm.

Le Kiosk, Marine Parade, Manly (tel. 02/977-4122), overlooking Manly's panoramic Shelly Beach, is not a French restaurant but a good and rather typical oceanfront eating spot. Housed in an imitation cottage, the place has rows of outside tables for sea-breeze dining, an extensive nonseafood menu, and wondrous ocean views. Seafood, of course, is the major drawing card for the multitudes who swarm in from their beach outings, making advance reservations advisable. The fish fare is good, reliable, and satisfying in an

A Dining Adventure

Only one restaurant in the whole of Sydney solely serves the food of the original Australians, or some of it, anyway. This is **Rowntrees,** 188 Pacific Hwy., Hornsby (tel. 02/476-5150). Here you can sample a few items of "bush tucker," the fare of the nomadic Aborigines, but in surroundings far removed from the natural setting. Chances are you've never tasted witchety grubs (rather like salty, crunchy shrimp), water-buffalo steak (like steak with a game flavor), lillipilli, or quandongs. Other house specialties are more familiar: filet of shark, grilled barramundi (but with rain-forest sour plums) or river crayfish, and Tasmanian smoked salmon. The point is that all these items, familiar or not, are sauced and seasoned with Australian spices and served up, very stylishly, with all-Australian vegetables. There is a striking contrast between the Rowntrees fare and the elegant decor that lends a certain piquancy to the setup, as does the choice all-Australian wine list (the restaurant is both licensed and BYO). The main thing, however, is the overall excellence of the fare, the imaginative use of the "wild" spices and vegetables. For a true eating adventure, Rowntrees is unmatched. It's also fairly pricey—your adventure dinner will cost around $40. Open seven days a week till 10:30pm.

unimaginative fashion. Ingredients are fresh, condiments familiar, sauces unobtrusive. The beach crowds who flock here get exactly the kind of fare they want. The dish most in demand is a perfectly enormous mixed seafood platter for two people, containing a good proportion of Australia's ocean denizens. Eating out in the garden is quite idyllic on sunny days and warm evenings. On Sunday the Kiosk puts on a famous buffet breakfast, for the sake of which many people cross the harbor. A three-course dinner will cost about $30. Open seven days a week till 9:30pm. The famed Sunday breakfast (with complimentary champagne) has a set price of $19.

A dreamy little enclave on the northern shore, Hunters Hill is full of colonial mansions hand-hewn in stone by convict labor, and one of Sydney's loveliest (and snootiest) residential areas. Here you have a restaurant in a *real* cottage—or rather, in three of them. **Carey Cottage,** 18 Ferry St., Hunters Hill (tel. 02/817-3643), is actually a trio grouped around a tree-shaded courtyard. The buildings date from the colonial era, have timbered walls and ceilings, and show display cases filled with antique cutlery, heirloom china, and hand-woven Irish table linen. Because of the number of cottages, dining areas are divided into small, intimate nooks that never get crowded, although advance reservations are advisable. Carey is BYO and concentrates on plain, wholesome, plentiful fare: steak and three "veggies," roast lamb with mint sauce, roast pork with applesauce and piles of crackling, with apple crumble and custard cream for dessert. The food fits the old colonial surroundings like a glove. Three courses for $34, and the place is open Tuesday through Saturday till midnight, on Sunday for lunch only; closed Monday. Take the little Hunters Hill ferry across from Circular Quay.

Sala Thai, 778 Military Rd., Mosman (tel. 02/969-9379). Few Thai restaurants have as yet penetrated the northern realm, so the Sala is something of a novelty in these here parts. Although it does have take-out service, in every other respect its image is as trendy as that of the entire neighborhood. Some, in fact, consider this to be the top Thai restaurant in Sydney, but these are biased North Shore patriots of course. No argument about the Sala's being supremely pleasant and comfortable. You can dine outside at sidewalk tables or inside amid Asian elegance, enjoying the smiling service as well as the lengthy (and pricey) wine list. Among the finest appetizers are the curried vegetable puffs—crisp on the surface, pungent beneath. The equally spicy fish soup makes a good alternative. After that, try one of the hot vegetarian specials, or by contrast, the cubed beef marinated in whisky. Whatever you order, make sure to conclude with the bananas in coconut cream, one of the richest, most flavorsome desserts I've ever tasted. You'll pay about $22. Open daily till midnight.

Amici Miei, 388 Pacific Hwy., Crows Nest (tel. 02/436-2991), is an Italian restaurant quartered in very large premises. You could easily dance between the tables, which makes for comfortable dining. Plants, greenery, bright furniture, and crisp table linen decorated with small vases of flowers give it the right Italian air to match the shingle. The menu appears on a blackboard and changes frequently. For appetizers, you can't do better than the homemade potato dumplings called gnocchi gratè, sprinkled with cheese and not at all heavy. After that, perhaps the grilled Italian sausages—spicy and succulent—or one of the special mountainous seafood platters. A three-course repast costs around $27. The place is licensed *or* BYO, and the only jarring note is the $2 corkage imposed on BYO patrons. Open Monday through Saturday till 10:30pm.

---

3. Budget Restaurants

Virtually all the places listed under this heading are BYOs, and many won't take table reservations. An amazing number of restaurants in this class thrive along **Oxford Street,** which runs from the center city through Darlinghurst.

Two restaurants, almost side by side, complement each other's menus. The first is the **Balkan,** 209 Oxford St., Darlinghurst (tel. 02/357-4970), Yugoslav to the backbone but with nary a trace of ethnic atmosphere. It has one dining room downstairs, another upstairs, and needs them both to accommodate the nightly throngs. It's a long narrow premises, with plastic tables, metal chairs, sliding doors to the street, and an open-grill kitchen in front sending out aromatic signals to your taste buds. Service is fast and usually breathless, the tables are usually packed, the ambience relaxed. "Hearty" is the only word to describe the fare. The Serbian bean

Dining Afloat

The following are Sydney's shipboard, or rather boatboard, restaurants that combine meals with scenic still-water cruises around the harbor. Both weigh anchor from Circular Quay, but serve slightly different purposes. Both require advance reservations.

The **John Cadman,** no. 6 jetty, Circular Quay (tel. 02/922-1922). A sleek white twin-funneled boat, beautifully illuminated, the *John Cadman* has a dance floor as busy as the dining salon (the music is *live,* not canned). Gleaming white table linen, intimate little "oil" lamps, and an array of nautical touches help the atmosphere. You can choose between lunchtime and dinner cruises seven days a week. Dinner costs $55 per head.

The **Sydney Showboat,** no. 2 jetty, Circular Quay (tel. 02/264-3510), is the oldest and simultaneously the newest of the floating restaurants: the oldest because there's been a showboat on the harbor for 40 years; the newest because this particular one was launched in 1987. Built to resemble the venerable paddlewheelers that used to chug around the waterfront, the *Showboat* is actually a large, 400-passenger luxury craft, elegantly fitted and elaborately equipped for different purposes. The upper deck is for observation and moonlight strolling; the three lower decks house a pretty good cabaret/vaudeville show, several bars, and the restaurants. The accent on board is on entertainment, as befits a showboat. Lunch is served from 12:30pm and dinner from 7:45pm every day. Call ahead for the show times. Costs $55 to $60 depending on the night.

There are about half a dozen other craft of various shapes and sizes on which you can eat while cruising, but they are first and foremost sightseeing or entertainment vessels, and we'll take a look at them in the appropriate chapters.

soup alone would make a meal. The other Balkan goodies are equally tasty and just as filling: plieskavica (a kind of Serbo-Croatian hamburger), chepavcici (beef, veal, and pork minced together and cooked on a barbecue), or raznici (tender chunks of pork cooked on a skewer). It takes a very hale appetite to manage more than one course here. Thick Turkish coffee is the indispensable finale. Main dishes run from $12.50 to $15. Open six days a week from 11am to 11pm; closed Tuesday.

The second is the **Balkan Seafood,** 215 Oxford St., Darlinghurst (tel. 02/331-7670). Decorated and run along the same lines as the first, it's equally popular, but with the accent on marine edibles. The two places frequently pool customers—if you can't get a seat in one, you wander into the other. Portions are equally huge, but the substance somewhat lighter. And in both establishments the food is consistently good, come rain, shine, or the chef's hangovers. Noisy, relaxed, and convivial, it's not a hideaway for an intimate rendezvous. For starters, try the baby calamari, with wonderfully tangy charcoal-grilled whiting to follow. Alternatively you can order most of the Slavic meat dishes available at the other Balkan bastion. Two courses come to around $21. Open Tuesday through Sunday till 11pm.

By way of contrast **Kim,** 235 Oxford St., Darlinghurst (tel. 02/357-5429), is a dainty little establishment serving Vietnamese morsels. Simple yet quite stylish, it has only 13 tables downstairs and upstairs, but wood-paneled walls, soft lanterns beneath a beamed ceiling, and the ambience produced by a mixture of Gallic finesse and Asian piquancy. The menu is printed in Vietnamese with English translations. You can go through any number of courses here. Goi tom is a starter salad of chicken, shrimp, and carrots with peanuts; mangtay, a classic asparagus soup made with chunks of crab. Main courses include sweet-and-sour squid (this may be a new one for you), and bean curd stuffed with onions and vermicelli. Several unusual desserts beckon as well, such as a pudding made of sweet corn and creamed rice and a surprisingly palate-pleasing jelly of seaweed. A three-course meal costs in the $14 to $16 range. Open six days a week till 10:30pm; closed Tuesday.

Darlinghurst and Kings Cross blend into each other without a dividing line. **Una's Espresso,** at 340 Victoria St., Darlinghurst (tel. 02/357-6885), could be in either. It bears a misleading name because this is actually an unconventional restaurant, open for breakfast, lunch, and dinner until midnight right through the week. The espresso bit is more of a sideline. There's a very small coffee bar and a much larger dining room, saved from plainness by pictures, candles on the tables, and a general air of neighborhood gemütlichkeit. Una's is thoroughly German in fare, cosmopolitan in clientele, heavy into the schnitzel line. You can start with strong beef broth, then choose either one of the half dozen schnitzel varieties, or perhaps the mildly spicy continental meatloaf. Outstanding Rösti potatoes come with every course, and a range of German pastry—*mit* whipped cream or ice cream—adds the finishing touch. Three courses cost around $12 or $13.

In the very center of Kings Cross, yet not *of* it, is the **Astoria,** 7 Darlinghurst Rd., Kings Cross (tel. 02/358-6327). This is an old-style Aussie diner, serving old-style food during old-style hours—and at very near old-style prices. With two rows of eating booths in a long and narrow dining room, plus a large standing fan, no space is wasted on decorative touches, but everything is spick and span, the service fast and efficient, and the no-frills fare cooked with a minimum of alien-spice additions. A typical meal would be barley broth, Irish stew or lamb cutlets with three "veggies" or roast pork with applesauce, concluded with ice cream or fruit salad. A three-courser runs an astonishingly low $7.50. But the place closes at 8:30pm sharp and stays closed on Sunday.

Hard Rock Café, 121 Crown St., Darlinghurst (tel. 02/331-1116), is the Oz version of the famed New York and London namesakes that are sending patrons into rapture or convulsions, according to taste. The Sydney replica is more of the same: the exterior graced by the butt end of an automobile, the interior devoted to rock memorabilia, the human traffic tremendous, and the sound level deafening. Leaving aside decor and decibels, however, the café provides good comestibles at modest prices. (Drinks tend to be costly.) There are hot or cold soups for starters, then either American hamburgers or English fish and chips, and excellent ice cream desserts; all are served up with polish and speed. The size of the portions is such that you're not likely to manage three courses, so your tab will be below the $14 mark. Open Sunday through Thursday till 11:30pm, Fridays and Saturdays till 2:30am.

Fatima, 296 Cleveland St., Surry Hills (tel. 02/698-4895), is a Lebanese BYO, long-established, sociable, and comfortable, that specializes in mixed plates of Middle Eastern favorites at painless prices. The platters come in small, medium, and large sizes, starting at $4 and climbing to $9. You can munch your way through the whole range of hummus, kafts, tabbouleh, Lebanese sausages, garlic chicken, and kebabs, served with olives and bread in pleasing quantities. Set menus that include coffee and ultra-sweet desserts range around $11. It's a good place to sit, nibble, and sip your (self-supplied) bottle of wine, because the Fatima stays open till midnight seven days a week. If you've never tasted the Levantine semolina pudding, try it here.

Kellett Café, 3 Kellett St., Kings Cross (tel. 02/358-4209). A spot for nightbirds and one of a row of four establishments catering to the late set, the Kellett doesn't start filling up until around 10pm. But it operates seven days a week until anywhere from 2 to 5 am, "depending on who's around." The café consists of a lengthy corridor connecting a charming streetfront garden with an equally charming courtyard eating area. There are modernistic prints on the wall and a rather intriguing and very mixed crowd of patrons at the tables, the kind once classified as "bohemian," but in any case folks

Graffiti Mansion

In the traditional Italian neighborhood of Leichhardt stands the only eatery that *invites* you to scribble on its walls. The **Titina,** 19 Norton St., Leichhardt (tel. 02/569-2959), uses graffiti for decor. Every available wall space and a fair portion of the ceiling is covered with slogans, mots, declarations, and exclamations ranging from a simple and puzzling "Victory!" (whose?) to the kind the management hastily blacks out. They make educational reading while you're waiting for the next course. The fare is good standard Italian, most of the main dishes priced between $7.50 and $10.50. Among the best is the gamberi alla griglia (barbecued king prawns) and the roast quail with spinach. For dessert try the profiteroles, as diet-wrecking as they should be. The Titina is both licensed and BYO, features a guitarist, and, no, the management does *not* supply you with magic markers. You'll have to bring your own. Open all week till around 11pm.

who can sleep late in the morning. The menu is very brief: you get a selection of tidbits plus chicken or pork pie, chili con carne, and various cheese melts. Two of these selections will set you back around $15.

No Name. Some confusion here because there are actually two places with the same label—one an offspring of the other. Neither has a name, but the one we're concerned with is known to patrons as Caesar's. Located at 2 Chapel St., East Sydney (tel. 02/360-4711), it has the reputation of being *the* prime budget eatery in Sydney (though you'll get arguments about that). Founded many years ago as an economy diner for young single Italian immigrants, it has long outgrown this limitation and now attracts vast crowds of every origin. It's a place for lining up (excuse me, queuing). You queue on the stairs, then share the first vacant table with whoever was in line with you. Many interesting friendships can be made in this manner. No decorations and a basic minimum of furniture here, but salad, milk or orange juice comes gratis with your meal, and the food is good and astonishingly cheap. Any two courses cost $11. Choices range from roast veal, boiled beef, and veal scallopine to beef stew or meatballs. Portions are generous, the vibes friendly, and the staff *very* busy, is also fast and amiable. For coffee you descend downstairs into the Arch Coffee Lounge. The No Name lies just off Crown Street and stays open seven days a week till the last hungry customer is sated.

Silver Spoon, 203 Oxford St., Darlinghurst (tel. 02/360-4669). Despite the veritable explosion of Thai restaurants in Sydney, the Silver Spoon is so popular that you'd better make reservations. If you enjoy the delicate heatwaves of Thai cuisine, this is the establishment to head for. It's a dainty and carefully groomed hostelry: furnishings look fragile (but aren't), decorations are lovingly and artfully arranged, and even the paper napkins greet you folded into floral patterns. There is an agreeable contrast between the gently spiced entrées and the robust heat of the curry main dishes, preparing your palate in stages, so to speak. Among the starters are plates of fishcakes and slightly sweetish coconut-cream soup. Then you have a choice of four main courses and an array of curry dishes (including a vegetarian one that really scorches). It's a good idea to follow the daily specials here, particularly in the seafood line, because they really *are* special. If you don't feel seaworthy, try the grilled chicken for a poultry dish that's really different. Three courses will cost $18 to $25. Open seven days a week till 10:30pm.

On the same thoroughfare is the **Tandoori Palace,** 86 Oxford St., Darlinghurst (tel. 02/331-7072). A palace it ain't, exactly, but the place is newly and tastefully decked out and boasts a very elegant cocktail bar—a rarity in Indian eateries. The fare offers specialties from half a dozen Indian regions and the menu is cleverly balanced between red-hot and mildly seasoned dishes. You can order an economy meal or a middling expensive repast, as your exchequer permits. Most of the main courses go for around $9 to $10. Among the lamb dishes, the saag gosht, cooked with spinach and spices from the proprietor's own recipe, stands out. On the mild side you have the beef badami, served in a creamy sauce with ground almonds. If you're a couple your best bet is the mixed platter for two; heaped with succulent chunks of chicken, lamb, and king prawns, roasted in a tandoor. At the finish try the homemade mango ice cream with pistachio nuts. Open all week till 11pm.

4. Old Standbys, Cafés, and Pubs

Sydney is literally entwined with chain restaurants, including the ubiquitous **McDonald's** and **Kentucky Fried Chicken** franchises, for which you'd need a separate alphabetical address appendix. Most of the chain establishments belong in the economy bracket, but there are certain exceptions. One is the purely Australian **Black Stump** series, specializing in prime steaks cooked to exact order, where a meal costs around $24. Others, like **Hungry Jack's,** dispense hamburgers throughout the continent but have only one Sydney outlet. This one is at 640 George St. (tel. 02/267-2816), and sells so-called Aussie burgers (with egg and beetroot) for $4.50.

Of the chains listed below, I'm giving only the addresses in reasonably central locations.

Pancakes on the Rocks, 10 Hickson Rd., The Rocks (tel. 02/27-6371), is one of the country's greatest business successes. The decor alone could keep you entertained, but for good measure the management also provides games of chess, backgammon, and Trivial Pursuit. The menu offers an immense array of pancakes from savory (like the Persian Tabriz) to sweet blintzes with cheese, brandied sultanas, and sour cream. They cost $5.05 to $10.25, the place stays open seven days around the clock, and the breakfast specials include "bottomless" cups of coffee. Other outlets are **Pancakes at the Movies,** 485 George St.; at 199 Military Rd., Neutral Bay; and 164 Campbell Parade, Bondi Beach.

Denny's, 334 Macquarie St., Liverpool (tel. 02/821-1222). These are very modern, highly functional fast-food places with large menus, swift service, and no ambience to speak of, but imbued with a great knack for catering to kids. They stay open 24 hours, and have spotless facilities and no-smoking sections. This chain features a three-course special that's hard to beat: you get soup, a choice between three main courses on the menu, and dessert for $11. These meals come with crackers and salad on the side, and the fish dishes are not only excellent but very ample. Other branches are at 486 Church St., Parramatta, and 296 King's Way, Caringbah.

Double Bay Steak Houses, 31 Market St. (tel. 02/29-6965), started out in Double Bay but have since spread all over town. And no wonder. The labels are misleading because these are not exclusively steak houses, but serve chicken, veal, and seafood as well. In all categories the helpings are very generous and include salad, garlic bread, and either baked potatoes or french fries. Prices depend on the day of the week. Four days it's $8.50; Friday, Saturday, and Sunday carry surcharges bringing it to around $10. The chain is fully licensed and serves wine by the glass. Other locations include 15 Knox St., Double Bay; 66 Spit Road, Mosman; and the corner of Campbell Parade and Roscoe Street, Bondi Beach.

Pizza Pizazz, 65 Bondi Rd., Bondi (tel. 02/389-4666). These places are best known for their delivery vehicles: pink mini-vans wearing top hats! You can't help noticing them even in dense traffic. The pizzas come in a fairly wide price range, which depends on the unusual number of choices in the toppings. They cost from $7 to $12 and range from just large to positively gigantic. Deliveries to inner areas are free. Other branches are at 242 Military Rd., Neutral Bay; and 323 Anzac Parade, Kingsford.

The above chain is frequently confused with the **Pizza Huts.** These, however, are located chiefly downtown, where they have acquired a reputation for quality. The Huts are licensed and in operation seven days a week till 11:30pm. You'll find them at 630 George St. and 238 Pitt St.

A CLUSTER OF CAFES

Nobody has come up with a precise definition of the term "café," not even the French who coined it. Whatever it may be, Sydney is full of the species. There are hundreds of them, ranging from lunch spots that close in the early afternoon to all-nighters that never close at all. Some prefer the hoary English label "coffee lounge"; other go by cutesy personal tags. They may serve snacks only or offer fairly elaborate meals. They may be totally devoid of character or breathe atmosphere. In any guise, they fulfill the vital function of providing rest for tired legs, closing the gap between dinner and bed, allowing you to imbibe a bit of local color. For although Sydney has no classified "café society," certain places get a regular and particular clientele that may tell you more about the neighborhood than any guidebook.

The spots listed below are merely a few samples, chosen from areas that visitors are most likely to wander in. A few are licensed; the majority don't handle liquor.

Frenchy's Café, MLC Centre, Martin Place. Right in the heart of downtown, this is one of the terrace cafés overlooking the lunchtime entertainment below. Sit under umbrellas in the open or behind sheltering glass on a raised stone piazza and order Devonshire tea with freshly baked scones and jam. Nothing remotely "Frenchy" about this place, which caters mainly to office workers. Closes at 8pm and stays closed Sundays.

Café Opera, 117 Macquarie St., is the svelte and ultra-chic coffeehouse of the Hotel Inter-Continental. Fully licensed, this is a cocktail as much as a coffee establishment, and "up there" on the price scale. Service has the velvety touch that goes with such elite surroundings. Open daily from breakfast (which costs $13) till midnight.

Hyde Park Barracks, on Macquarie Street, may sound like an odd name, but this really was the barracks of the New South Wales regiment back in the convict days. You sit in what used to be the officers' mess, overlooking the parade ground outside. A tourist landmark, often difficult to get into, the Barracks serves a set menu as well as between-meal bites. The fare is fine (sandwich platters for $8 to $10), the coffee the weakest link. Better stick to tea or something stronger—the place is licensed. Open seven days till 5pm.

Roma, 189 Hay St. Located at the other end of the center city, near Chinatown, the Roma fills a double role as an inexpensive Italian restaurant and a superlative—and equally Italian—café. It's tremendously popular in both roles, particularly with family groups at weekends. Apart from good solid food, the Roma serves some of the finest Italian pastries and cakes you've ever munched, for about $3 each, accompanied by a dozen varieties of coffee, all outstanding. The only possible complaint is with the closing time: Monday through Friday it's 5:30pm, and on Saturday, 3:30pm; closed Sunday.

Over to Kings Cross, where the hours suit the nightbirds.

Café at the Fountain, Darlinghurst Road, Kings Cross. Directly opposite sparkling El Alamein Fountain, the heart of the Cross, this place offers a grandstand view of the nocturnal action all around. With a plain interior, but a vast expanse of outdoor tables and umbrellas, this is the prime rendezvous spot of the area. The iced coffee (at $2.50 a tall glass) is the best in Sydney. Open seven days until around 2am.

Sweethearts, 40 Darlinghurst Rd., Kings Cross, was the inspiration for the hit song "Breakfast at Sweethearts," by the Australian rock group Cold Chisel. You can have breakfast or any other meal there because Sweethearts is open around the clock, seven days a week. Meals are light, but the selection is large and inexpensive (Spanish omelet for $5.50), and the espresso first-rate. This is chiefly a hangout for locals, so you can observe real slices of Kings Cross life while sitting there. Strictly indoors and no decor to speak of, but the street windows offer a regular roadshow.

Geoffrey Café, 1B Roslyn St., Kings Cross, has another plain interior, but a lovely tree-shaded patch of corner pavement for outdoor sitting, as pleasant for breakfast as for night observations. Frequently there's a street performer (juggler, singer, dancer, fire-eater) in action on the street corner. The coffee is good and strong, and most of the main dishes go for around $7.50. Hours are somewhat erratic: sometimes till midnight, sometimes till 3am.

Bar Coluzzi, 322 Victoria St., Kings Cross is sadly misnamed, since it serves no liquor, but is one of Sydney's prime cafés. Bar Coluzzi always has a crowd spilling out on the sidewalk, always has flirtations or debates in progress, and yet has enough sheltered corner tables to let patrons read books, write letters, or just study the scene. It serves what may be the finest coffee in the southern hemisphere, as well as a limited array of scrumptious Italian pastries. Opening hours extremely flexible—let's say from early in the morning till mid-evening.

Dean's Café, 1 Kellett St., Kings Cross, is a coffeehouse cum BYO tailored for nightbirds and insomniacs, of which the Cross has a vast supply. The interior is so dark that you have to find a table by touch. You could spend hours in there without knowing what the decor is like. But both service and clientele are amiable, immense bowls of nachos come for $9, and the homemade Cointreau cake is in a class of its own. Dean's doesn't start filling up until around 10pm, but stays open till 3am on weekdays, till 5am Saturdays and Sundays.

Badde Manors, 37A Glebe Point Rd., Glebe, despite the dreadful pun of a name, is a cozy and interesting place. Vegetarian by persuasion, but BYO, the Manors serves such items as eggplant cutlets and lasagne besides excellent coffee and various herbal teas. The clientele is young, mainly local, and an intriguingly mixed bag of college students, journalists, and artists. Open till 1am weekdays, till 5am on weekends.

Harry's Café de Wheels, 1 Cowper Wharf Rd., Woolloomooloo. This isn't a café at all but an institution, the scene and subject of countless semi-true anecdotes dispensed by stand-up comics. It's a pie caravan, successor to the original Harry who fed sailors and wharf laborers in dawn's early gray for 40 years. Now the pie wagon is a magnet for platinum night owls and visiting celebrities who wait patiently in their limos until their turn comes for a wedge of steaming-hot pie and a thick cuppa. Doesn't have a telephone, but stays in operation till 3am, seven days a week.

Good Health Café, 185 Avenue Rd., Mosman. Don't be put off by the name; this place is an absolute charmer. Very small, tastefully furnished, with a special corner for kids, the café isn't *quite* vegetarian: it does serve chicken and seafood. But most of the patrons come because of the superb open sandwiches on whole-meal bread, and the even better cakes. The orange and almond tortes are positively poetic. There is a selection of herbal teas, fresh fruit juices (squeezed before your eyes), and some of the finest, strongest coffee served in Sydney. The cakes are made from flourless recipes, the ingredients used in the hot dishes so fresh you can taste the countryside. The only drawback is the hours—the café closes at 5pm six days, and stays closed on Monday.

The **Good Day Café,** 222 Glenmore Rd., Five Ways, Paddington, overlooks a road junction with the ambience of a village square and blends in perfectly. Small, simple, with deliberately understated decor, this daytime snack shop and local rendezvous spot depends on first-rate modern art pieces—silkscreens, portraits, and still lifes —for ornamental effect. The taped background music consists mainly of jazz classics kept low enough to permit table talk. Menu offerings run from $3.60 to $6. For an excellent light lunch try the open focaccia with homemade pizza sauce and salad garnish followed by the fresh fruit salad. The café is open from 8am to 5:30pm Monday through Friday, and till 3pm Saturday; closed Sunday.

If you feel a craving for those delicately symphonic open Swedish sandwiches that always make you wish for a couple more, drop in at the **Skandic,** at the corner of Crown and Cathedral streets, Woolloomooloo. This regular rendezvous for Sydney's Scandinavians dishes up a mouthwatering selection, the concoctions piled high on white, black, or cracker bread. Combinations like herring, cucumber, tomato, and lettuce cost around $3.50, but you need several for a meal. Coffee and tea are both excellent, but the hours far too brief: 7am to 3pm Monday through Saturday.

. . . AND A PATTERN OF PUBS

Under the dead hand of wowser dominance Sydney's "hotel" cuisine achieved truly impressive depths. You ate plastic food off plastic tables and washed it down with beer. The result, of course, was that no one who valued his or her stomach had a meal in a pub. When the Great Culinary Revolution swept Australia, publicans became aware that they were losing a great deal of money in the upheaval; licensed and BYO restaurants were drawing off thousands of patrons who once frequented "hotels." The publicans (at least a good many of them) reacted by taking in first-rate chefs as business partners. They had the advantage of owning licensed premises, whereas restaurants had to go through the liquor rigmarole before opening their doors. The result of this belated alliance is that certain pubs today offer some of the best and most atmospheric meals extant. As a general rule they offer lunch at lower prices and serve dinner till 10pm. The survey below includes only a few of the possibilities. But any cab driver or hotel clerk will gladly add to your list; most of them have their own particular favorites.

Agincourt Hotel, at the corner of Harris Street and Broadway (tel. 02/211-4375), is an elderly Victorian structure with an unpretentious bar downstairs. But the Sri Lankan Room upstairs ranks high among fans of the cuisine of Sri Lanka. If you haven't sampled the cuisine before, this is an experience. The menu is huge, including delicacies like spiced (very) meatballs, marinated lamb shanks, honeyed chicken basted in aromatic herbs, and gently fiery Sri Lankan sausages. A new dish is featured every month. For teetotalers, the restaurant offers large carafes of unsweetened apple juice. Open five days till 10pm; closed Monday and Tuesday.

Tilbury Hotel, at the corner of Nicholson and Forbes streets, Woolloomooloo (tel. 02/357-1914). My, how that once notorious dockside district south of Kings Cross has changed. Spike's Brasserie, housed inside the hotel, is now a major draw. The reason is partly the fare, partly the entertainment. On weekdays you can get an excellent meal selecting from among marinated king prawns, house pâtés, American spare ribs, quail, and quite a superlative chocolate-cream pie. A three-courser will run $18. On Sunday it's a grand-slam buffet. There's a garden for summer dining, open fireplaces for winter coziness. On Thursday, Friday, and Saturday evening Spike's puts on "cabaret" shows ($5 to $7 cover)—a nice, vaguely open-ended label that can cover just about anything. But every Sunday afternoon there is a not-to-be-missed chamber music ensemble called Mozart and his Mates that starts at 1pm and has music lovers flocking in from all over town. As I said, the Loo *has* changed! Open Monday through Saturday till 10pm, on Sunday till 8:30pm.

London Tavern, 85 Underwood St., Paddington (tel. 02/ 331-1637). The hotel was built in 1875 as a blue-collar beer palace and is going strong more than a century later, but in a somewhat

Drinks in a Brewery

The name of **Tommo's Pub Brewery,** 116 Victoria Rd., Rozelle (tel. 02/810-7666), is a traditional joke around Sydney, where every kid knows that "Tommo's" denotes an illicit floating two-up game, spinning coins at a different location each night. Proprietor Rod Thomas cashed in on the tradition quite legitimately by calling his pub after himself. It attracts a lot of customers, but does lead to a certain amount of confusion because no two-up game is conducted on the premises—nor in the back.

But Tommo's has other claims to fame. The pub actually incorporates a brewery, separated from the splendiferous bar by a glass wall. You can watch the beer being brewed while sipping the end product. You can also ask for one of the "special" home brews, but not if you're driving. Their alcohol content is a military secret. Apart from all that, Tommo's has a leafy beer garden and a smart bistro section. The fare is good, simple, and inexpensive, built around standard favorites like steaks and salad, roast beef, and schnitzels. In case you don't wish to breast any bars, the entire boutique brewing action can be followed on the specially installed closed-circuit video system. Open daily till 10pm.

different guise. Now very much a watering hole for youngish execs of both sexes, the London houses La Trattoria—and they don't come much more Italian than that. Stimulate your appetite with baby squid in fettuccine, proceed to a main course of, say, pollo valdostana (with ham and mozzarella in white wine), and finish with a cream Napoleon dessert. The feast will cost you $19 and is available seven days a week till 10pm.

Dolphin Hotel, 412 Crown St., Surry Hills (tel. 02/357-5614). A sizable group of aficionados swear that this place serves the top "pub grub" in Sydney. It certainly does so in exceptionally pleasing surroundings. In good weather it's imperative to make reservations, because the Dolphin's tranquil and romantic garden terrace fills up fast. The salad here is famous—you can pile up as much and as often as you desire for $5. Accompany this with seafood quiche or the exceptionally thick and juicy steak from the grill and you'll have an eminently satisfying meal for around $13. Open seven days a week, on Monday and Tuesday for lunch only.

Hero of Waterloo, 81 Lower Fort St., The Rocks (tel. 02/27-8471), is the oldest pub in Sydney Town. Originally built as a jailhouse in 1804, the little sandstone building was licensed as a "common and public tavern" in 1815, just after the Battle of Waterloo. It enjoyed an evil reputation during the windjammer days—drinkers would make involuntary exits through a trapdoor in the floor and wake up doing deck duty on some undermanned coffin ship sailing for China. Today this colonial relic is a *must* for visitors (the trapdoor no longer functions) and its restaurant, the Duke's

Room, is full of nostalgic atmosphere with hanging gas lamps and polished brassware. It serves items such as veal in cream of mushroom sauce, chicken breasts in tarragon, and crumbed brains with lemon, alongside a good selection of Australian wines and beer. On Friday, Saturday, and Sunday there's entertainment in the form of old-time and folk music played with nostalgic fervor.

Sir John Young Hotel, at the corner of George and Liverpool streets (tel. 02/267-3608). Despite the hotel's British name, its restaurant, the Grand Taverna, is genuinely Spanish, as are many of the customers. Stone archways, wood paneling, and guitar background music set the tone. The menu reinforces it. Saffron-hued paella, grilled bream, roast kingfish, with caramel flan for dessert, for about $14. Lunch is served Monday through Saturday; dinner, Monday through Thursday till 9:30pm; closed Sunday.

Royal George Hotel, 115 Sussex St. (tel. 02/29-2285), is a very old watering hole turned into a retreat for trendies, who come in droves. The restaurant here, Enzuccio, has a delightfully split personality. Downstairs, the bistro portion is casual and economical, with an adjoining open courtyard where you can sup and sip while enjoying a ringside view of Darling Harbour. This section specializes in barbecues, pasta, and salads, with meals costing around $8. Upstairs, the "ristorante" is more formal, with à la carte dining and menus that change daily. The fare is first-rate Italian, particularly the antipasto and those mouthwatering little dumplings called gnocchi. Open seven days till 10pm. The disco on the premises operates Wednesday through Saturday till 3am.

Royal Hotel, 237 Glenmore Rd., Paddington (tel. 02/331-2604), is another "royal" and another of the legion of old-time pubs refurbished and face-lifted—but only on the inside, so as to retain the exterior patina. The downstairs bar now looks downright regal, with stained-glass windows and leather lounges. Upstairs, you can dine on an authentic Victorian balcony, wreathed with the delicate wrought ironwork called "Sydney lace." The menu here includes an outstanding bell-pepper, olive, and anchovy tart as an appetizer, and whole grilled and marinated spatchcock as a main course. A three-course dinner costs around $22. Open seven days: till midnight during the week, till 8pm on Sunday.

Lords', 79 Bayswater Rd., Rushcutters Bay (tel. 02/331-2520). Calling itself "The Tavern with No Peers," this establishment stands just beyond Kings Cross and serves some of Sydney's most unusual dishes. One of the house specials is crocodile steak, at $19.50 a plate, and a number of patrons come a long way just for that. You can also get Northern Territory buffalo steak for $12.50. The hotel also features more mundane fare, like lemon sole and superb fresh rhubarb mousse with custard for dessert. On Friday night you can hear some very fine live jazz here. Open noon to midnight, seven days.

Hotel Bayswater, 100 Bayswater Rd., Rushcutters Bay (tel. 02/331-2941), is a very "in" gathering spot for the young party crowd of the eastern suburbs, but likewise is esteemed by serious gourmands who meet here every month for a formal food- and wine-tasting luncheon, with guest speakers who are intimidatingly knowledgeable on both subjects. The dining room has an air of cool simplicity and the wine list is impressive. Several wine companies use the special gourmet lunches here to introduce newly released vintages. Outstanding dishes include rack of lamb and the grilled quail forestière. A three-course meal costs around $23 and the restaurant is open Monday through Saturday till 10pm.

Coogee Bay Hotel, 237 Coogee Bay Rd. (tel. 02/665-8975). This was the only hotel I discovered with a BYO restaurant on the premises. The restaurant is Renato's, and you can buy your bottle in the same house, then take it to your table. The hotel is a landmark in one of Sydney's most popular beach suburbs and is usually crammed with the surfing fraternity. The restaurant proclaims itself a pizza place, but actually offers a wide, very good, and economical range of Italian favorites. The pasta is freshly made, the fried calamari succulent and tender, the scaloppine asparagus richly flavorsome. Desserts are ordinary, but the espresso is quite outstanding. A three-course meal costs around $17. Open till 11pm seven days.

Geebung Polo Club, 106 George St., Redfern (tel. 02/699-6381). As far as I know, this is the only pub in town named after a poem. The verses were penned by Australia's national bard, "Banjo" Patterson, a century ago, but the original Geebung Polo Club was a famous jazz dive of the '60s. The current bearer of the title is an elderly hotel, refurbished into a chic, colonial-style drink-establishment with stained-glass windows, red cedar flooring, elegant wood paneling, and walls hung with horse prints and polo mallets. The place consists of the spacious downstairs bar and an upstairs entertainment venue. An adjoining bar caters to pool and jukebox buffs and holds regular pool competitions. The restaurant menu is short and inexpensive: you get rump steak or pasta dishes for around $9, plus endless helpings at the self-service salad bar. The wine list, on the other hand, is extensive and of a high standard. Entertainment here runs from jazz pianists and jazz combos to rock groups and—once a week—male strippers. On band nights there's a cover charge. Open seven days till midnight.

Burdekin Hotel, 2 Oxford St., Darlinghurst (tel. 02/331-1046). A classic example of the split personality that haunts so many Sydney watering holes . . . and makes them interesting. The downstairs bars are quite pedestrian, the building medium-ugly. But the fourth-floor dining room is an intimate little gem, done in art deco style, agleam with starched-linen whiteness and crystal glitter. It serves what many knowledgeable food-lovers rate as the finest pub fare in town—you have to book a day in advance to make sure of a table. The wine list features some of Australia's proudest vintages and the service has the friendly, assured polish of a first-class country inn. The menu is based on seafood (try the Jervis Bay mussels in saffron butter) but reinforced by dry land specials like steak tartare and roasted spatchcock, accompanied by potato chips that make you realize how delicious they can taste *if* prepared properly. Dinner here will cost you around $36 and is served Monday through Saturday till 10:30pm.

Woolloomooloo Bay Hotel, 2 Bourke St., Woolloomooloo (tel. 02/357-1928), is yet another symbol of how the vibes have changed in "the Loo." A decade or so ago this hotel bore a different name and they used to raffle off girls. Now this once-infamous spot is a mecca for the upwardly mobile of all sexes and winner of the coveted 1988 Best Hotel tourism award. The *pièce de résistance* here is the bistro, an in- and outdoor affair with atrium roof and colored umbrellas, a view of the bay, and a celebrated pianist who tickles the baby grand at night. The bistro's blackboard menu offers stir-fried squid, chile crab, char-grilled steaks, and a mountainous mixed seafood platter ($20). Open seven days till 9pm.

Pub Entertainment

Pubs are the main venues for Sydney's rock bands and a few of these will be discussed in "Nightlife," Chapter XI. The groups— scores of them—run the gamut from delirious to disastrous. Unless you're familiar with the local music world, catching any particular category is a matter of luck. The only guideline is that a cover charge of around $5 usually means a popular outfit.

A handful of hostelries feature tacky amusements like ladies' mud wrestling or bosom-painting contests (dwarf-throwing is *out).* The vast majority, however, rely on pastimes that don't require paid performers. One of them is Sky Channel, a satellite television service devoted almost entirely to sports, and screened simultaneously on sets strategically placed so there's no escaping them—guaranteed to paralyze any attempts at socializing.

Sky Channel comes gratis, but the special pub poker machines cost 20¢ per hand. These are TV screens that flash up poker hands on which you can bet. Winnings are paid out in beer, occasionally in cash.

The two traditional tavern games, darts and pool, are usually played for "shouts"—that is, the loser pays for a round of drinks. Pool-table etiquette is a mite tricky: every pub seems to have its own rules. Make sure to have them explained to you before you start rolling the balls.

Streetcar Dining

A quite unique brasserie/nightspot in the eastern suburbs, the **Maroubra Junction Hotel,** 199 Maroubra Rd. (tel. 02/349-1174), is based around an authentic 1924 model Melbourne tram (streetcar to you, mate). Tram no. 411 has been converted into a 34-seat dining car with tapestry seats and dainty lace curtains. The remainder of the stylishly refurbished hotel is more or less an adjunct to the ancient vehicle standing in motionless splendor, flanked by two skylights. The tram menu includes seafood in Pernod sauce, pepper steak, first-rate vegetarian platters, and chicken filet stuffed with prawns, Camembert cheese, and garlic. Main courses cost around $13. Entertainment features a Wurlitzer baby grand (historically in tune with the tram), weeknight vocalists, and 1920s jazz on Sunday. Open seven days a week till 10pm.

THE SIGHTS OF SYDNEY

This chapter posed some organizational difficulties because so many of Sydney's attractions—like its beaches—aren't "sights" in the strict sense. A harbor cruise, on the other hand, is very much a sight, but not in the same way as a historic edifice. And how do you classify a quite colossal, multilayered creation such as the Darling Harbour Project?

I have, therefore, adopted a rather freewheeling method, regulated more by taste than by category. All the beaches come into a bracket of their own. Art museums and exhibitions get a separate chapter (see Chapter VIII), as do the organized sight-seeing tours that will enable you to take in most of these attractions in a couple of packaged swoops (see Chapter VII).

I've made no attempt to arrange the sights in order of importance—I wouldn't know how. But we'll start off with one I can call the top draw without fear of contradiction.

1. The Top Attractions

THE OPERA HOUSE

No city ever consciously created its symbolic landmark—it just happened to become one, often in the teeth of fierce public antagonism. Most Parisians detested the Eiffel Tower when it first went up. While Sydneysiders weren't exactly opposed to the Opera House, they viewed the project with considerable cynicism. The general opinion was "It'll never fly." The cynics very nearly proved right, because everything that could possibly go wrong with the enterprise followed Murphy's Law and did so.

The project was conceived in 1954 by a group of prominent citizens who selected a suitable site, a derelict trolley depot on Bennelong Point. In 1957 the Danish architect Joern Utzon won the international competition for a design of the building with his revolutionary sails-on-the-harbor effect, and the actual work began. The enormous projected budget of $7.2 million was easily funded by means of a state lottery. But now the troubles began. The first major lottery winner became the victim of Australia's first kidnap-murder—his young son was killed by the ransom kidnapper. In 1966 Utzon, fed up with bureaucratic and union troubles, withdrew from the project and went home.

The plans he left behind were full of untried techniques and daring innovations, and the people who tried to put them into practice fell from one blunder to the next. They left out vital staircases, they left out parking lots, they forgot about fire exits, about elevators, and half a hundred other trifles. Work had to be redone, patched up, overhauled, modified—and this in the face of countless stoppages, strikes, and on-site labor disputes that slowed proceedings still further.

For years the skeptical populace watched the skeleton that never seemed to put on flesh and coined cute little nicknames. "The Hunchback of Bennelong Point," they called it; the "New South Whale," "a haystack with a tarpaulin," and "a pack of French nuns playing football." Meanwhile the budget allocations went up and up, to $50 million, $110 million, and still the thing wasn't finished.

And then one day it was. People rubbed their eyes, looked again, and saw a pearl-pale sculpture, grandiose yet fragile, floating above the water against a background of blue that set it off like a painting. It was a masterpiece, the most beautiful creation of its kind in the world. No other could match it. The London *Times* called it "the building of the century," and even the most sardonic locals realized that they had a national symbol on their foreshore. When Queen Elizabeth cut the ribbon in October 1973, everybody, even those who didn't give a hang about music, was aware that Sydney had entered a new era.

The Opera House is far more than simply a building housing an opera company. It's a pleasure complex in the best sense of the word. Apart from the magnificent main auditorium, the building contains three performance halls (within a total of 980 rooms): one for concerts, one for drama, and one for more intimate recitals. Aside from grand opera, ballet, and symphony, it's an acoustically perfect showcase for pop groups, comedians, and experimental stage productions. People flock to all of them with unabated enthusiasm. The Bennelong sea monster, 30 years in the hatching, has been turned into a prince by public embrace. You can eat and drink there as well—and *very* well—and during the intermissions, walk out on the promenade and stroll by the water, with yachts and ocean liners sailing by. You don't have to attend a performance to admire the interior: the timber panels, the tinted glass merging into the sea beyond, the modernistic murals, the curtains woven in the bold hues of the Australian day and night. Tours are conducted daily from 9:15am to 4pm. Adults pay $4.50; children, $2.30.

THE ROCKS

Northwest of the central city area lies the cradle of Sydney Town. The Rocks, between Sydney Cove and Darling Harbour, were the site of the colony's first permanent buildings, including the first hospital, church, tavern, military barracks, and jail. A little later the upper-class citizens built imposing mansions in the higher rock region and poured their wastes on the lesser mortals dwelling below. The ramshackle terraces in the lower reaches became a Barbary Coast strip—a place for cheap liquor and prostitutes for visiting sailors.

Today the area has been lovingly restored and ranks as Sydney's second-strongest tourist magnet. You can spend a couple of hours or a couple of weeks exploring it, because it also contains some of Sydney's finest hotels, pubs, restaurants, and nightspots.

The logical starting point is the **Information Centre,** at 104 George St. There you can pick up a handy map/guide and simply follow the route indicated. Stops along the way might be:

The **Argyle Arts Centre,** 18 Argyle St., a complex of workshops, art galleries, stores, and courtyards housed in a handsome three-story warehouse, convict-built in 1820 of durable sandstone and hand-hewn timber. You can watch various craftspeople in action (the crafts change, the beards seem permanent). Buy something or just wander around, perhaps taking in a free film show at the **Ampol History Centre.** For lunch or tea, stop at **Mary Reibey's Parlor.** Mary was transported at the age of 13 for stealing a horse (and was mighty lucky not to be hanged for it). She died 60 years later, richer by seven children and £120,000 sterling, most of which she acquired by trading in the rum stored in the cellars below.

The Argyle Cut is a 300-foot tunnel hollowed out of the solid rock to give direct access to Millers Point from Circular Quay. It was begun by convict laborers in 1843, and you can still see the prisoners' marks on the granite. The cut region was possibly the toughest scene in the southern hemisphere. This is where the thugs, sailors, whalers, harpies, and sharpies gathered after dusk to exchange gossip, cash, women, or a little friendly knifeplay. The infamous Sydney Ducks were reigning princes here, and every morning the garrison soldiers picked up a few bodies for burial.

The **Mining Museum,** 36 George St., offers considerably more than exhibits of minerals and excavation methods. The imaginatively and lavishly staged shows take visitors on a journey through the formation of the earth's crust. Several floors of the building are transformed into a realistic coal mine, and you follow not only the mining processes but the uses to which the earth's treasures are eventually put. By means of interactive video equipment and computers, the museum simulates earthquakes and pretty scary volcanic activities. Admission is free. Open Monday through Friday till 4pm, on Saturday from 1 to 4pm, and on Sundays from 11am to 4pm.

Now covered by the southern end of the Harbour Bridge, **Dawes Point** was named after Lt. William Dawes, who operated Australia's first observatory here. This was also the location of the colony's first defense battery, consisting of 14 guns each weighing four tons. Five of these cannon still stand in the park. They were originally intended to ward off French enemies, later a possible raid by Russian warships. Neither foe ever appeared. By the time the real enemy arrived—Japanese midget submarines during World War II —Sydney's defenses had been shifted elsewhere, so the guns never served any but ornamental purposes.

Cadman's Cottage, at 110 George St., is the oldest dwelling in Sydney. Constructed by Francis Greenway, the colony's first architect (likewise a convict), it went up in 1815 and now houses the National Parks and Wildlife Association. A historical display center downstairs is open to the public and can be viewed Monday through Friday from 9am to 4pm. The **Colonial House Museum,** at 53 Lower Fort St., isn't a museum in the usual sense. It's a period home —or actually two floors of a four-story terrace residence. The six museum rooms, furnished with 19th-century elegance, look so lived-in that you can almost see some affluent Aussie forebear strolling through the plush. There is a complete photographic record of The Rocks from 1880 to 1901, giving you a glimpse of the many buildings that were demolished when the approaches to the Harbour Bridge were built. Open daily from 10am to 5pm. Admission is 90¢ for adults, 40¢ for children.

If you don't feel like tramping up and down the hilly Rocks, you can ride in correct period style. The **Horse and Carriage Company,** with a rank at 101 George St. (outside the Old Police Station), operates a fleet of enclosed hansom cabs and open wagons, drawn by fine horses and piloted by nattily dressed coachmen (and women). Hansom cabs (for two persons) cost $20 for a tour of the region, with the same charge for four in an open wagon. You can rent a carriage from the stand or call the company's reservations office (tel. 02/27-3181).

The tip of the Rocks lies underneath the Sydney Harbour Bridge. The southeast pylon of the bridge has been turned into the **Pylon Lookout.** All four of these massive structures are used as storage chambers (during World War II they also supported antiaircraft guns). Getting to the top of the pylon means climbing some 200 steps, but the view from the peak is worth it. The whole expanse of the harbor lies at your feet. Admission is free and the lookout is open daily from 10am to 5pm.

Below the Rocks, underneath the southern end of the Harbour Bridge, lies **Pier One** (the official address is Hickson Road, Walsh Bay, but nobody has ever heard of it). Pier One is a multitiered, very commercial entertainment center, not exactly stylish, but loads of fun if you're in the right mood. A kind of merry mélange of amusement park and San Francisco's Cannery, Pier One has so many attractions that you'd have to list them alphabetically. Clustered in a row of converted warehouses are bumper cars, merry-go-rounds, a movie theater, an excellent bookstore (John Cookson), market stalls, shops selling everything from jewelry to junk, a colonial vil-

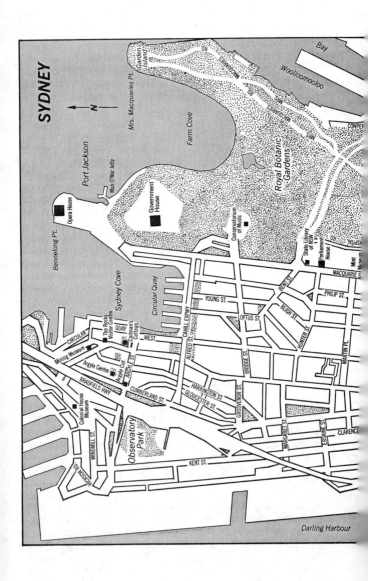

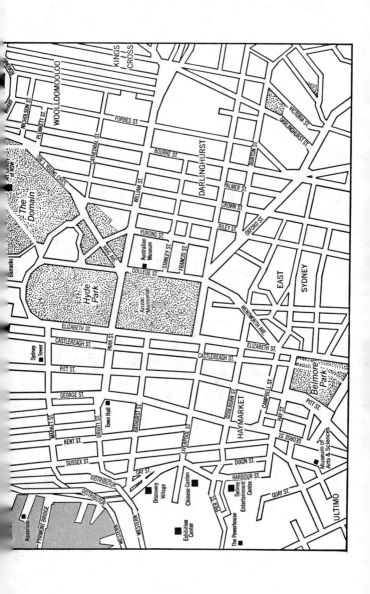

lage from the turn of the century, and a strange but fun amusement park ride called the Gravitron. Restaurant outlets range from little seafood stalls to glassed-in mansions with gourmet ratings. Also cafés, snack bars and ice-cream booths, and candy stores. The harbor views are spectacular from all levels, the offerings wildly cosmopolitan, and on sunny days the place is sheer delight. Entertainment is supplemented by strolling minstrels, jazz musicians, folksingers, and earnest municipal bands. The fun goes on seven days till 5 or 6pm.

FORT DENISON

You can't miss the little mount of rock with the round tower that looks rather like a squat submarine anchored in Sydney Harbour. Officially named Fort Denison, it was known, and dreaded, by the convicts as "Pinchgut Island," the punishment rock where you were confined on "tight rations" (meaning starved to a skeleton). A woeful ballad of the period ran:

> Carve yer name into me backbone,
> Stretch me skin across a drum;
> Iron me up on Pinchgut Island
> From today till Kingdome Come.
> I will eat yer Norfolk dumpling
> Like a juicy Spanish plum,
> Even dance the Newgate Hornpipe,
> If ye'll only give me rum.

("Norfolk dumpling", for your information, was prison gruel, and dancing the "Newgate Hornpipe" meant getting hanged.) Escape from this miniature Devil's Island was virtually impossible because the harbor then was full of sharks (hunting and oil slicks have driven them away). Built and armed to protect Sydney from invasion (which never came), Fort Denison today is a tide observation station as well as a landmark. The round Martello Tower still houses the six muzzle-loading cannons, which were never fired. But the "one o'clock gun" booms out from the fort every day on the dot— you can set your watch by it. The Maritime Services Board arranges tours of the island, but you have to make reservations ahead by calling 02/240-2111, ext. 2036. The tours take about 1½ hours and cost $7 for adults, $3.50 for children.

TARONGA PARK ZOO

Located across the harbor in Mosman, the Taronga Park Zoo has the most beautiful natural setting of any zoological garden in the world. Perched on a hillside 12 minutes by ferry from Circular Quay, it offers harbor panoramas together with the animals and 75 acres of bushland park. Take the ferry from no. 5 wharf (adults pay $1.20; children, 60¢), then the waiting bus to the top of the hill and sight-see downhill all the way back to the ferry stop. See the koalas at their own treetop level in their specially designed enclosure. Check out the platypus house (you can watch it underwater), the rain-forest aviary (where you walk through the cage and have the birds fly above and around you), and the Friendship Farm, where you can pet a lamb and stroke a wombat. In the underground building, where special lights turn day into night, you can watch the nocturnal creatures of Australia and New Guinea at their busiest (watch for the huge Queensland fruit bats called flying foxes). Plus there are the inevitable lions, tigers, elephants, gorillas, bears, and monkeys. Admission is $11 for adults, $5 for children, and the zoo is open from 9am to 5pm seven days a week.

DARLING HARBOUR

This, the greatest urban redevelopment project in Australian history, covers the western dockside region and adds a new dimension to the downtown area. Darling Harbour used to be Sydney's tradesman's entrance, a wilderness of cranes and warehouses that fell into idle decrepitude when container shipping came in. Now the entire expanse has been transformed into a gigantic pleasure and cultural complex, with parks, gardens, and promenades thrown in as well as a monorail system to connect it with the center city.

Matters did not go altogether smoothly with this marvel; they rarely do in Sydney. It was to have contained the first *legal* gambling casino in the state (as distinct from the scores of illegal little dens now thriving). But someone discovered that the entrepreneurs involved had the wrong kind of business connections, and in the resultant uproar the casino project got shelved. It may yet reappear one day, but don't hold your breath. There are quite enough attractions to go on with in the meantime.

Harbourside Festival Marketplace is a huge, bustling, flag-fluttering marketplace, partly roofed against rain and festive with clowns, jugglers, dancers, and strolling musicians. It contains more than 200 shops and 9 restaurants and bars, as well as a disco.

Directly in front stands the **Sydney Maritime Museum** (tel. 02/552-2011), displaying historic ships and nautical equipment. The grandest exhibit is the 1874 vintage square-rigger *James Craig,* completely restored and equipped with a 24-projector audiovisual apparatus that gives you the thrill of a rough ocean voyage under canvas without the seasickness. Adults pay $4, children $2, and the place is open seven days from 10am to 6pm.

The Aquarium, Pier 26, simulates a trip to the bottom of the sea by means of two floating oceanariums and 50 tanks depicting aquatic environments around Australia. You get eye-to-eye encounters with sharks, stingrays, and giant eels; watch octopuses and deadly poisonous stonefish; and come within a couple of glass-partitioned inches of saltwater crocodiles grinning through barricades of teeth. Tickets $10 for adults, $5 for children. Open all week from 9:30am to 9pm.

The **Powerhouse Museum** (tel. 02/217-0111) has a misleading name because the exhibits are only indirectly linked to electricity. Primarily it tells the social history of Australia by showing the machines, the buildings, tools, and artifacts that made the country. The building is huge—large enough to display complete aircraft, locomotives, and houses. Many of the machines and gadgets are push-button affairs that can be worked by the visitors. Others show slices of everyday life, such as an old "picture palace" from the silent days, a bush squatter's hut, and a suburban grocery. Too much to see and play with for one visit; plan on coming back to see the rest. Free admission, and the hours are 10am to 5pm all week.

The **Chinese Garden** is an exquisite piece of horticultural craftsmanship, designed by specialists from Guangdong Province, and the the largest and most elaborate such garden outside China. Linking Chinatown with Darling Harbour, the complex centers on a two-story pavilion surrounded by a pattern of interconnected little lakes and waterfalls, spanned by bridges and laced with dreamily secluded walkways. Open daily till sunset. Admission is $2 for adults, 50¢ for children.

The **Exhibition Centre** is a huge edifice with a great roof canopy suspended from steel masts. Seven stories high, with an enormous interior expanse free of obstructing columns, the center holds a banqueting hall designed for 5,000 guests, and has changing exhibitions—the one I saw re-created the world of dinosaurs in all their reptilian splendor.

These are by no means all the attractions of Darling Harbour. There is also Australia's biggest **Convention Centre;** the entertainment-lined, carnival-style **Darling Walk;** and the restored, decorated, and illuminated **Pyrmont Bridge,** linking the center city with the project.

Transportation to and from is provided by the **Monorail,** which is an extremely touchy subject with Sydneysiders. The controversial apparatus glides silently above all traffic snarls, but possibly creates even more of them with the massive support pillars anchoring the rail to the streets below. Start talking monorail to a local and you can really buy into an argument. Rides cost $2. That part, at least, is unarguable.

2. More Attractions

SIGHTS IN THE CENTER CITY

The chief landmark in the central downtown region is **Sydney Tower,** one of the tallest structures in the southern hemisphere. It's a giant silver needle stabbing 1,000 feet into the sky, secured by steel cables and crowned with a shining gold turret. The tower, which looks incredibly slender from a distance, rises at the Centrepoint Arcade, 100 Market St., a maze of shops and boutiques that seems like a city of its own. The tower's Observation Platform offers stupendous views of the entire city area and beyond. High-speed elevators whisk you up—leaving your stomach somewhere below—and high-powered telescopes let you see still farther. The tower also con-

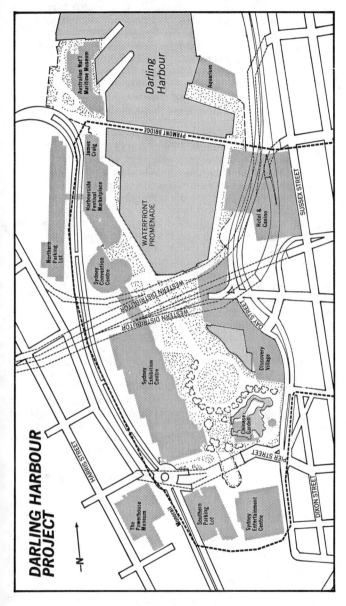

DARLING HARBOUR PROJECT

—N→

Darling Harbour

Australian Nat'l Maritime Museum

Aquarium

PYRMONT BRIDGE

James Craig

Harbourside Festival Marketplace

Northern Parking Lot

WATERFRONT PROMENADE

Hotel & Casino

SUSSEX STREET

Sydney Convention Centre

WESTERN DISTRIBUTOR

DAY STREET

WESTERN DISTRIBUTOR

Discovery Village

Sydney Exhibition Centre

Chinese Garden

HARRIS STREET

PIER STREET

DIXON STREET

The Powerhouse Museum

Monorail

Southern Parking Lot

Sydney Entertainment Centre

tains two restaurants (one revolving) at cloud level, reached by other elevators. Admission costs $5 for adults, $2 for children. The tower is open seven days till 9:30pm.

Parliament House, on Macquarie Street, seat of the New

South Wales state legislature and the oldest legislative building in Australia, was once the so-called Rum Hospital, origins which have given rise to countless jokes at the expense of the politicians who now occupy it. A beautiful piece of colonial architecture, with timber verandas and colonnades, the building can be inspected Monday through Friday from 10am to 3:30pm. On days when Parliament is in session, visitors are admitted to the galleries during Question Time, on Tuesday and Wednesday at 1:15pm and on Thursday at 9:30am. What you hear is not always edifying, but usually illuminating.

Next door to Parliament stands the **State Library of New South Wales.** Mount the impressive stone steps to the Dixson and Mitchell Galleries. A repository of papers, prints, paintings, and proclamations connected with the early settlement of Sydney, the galleries mount various showings of the trove. The items vary. If you're lucky you can see some of the wordless but graphic cartoons issued by colonial governors for the benefit of the Aborigines. The promises implied weren't always exactly sincere, but their meaning was clear enough. The galleries are open from 10am to 5pm Monday through Saturday and 2 to 6pm on Sunday.

The **Australian Museum,** at the corner of William and College streets (tel. 02/339-8111), is the largest museum of natural history on the continent, and also houses an impressive section on Aboriginal and Pacific Islands anthropology, including replicas of New Guinea villages. There are gigantic whale skeletons, models of sharks and other marine creatures, and hundreds of tribal weapons, artifacts, and ornaments. Admission is free and the museum is open seven days till 5pm.

Hyde Park Barracks, Queen's Square, Macquarie St. (tel. 02/217-0111), is another of the beautiful Georgian-style public buildings designed by the prolific convict-architect Francis Greenway. Completed in 1819 as a military barracks, the building is now partly a museum. The museum rooms trace the social history of Australia, starting with the convict room and concluding with the pretty dismal period style of the 1950s. Look for the special exhibitions arranged by this museum; some of them are highly original and all are arranged with painstaking care and knowledge. Admission is free. The barracks is open Wednesday through Monday from 10am to 5pm, on Tuesday from noon.

The **Mint Museum,** Queen's Square, Macquarie St. (tel. 02/217-0111), is the other wing of the old Rum Hospital, partly given over to the state legislature. The colony's coins used to be minted here, but now the rooms serve as a showcase for Australian decorative arts—a good choice, because the building is itself a work of art. Admission free, the museum is open daily from 10am to 5pm.

The Royal Botanic Garden (tel. 02/231-8111), stretching out for miles to the east of Queen's Square, forms the greater portion of an almost unbroken green quilt that starts at the Farm Cove, harborside in the north, and merges into **Hyde Park** to the southwest. The enormous expanse of greenery contains a glass pyramid of tropical plants, vast flower beds, duck ponds, secluded walkways, an open-air garden café, and a restaurant.

At the edge of the garden stands the **Art Gallery of New South Wales** (see Chapter VIII) and the oddly medieval-looking **Conservatorium of Music.** Inside the garden, on high ground, stands **Government House** (no, you can't get in there).

To the south, the Botanic Garden becomes the open grassy **Domain,** which was once one of Sydney's major Sunday entertainment areas. The Domain is a free-speech forum—anyone can mount a soapbox or its equivalent and bellow out orations on any subject. In prevideo times the Domain was populated by masses of leather-lunged orators declaiming on subjects ranging from industrial syndicalism to the removal of gallstones by means of prayer. Some were highly skilled in dealing with hecklers and keeping audiences amused. Nowadays their numbers have shrunk to a determined handful and most of the excitement has gone, but they still provide an intriguing interlude on a Sunday-afternoon stroll.

Sydney Entertainment Centre, Harbour St., Haymarket. Well, a thing of beauty it ain't, made no more so by the gigantic and fabulously tasteless billboard across the road. But this is Australia's largest auditorium and, though it looks like an outsize airport terminal, a marvel of interior flexibility. Four different layouts allow the center to be used for solo performers, theatrical productions, or big sporting events. It can hold from 3,500 to 12,000 people with not a single pillar to block anyone's view of the stage.

SIGHTS BEYOND THE INNER CITY

A living history of Australia's military forces, **Victoria Barracks,** Oxford St., Paddington (tel. 02/339-0455), built largely by convict labor and finished in 1848, was designed to house one regiment of British infantry. British garrison troops were withdrawn in 1870, since there was no conceivable enemy that couldn't be handled by the Royal Navy. Since then, Australia's own forces have occupied the barracks, which today are the hub and command post of the Commonwealth's field and supporting units. The building is a splendid example of late Georgian architecture, crammed with military memorabilia. Every Tuesday at 10am (except in December and January) there is a ceremonial changing of the guard, impressive to watch; following this, the premises are open to tours. Admission is free, and you can call ahead to make arrangements to visit.

Elizabeth Bay House, 7 Onslow Ave., Elizabeth Bay (tel. 02/358-2344), is an enchanting period mansion built for the colonial secretary of New South Wales in 1838. This is Australia's finest remaining "stately home." Laid out around a superb central staircase lit by an oval lantern from above, the white Grecian villa shows in what tasteful splendor the colonial upper classes dwelled at a time when Australia's lower orders were somewhat less stylishly housed. The furnishings have the typical elegant simplicity of the Georgian era (which was soon to be obliterated by the overstuffed red-brick monstrosities of the Victorians). Apart from the original furnishings, the mansion also displays changing exhibitions. It's open Tuesday through Sunday from 10am to 4:30pm. Admission is $3 for adults, $1.50 for students.

Sydney Agrodome, Dalgety Centre, RAS Showground, Paddington (tel. 02/331-7279), is a patch of rural Australia right in the city. Located at the Showgrounds of the Royal Agricultural Society, the Agrodome introduces you to a parade of famous sheep breeds, stages shearing exhibitions, and displays the process that transforms the rough and dirty fleece into finely spun wool. The best part of the show is the wonderfully photogenic sheepdog trial, in which the highly skilled pooch keeps control over a dozen woolly charges by responding to whistle signals from its master. The restaurant on the grounds serves traditional Outback lunches and the $9 admission ($4.50 for children) entitles you to billy tea and genuine bush dampers (unleavened strips of dough baked in campfire ashes). Shows at 9am, noon, and 2:30pm.

Children's Treasure House, 19 Beesan St., Leichhardt (tel. 02/560-2044), is a small museum of children's toys from the 1880s to the present. They range from the tin-clockwork mechanical contraptions of the early 1900s to the streamlined battery-operated gadgets of today. The best part, though, is the large collection of teddy bears, most beloved of all nursery companions. Admission costs $2 for adults, $1 for children. Open Monday through Friday from 10am to 4pm.

The **Hall of Champions,** State Sports Centre, Underwood Rd., Homebush (tel. 02/763-0111), is a memorial for the greats of Australian sports. Displays include hundreds of photos and books, plus memorabilia such as tennis rackets, cricket bats, boxing gloves, and football boots that belonged to the heroes. Admission is free. Open seven days 9am till 5pm.

Vaucluse House, Olola Ave., Vaucluse (tel. 02/337-1957), is another lovingly preserved stately home, formerly the property of explorer-statesman William Charles Wentworth (you'll find reminders of his name all over New South Wales). Completed in the 1830s, the house is surrounded by superbly landscaped grounds and crammed with antique furniture, somewhat gloomy oil paintings, and acres of period ornaments. There is also a costume room, a very impressive wine cellar, and a tearoom serving—what else?—afternoon tea as well as pretty lavish picnic hampers. Open Tuesday through Sunday from 10am to 4:30pm. Admission is $3 for adults, $1.50 for children.

3. Beaches

There are 34 glorious ocean beaches within Sydney's city limits. No other place on earth can boast anything like that number. They form golden dashes along an undulating path stretching from Port Hacking, 30 miles south of Sydney, to Palm Beach, 20 miles north. The average annual water temperature is 68° Fahrenheit, the sand is as fine as facepowder, and the surf ranges from fair to spectacular. All the beaches are shark-netted and regularly patrolled (there hasn't been a shark attack since netting started some 30 years ago). The beaches are Sydney's most popular summer form of mass entertainment, but there are so many and they're so large that all you have to do is venture a bit farther out to find some relatively uncrowded ones.

Sydneysiders worship their beaches—surfing, swimming, or just roasting their skins for entire weekends. With the exception of certain Pacific islanders, probably no one spends so much time just lying on sand with their eyes closed. The only difference the skin-cancer scare has made to this habit is that they now spray themselves with protective lotion beforehand.

The most popular beaches are the closest: **Bondi, Coogee, Maroubra, Bronte,** and **Cronulla,** all easily reached by public transport from downtown. **Manly** follows close behind, although it involves a ferry ride. **Whale Beach, Avalon,** and **Bilgola** are somewhat less crowded because they lie farther out. To survey the northern shore beaches, you can catch bus 190 behind Wynyard Station to **Palm Beach,** which skirts approximately 26 miles of shoreline.

BONDI

To reach Bondi, the closest beach, catch bus 380 from Elizabeth Street in the center city. Bondi is vast, but it does get packed on summer weekends. In those periods, do yourself a favor and *don't* drive there, because then Bondi has only three kinds of parking facilities: illegal, impossible, and somebody else's. In every other respect Bondi is richly supplied: scores of restaurants, cafés, and snack bars; a famous Beach Pavilion for nighttime entertainment; toilets and shower rooms; surfboards and rafts for rent at nominal rates; and more beautiful bodies than you're ever apt to have seen in one place.

A final word about the beaches: They can, on occasion, be dangerous. The signs BATHE BETWEEN THE FLAGS are not put up for fun. Obey them! Even shallow water can be rent by powerful currents. Some of the dramatic rock outcrops can be absolutely lethal unless you're familiar with the water conditions around them. And while sharks are not a menace on netted beaches, schools of stinging jellyfish are. When you see a warning notice, don't go in—I hate to lose readers.

The Lifesavers

If Australia has produced a folk-hero image equivalent to the American cowboy's, it is those bronzed young men in multicolored swimsuits who look as if they had leaped out of Olympic Games posters onto the beaches. They are members of the **Surf Lifesaving Association,** the most prestigious bunch of volunteers in the country. Oz people consider it downright decadent to hire paid lifeguards, as most other countries do. Here the task of safeguarding the beaches is performed by the 60,000 volunteer lifesavers who not only rescue swimmers in distress but perform duties left to the police elsewhere. The lifesavers are the main reason why Australia gets so little of the beach violence and vandalism that troubles America. The lifesavers are *big* guys and they settle outbursts of hooliganism very quickly.

They got their historic start in a characteristic clash with Australia's ubiquitous wowser element. In 1906 the young rector of Sydney's St. Mary's church was arrested for "surfing during daylight hours while dressed in flimsy garments" (to wit: a neck-to-knee swimsuit). This prosecution sparked off a tidal wave of protests that resulted in not only a change of beach laws but also the formation of the Bondi Surf Bathers Lifesaving Club—the first such outfit on the continent.

Sydneysiders then flocked to their beaches by the thousands, and the new lifesavers soon acquired an almost legendary reputation. In those early days they were frequently the only strong experienced swimmers on the entire beach. And they produced such local heroes as Harald Baker, who personally accounted for more than 100 rescues. On one occasion he hauled out three girls who had been caught in a treacherous undertow. The girls were frantically clinging to him, threatening to pull him under. Harald clipped each of them neatly on the jaw, knocking them unconscious, then floated them to safety. On such exploits the lifesavers' prestige was built.

As stated before, they are unpaid in terms of cash, but get more than their share in other compensations: the young women flock around them in swarms, people implicitly obey their instructions, and at the **Surf Carnivals** they are the undisputed glamour boys. These carnivals, which take place at one Sydney beach or another every summer weekend, are a uniquely Australian ritual, quite apart from being wonderful spectacles and thrilling to watch. Make a point of seeing at least one of them. They start with parades by the various lifesaving clubs, carrying their rescue gear and using the peculiar high-stepping gait that enables them to march in soft sand. Then come demonstrations of skill—surf-boat races, in which the specially constructed, oared boats have to maneuver over the crashing waves; competitions between surf reel teams in rescuing "drowners"; demonstrations of first-aid techniques and sand-buggy driving—and the final parade, with bands blaring and club flags flying amid the cheers of the spectators. It's a memorable blend of sporting prowess and almost military precision.

MANLY

A resort area and world of its own, dedicated to sand, surf, and sun (plus tourist dollars), Manly has four ocean beaches, six calm harbor beaches, and two ocean swimming pools. It also offers more than 700 other attractions, including first-class restaurants, several nightclubs, hotels, shops, boutiques, seaside promenades, and fun-park entertainments, as well as shady parks, gardens, and museums. Pride of place goes to the beach promenade lined with towering Norfolk Island pines along a seemingly endless boardwalk that follows the curves and indentations of the vast ocean beach.

The most pleasurable way to and from Manly is by two different modes of transportation. When it's early and you're raring to go, speed the seven miles across the harbor in 13 minutes via **hydrofoil** from no. 2 wharf, Circular Quay. The cost is $4. Coming back, surfeited with saltwater and sun, take the leisurely **ferry** cruise. The ferries commute between Manly and no. 3 wharf, Circular Quay. It's a wonderfully scenic and relaxing chug, taking 35 minutes and costing $2.20 for adults, 55¢ for children.

Manly has a **Fun Pier** with various shrieking, whirling, and spinning rides, and a **Waterworks** across the park from the ferry wharf consisting of four giant waterslides that sluice you down from considerable heights. **Marine Land** has a 250,000-gallon tank, which can be viewed from above and from three depth levels. The pool is swarming with thousands of ocean denizens, from tiny rainbow fish to enormous sea turtles and torpedo-shaped sharks, giant groupers, stingrays, and razor-toothed eels. At feeding time divers descend into the tank with food sleighs and actually hand-feed the inhabitants. How they manage not to get their hands snapped off is one of the permanent puzzles and special thrills of the place. Admission is $10 for adults, $5 for children.

The Museum and Art Gallery, West Esplanade, Manly Cove (tel. 02/949-1776), has a collection of permanent works, plus changing exhibitions by local artists, whose talents range from fine to middling-mediocre. Admission is free, but donations are welcome. It's open Tuesday through Sunday from 10am to 4pm.

NUDE BEACHES

All of Sydney's beaches are topless by custom and general consent. Only two, however, let you go barefoot up to your chin. These official nudist havens are **Lady Bay** and **Camp Cove,** both situated at the end of Cliff Street, Watsons Bay. Oglers can't get a glimpse, and in the sand nobody bats an eyelid at the gallery of Adams and Eves. But caution is advisable for sensitive derrières; otherwise you'll be eating your meals standing up for the rest of your trip.

---

4. Day Trips from Sydney

Just 18 miles north of central Sydney lies the **Ku-ring-gai Chase National Park** (tel. 02/457-9322). Part nature reserve, part flower garden, part picnic ground, this is an idyllic escape from the urban rat race. Ku-ring-gai has everything to gladden the hearts of nature-craving city dwellers: wildflower sanctuaries, hiking trails, rocks for climbing, panoramas for viewing, boats for rent, tent areas to spend the nights. Some of the region is virgin bush, but there are also restaurants, tearooms, and kiosks for those who prefer roughing it with a knife and fork. Take the train to Turramurra station, then the connecting bus to the park entrance at Bobbin Head. If you drive, there's an admission price of $4 per car.

Waratah Park, Terry Hills (tel. 02/450-2377), isn't really a park but a wonderful patch of bushland carved out of the edge of Ku-ring-gai Chase, about half an hour's drive north of Sydney. This is mainly an animal reserve and most of the fauna—wallabies, emus, koalas, wombats—roam around freely. Kangaroos and wombats are gentle critters, but emus—the ostrichlike flightless birds of Australia—can be ill-tempered at times, so be cautious about petting any. Other Oz natives, such as dingoes and Tasmanian devils, you can watch through wire mesh. Tasmanian devils, although only the size of terriers, are ferocious carnivores that will tackle and devour game three times their size. If you watch one feeding, you'll know how it got its name. Waratah is the home of one of Australia's top television stars, Skippy the Bush Kangaroo, who loves meeting his fans and has never been known to throw star tantrums. Admission is $8 for adults, $4 for children. Open seven days from 10am to 5pm. For tourist coach reservations, call 02/241-1636.

Australian Reptile Park, Pacific Hwy., Gosford (tel. 043/28-4311), offers you a close look at some of the less cuddly Australians: tiger snakes, taipans, death adders, crocodiles, giant pythons, and the large dinosaurian lizards called goannas. Some of these creatures are quite harmless (pythons, in fact, make good pets), but the taipans and tiger snakes count among the most venomous reptiles on earth. You can watch them being milked of their venom, which forms the basis of snakebite serums, by highly skilled keepers. Open seven days from 9am to 5:30pm. Admission is $6 for adults, $2.50 for children. Take the train to Gosford.

Also on Pacific Highway, at Somersby, stands **Old Sydney Town** (tel. 043/40-1104), a major attraction for interstate and overseas visitors. This is a fairly faithful replica of colonial Sydney, circa two centuries ago. Houses, workshops, taverns, barracks, churches, and government offices have been re-created as close to the originals as possible. And so have the events. You can hear a town cryer bellowing out the news, watch a display of military drill, or witness a colonial magistrate's court in action. (The main historical deviation here is that all participants are stone cold sober.) The spectators (including you) take part in the action—at least in the sound effects. You see the convicted culprit marched to a public triangle and given a flogging with a cat-o'-nine-tails (not for the squeamish). After that you can take a break by attending a Punch and Judy show. Open Wednesday through Sunday from 10am to 5pm. Adults pay $10.80, children, $5.90.

Australiana Park, Camden Valley Way, Narellan (tel. 02/606-6266), is an area of landscaped gardens and rolling bushland filled with a happy grab bag of animal shows, thrill rides, fun vehicles, shops, and restaurants. Impossible to put under one label—there are horse-breeding paddocks and a banked race-car track, pettable wombats and kangaroos, and a shriek-inducing "twister" ride, sheepdog demonstrations, water slides, a Puffing Billy train, and an 1880s stagecoach. In the evening a superb performance by Andalusian dancing stallions takes place in a floodlit arena. There are also picnic grounds, barbecue sites, a vaguely rustic eating house, and an air-conditioned restaurant with a sumptuous spread of smörgåsbord. Admission is $10 for adults, $5 for children. Take the train to Campbelltown station, where the special park bus departs daily at 10am. Open all week from 10am to 5pm.

Featherdale Wildlife Park, Kildare Rd., Doonside (tel. 02/622-1644). About an hour's travel time west of the center city, this compact wildlife reserve harbors all the well-known—and some very obscure—Aussie animals. The less familiar ones include awesome-looking (but quite innocuous) frilled lizards, wonderfully multicolored parrots, the little spiny ant-eating echidnas, flying squirrels, strutting brolga birds, and miniature rat kangaroos. But the top attraction is the large walk-in koala enclosure, where you can roam around, photograph and cuddle the inhabitants, and generally discover what a koala is all about. They may resemble teddy bears, but are actually marsupials, carrying their young in pouches, like kangaroos. Koalas eat nothing but certain types of gum leaves, don't drink water, rarely come down from their trees, and have *very* placid dispositions. They smell strongly of eucalyptus, and while in no way vicious, have been known to well—er—urinate on whoever is holding them (including, on one regal occasion, Queen Elizabeth).

The most illustrious citizen here is Sydney, the Qantas koala and star of prizewinning TV commercials. Sydney, as you may recall, *hates* Qantas for bringing all those pesky tourists to his home habitat.

Get to Featherdale by taking the train to Blacktown, then bus 211 from the station. Open seven days from 9am to 5pm. Admission is $6 for adults, $3 for children.

African Lion Safari, Marsh Rd., Warragamba (tel. 047/74-1113). You need a car to get the full benefit of this attraction, a few miles west of Liverpool. It's an open reserve for strolling lions, tigers, and bears, with nary a fence between you and them—except the steel shell of your car. You'll get some terrific photos to take home, as long as you remember to follow the warning signs and *don't* leave your car. The place also contains considerably safer performing sea lions and dolphins, a trained-parrot show, gently nibbling kangaroos, and a pettable-pets corner. Nearby is the impressive **Warragamba Dam,** source of Sydney's main water supply and a beautiful area for picnics. The safari park is open Wednesday through Sunday from 10am to 4pm. Admission is $9.50 for adults, $4.50 for children.

PARRAMATTA

Although Parramatta today is simply one of Sydney's western suburbs, the town was actually intended to be the capital of New South Wales. Most of the early colonial governors resided there, while Sydney Cove was used merely as a cargo port. Gradually the advantages of a coastal town became obvious and the seat of government shifted to Sydney for good. But Parramatta remains a historic site, lovingly preserved by its citizens, and still looks and acts as if it weren't part of the metropolis at all, but an entity of its own. Which, in a fashion, it is. You get there simply by boarding a train at Central or Wynyard Station and riding some 18 miles westward.

A characteristic token of independence is the **Tourist Information Centre,** Market St. (tel. 02150/630-3703), which will give you free maps and brochures, plus as much verbal information as you can handle. Among the city's chief attractions are the various historic houses dating from Parramatta's governmental period. **Old Government House,** Parramatta Park (tel. 02150/635-8149), was begun modestly in 1790 and completed sumptuously in 1816. As the residence of several governors, the mansion is equipped with exquisitely crafted early colonial furniture, superb mirrors, grand staircases, and the type of representational artwork that viceroys love to surround themselves with. Admission is $4 for adults, $1 for children. The house is open four days a week from 10am to 4pm; closed Monday, Friday, and Saturday.

Elizabeth Farm, 70 Alice St. (tel. 02150/635-9488), is the oldest existing farmhouse in Australia, but not by any means a typical one. Built in the 1830s by one of the founders of the Australian wool industry, this was a rich man's spread and for a long time the center of the colony's social life and agricultural planning. Most of the time it was run by a woman, Elizabeth Macarthur, who furnished it tastefully and ruled with a *very* firm hand. The guided tours of the place are exceptionally informative. Adults pay $3; children, $1.50; and the premises are open Tuesday through Sunday from 10am to 4:30pm.

Linden House Museum, at the corner of Smith and Darcy streets (tel. 02150/635-7288), is in what used to be the military barracks of Parramatta. The barracks, in fact, are still occupied by soldiers, so only the museum wing of the sandstone building is open to the public. You'll see a colorful array of uniforms and many of the crude but fatally effective muskets and bayonets with which the colonial units were equipped. (Take a look at the size of those old musket balls.) Adults pay $1; children, 50¢. Open on Sunday only, from 11am to 4pm.

Notre Dame, Mulgoa Rd., Mulgoa (tel. 047/73-8599). The only way to describe this place is as a cross between San Simeon and Disneyland. Created as a millionaire's estate home, it contains a wild mixture of art treasures and entertainment facilities. There is a priceless collection of French antiques, a private zoo, a giant equestrian arena (with Andalusian dancing horses), a Japanese Shinto shrine, a patch of tropical rain forest, and a formal English garden. Good for a whole afternoon. Adults pay $10; children, $5. Open Wednesday through Sunday from 10am to 4:30pm.

Koala Park Sanctuary, Castle Hill Rd., West Pennant Hills (tel. 02/875-2777). One train stop north of Parramatta, this was the first private sanctuary for koalas founded in the state. The main theme here is the breeding of future koala generations, and you get some of the animal's habits explained to you by knowledgeable hostesses. Also present are wallabies, dingoes, wedgetailed eagles, and wombats. Open seven days 9am till 5pm. Admission is $6 for adults, $3 for children.

Australia's Wonderland, Wallgrove Rd., Minchinbury (tel. 02/675-0100). Although this vast spread is known as the largest theme park in the southern hemisphere, it's hard to make out any "theme" except fun. Wonderland is a grand-scale amusement area, beautifully landscaped, filled with snack bars and game areas, and filled with imaginatively named rides such as the Bush Beast and an immensely long and thrilling roller-coaster ride. You can also see acrobatic shows. The entire setting is far more scenic and eye-pleasing than you usually find in such locations. Admission prices here include *all* the rides: $17.95 for adults, $12.95 for children. Open all week till 6pm.

Before leaving Parramatta, you should know that the above attractions are merely some of the highlights of the town. There are also first-rate hotels and restaurants, an elaborate waterslide, and an 1890s vintage steam trolley, which, unfortunately, only runs on Sunday.

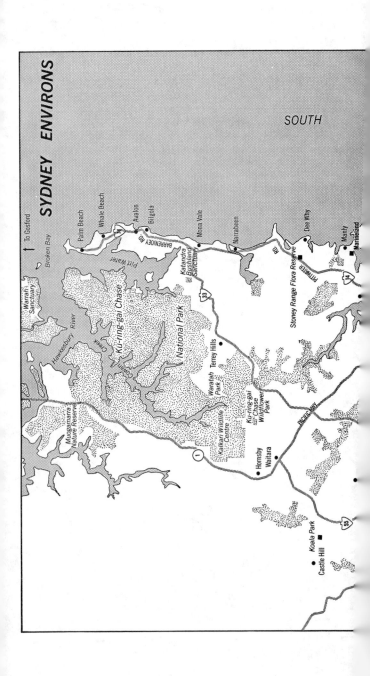

SYDNEY ENVIRONS

SOUTH

To Gosford

Broker Bay

Warrah
Sanctuary

Pitt Water

Hawkesbury River

Palm Beach

Whale Beach

Avalon

Bilgola

BARRENJOEY RD.

Mona Vale

Katandra
Bushland
Sanctuary

Narrabeen

Dee Why

Ku-ring-gai Chase

National Park

33

Stoney Range Flora Reserve

PITTWATER

Manly

14

Marineland

Muogamarra
Nature Reserve

Waratah
Park

Terrey Hills

Ku-ring-gai
Chase
Wildflower
Park

Kalkari Wildlife
Centre

1

Hornsby

Waitara

PACIFIC HWY.

Koala Park

Castle Hill

55

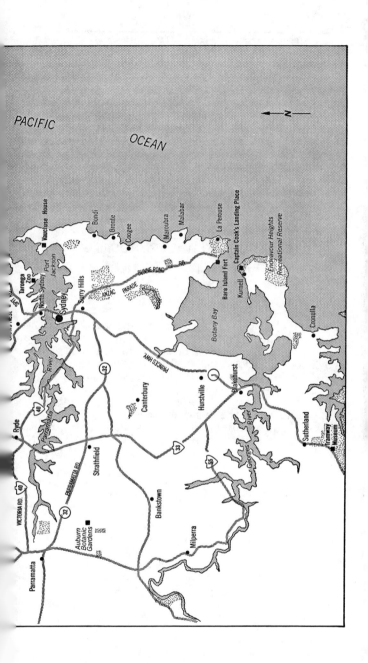

VII

TOURS, CRUISES, AND AIR ADVENTURES

1. ORGANIZED SIGHT-SEEING TOURS
2. HARBOR CRUISES AND RIVER RUNS
3. AIR ADVENTURES
4. SELF-GUIDED WALKING TOURS
5. A DRIVE-YOURSELF TOUR

Commercial sight-seeing tours seem to be one of Sydney's major industries. Organizers show you the sights by every means of locomotion, from coaches and limousines to small cars, pedicabs, and on foot. Therefore, again, the organized tours mentioned below are merely some samples from the vast selection at your disposal.

For those who prefer to go out on their own rather than taking an organized tour, I've also included in this chapter several do-it-yourself walking tours of Sydney's tourist areas, as well as a self-drive car tour through the North Shore and Ku-ring-gai Chase National Park.

1. Organized Sight-seeing Tours

Many of the sight-seeing companies feature tours that include trips through the rest of New South Wales and other Australian states. In fact, you can see most of Australia with them. Get their brochures for complete listings and prices.

Australian Pacific Tours, 84 Pitt St. (tel. 02/252-2988), features a daily tour that includes a guided tour of the Opera House, a hydrofoil trip to Manly, a ride across the Harbour Bridge, and a ramble around Darling Harbour. With free courtesy pickups at your hotel, the tour starts at 9am and returns at 5:30pm. Tickets cost $54.50 for adults, $48 for children.

AAT King's Tours, Shop 12, no. 6 wharf, Circular Quay (tel. 02/252-2788), has a morning jaunt that shows you the North

Shore beaches, Manly, Taronga Park Zoo, and the scenic Spit Bridge. A harbor ferry trip and the zoo admission are included in the overall price of $27 for adults, $24 for children. The tour leaves daily from the Circular Quay at 9am.

Third Dimension Tours (tel. 02/938-1931) specializes in individually tailored sight-seeing for no more than eight participants riding in air-conditioned mini-coaches. There are deluxe cruises with first-rate restaurant meals (including excellent wine selections) around Sydney Harbour, helicopter hops, balloon rides, and seaplane flights above the city. You can choose from four tours with prices from $110 to $230 for a full day of pampered viewing.

Sydney After Dark (tel. 02/27-2721), one of several nocturnal swings around the bright lights, is conducted in a scarlet doubledecker bus (try to get a seat on the upper deck) narrated by a charming hostess. The tour includes a three-course dinner at the Sydney Tower Restaurant, a visit to China Town, a nightclub show, and a (somewhat cursory) glimpse of the night activity in Kings Cross. Courtesy pickup at your hotel. The tours operate Tuesday through Saturday nights, starting at 7pm, and cost either $55 or $68, depending on the night. You can make reservations through the Travel Centre of New South Wales or by calling directly.

Newmans, Shop 2, Overseas Terminal, Circular Quay West (tel. 02/225-8061), operates a full-day Country Life tour every Wednesday and Friday. The destination is the historic Gledswood Homestead, a beautiful rustic spread southwest of Sydney. You sample country hospitality, watch sheepdog mustering and sheep shearing, learn to throw a boomerang, inspect the wine cellars, and make friends with the homestead animals—which include kangaroos. Hunger pangs are kept at bay by means of a sumptuous barbecue lunch, the steaks cooked to taste. This is followed by a visit to the Australian Wildlife and Reptile Park. The tour leaves at 8:45am, returns at 5:30pm. Adults pay $59, children $49.

For a highly informative **Guided Walking Tour,** contact Neville Mignot at 02/660-0860. These strolls leave from Sydney Town Hall at 2:30pm on Monday, Thursday, and Saturday and end at Sydney Cove two hours later. En route, at a leisurely pace, you see many of the city's most famous buildings, gardens, and statues and hear about the historic figures who shaped the city's past, including Captain Phillip, who commanded the First Fleet; Francis Greenway, the great convict-architect; Governor Macquarie; and the ill-starred Captain Bligh, who experienced his second mutiny here. The tour costs $7.50 for adults, $3.75 for children.

The Sydney Explorer requires no reservations or other preparation—it's pure impulse touring. These distinctive scarlet Mercedes buses are operated by the Urban Transit Authority and run a daily 13-mile circuit around Sydney's major attractions. The stops are clearly marked all over town, and the buses follow each other at half-hour intervals from 9:30am to 5pm. You can get off at any or all sights, look around for as long as you like, then catch the next Explorer and continue the trip. You get an entire day's touring for one price: $10 for adults, $5 for children. Attractions en route include Circular Quay, the Opera House, Botanic Gardens, Parliament House, State Art Gallery, Elizabeth Bay House, Australian Museum, Chinatown, the Argyle Cut, and Pier One.

Tourist Newsfront, 22 Playfair St., The Rocks (tel. 02/27-7197), is an extremely versatile outfit that acts as a reservations agency for sight-seeing trips around Sydney, around New South Wales, and around Australia. Apart from standard packaged tours, the managers, Molly and Peter Gregory, will accommodate specific itineraries or arrange for chauffeur-driven or self-drive tours. Unlike most agencies, they can quickly make up a schedule to meet your individual needs.

2. Harbor Cruises and River Runs

Few people revel in their watery surroundings like Sydneysiders. They're constantly sailing on it, swimming through it, or diving under it. The ragged configurations of the coastline, the countless peninsulas, bays, narrows, inlets, and river mouths offer almost unlimited mooring facilities for small craft of every description. In order to really see Sydney you must take to the water, and there is a staggering choice of marine transportation at your disposal. They range from ferries to windjammers and every variation in between. The samples cited below are merely that—samples.

CRUISES

The most economical cruises are offered by the Urban Transit Authority, which operates the harbor ferries. Their **Tourist Ferry** from no. 6 wharf, Circular Quay (tel. 02/27-4738), takes you on a cruise covering five harbor islands (including Fort Denison) for just $10 per adult passenger, $5 per child. A detailed commentary explains the sights, and refreshments are available on board. The Tourist Ferries run seven days a week, four times a day.

Captain Cook Cruises, no. 6 wharf, Circular Quay (tel. 02/251-5007), are more elaborate. Apart from harbor tours, this company has an afternoon Coffee Cruise, lasting 2½ hours, in which you take your coffee break on board a sleek white luxury cruiser and head deep into the upper reaches of the Middle Harbour. It sails twice a day and costs $20 for adults, $12 for children. The Luncheon Cruise includes an excellent buffet lunch (oysters and all), lasts 1½ hours, and costs $30. Then there's the romantic specialty—the Candlelight Dinner Cruise, departing at 7 and returning at 9:30pm. You'll need reservations for this one, which includes a sumptuous dinner, complimentary cocktails, and dancing on the upper deck, costing $50 (no guaranteed moonlight).

Another night cruise utilizes a standard Transit Authority ferry. The **Harbor Lights Cruise** leaves from no. 4 wharf, Circular Quay (tel. 02/27-4738), every evening except Sunday and gives you a breathtaking view of light-flooded Sydney from the harbor. No cocktails or candlelight, but the intriguing commentary and grand spectacle cost only $7.50 per adult, $4.50 per child.

If you prefer to cruise under sail you can do so on the ***Bounty;***

at least on the replica of the famous ship, which starred in the 1960s film *Mutiny on the Bounty.* Built as an exact copy of the 18th-century two-master, it is a beautiful vessel of 363 tons, unfurling 8,000 square feet of canvas, equipped with a dining salon and bar, and holding 49 passengers and a crew of 20. The skipper, however, is no Captain Bligh (who wasn't a captain but a lieutenant and, although he could handle ships brilliantly, couldn't handle men). The modern *Bounty* sails out five times a week, twice daily, and the passage rates include a lavish buffet meal with wine. Adults pay $65, children $39. Book your berth by writing The Bounty, G.P.O. Box 3797, Sydney, N.S.W. 2001, or by calling 02/251-6568.

A RIVER RUN
Get away from the harbor and onto a river for one of the most popular water excursions in all Australia. The **Riverboat Mail Run** (tel. 02/455-1566) is the last remaining river postman on the continent, and you can ride along while the little craft delivers letters, milk, groceries, and newspapers to the population along the scenic Hawkesbury River. It's a leisurely and wonderfully relaxing ride (*you* don't have to do any of the work involved), starting at 9:30am and returning at 1:15pm. Catch the connecting train at the Central Station at 8:15am and be on the mail boat at Brooklyn wharf any day, Monday through Friday (when there's mail delivery). The ride costs $14 for adults, $7 for children, and you can reserve ahead of time (call the number above).

---

3. Air Adventures

There are a variety of ways of seeing Sydney from the bird's-eye view: by luxury executive plane, by seaplane, or by helicopter. The deluxe flights include a limousine drive to the airport and a glass of champagne while flying. You can arrange for them by calling 02/558-0298. The seaplane service operates from Rose Bay and Palm Beach, is run by **Aquatic Airways** (tel. 02/919-5966), costs around $45 per passenger, and flies seven days a week. The **Sydney Helicopter Service** (tel. 02/690-1747) uses a chopper that can seat four passengers and does hover flights over Sydney Harbour lasting half an hour. The helicopters arrive and depart from a platform at Pyrmont Wharf 20 and charge $300 per trip.

BY BALLOON, BLIMP, OR "RED BARON"
You can choose from any number of aerial rides over Sydney, but the following are perhaps the most unusual available anywhere.
Balloon Sunrise (tel. 02/818-1166) has a fleet (armada? squadron?) of hot-air balloons based in the Camden Valley, outside Sydney. Manned by skilled balloonists, these silent pear-shaped bulbs waft over the rolling hills with the breeze, enabling passengers to take some memorable pictures of the landscape below. Special midweek flights for visitors to Sydney include transportation to Camden from your hotel early in the morning and back in the eve-

ning. Also includes a champagne brunch after the flight. Call for reservations and prices.

Thomas Cook Skycruise (tel. 02/234-4000) offers aerial sight-seeing by blimp or airship. Two of these midget zeppelins, each seating a dozen passengers, cruise slowly over Sydney to the tune of their characteristic bumblebee propeller hum. They look wonderfully archaic and are considerably more comfortable than heavier-than-air excursion planes. They also fly much more slowly and lower, so you can identify individual rooftops. Flights operate seven days a week, taking about 1¼ hours to complete. Most enjoyable, though not exactly cheap—adults pay $200. Call for flight times and reservations.

Red Baron Flights (tel. 02/709-5943), is the most unusual of all. You're not exactly in a World War I Fokker triplane, but a fair facsimile—a bright-red Tiger Moth of one world war later. You get a leather helmet and goggles before climbing into the open passenger cockpit. Only the twin machine guns are missing. You can choose the kind of flight you want—a "patrol" over Sydney or a more daring hop involving some mild aerobatics, for which this prop trainer is ideally suited. It's not for delicate stomachs, though. Flights cost $150 for one hour and operate seven days a week. Reservations are advised. Sometimes the "Red Baron" answers in person.

4. Self-Guided Walking Tours

These are among the very best ways of seeing Sydney. You can set your own pace, pick your own points of interest, stray in any direction you want, and linger anywhere you feel like lingering. All they require is a decent map, a sturdy pair of shoes, and a certain degree of self-discipline. Since nobody shepherds you along, there's nothing to stop you from having a few drinks en route, which will naturally affect the amount of territory you cover. The following suggestions for strolling are designed for three to four hours of walking, roadside refreshment stops not included. They cover areas of central Sydney that are generally flat; the only exceptions are the Rocks and the downhill hike from Kings Cross to Elizabeth Bay.

WATERFRONT WALK

You start at the **Overseas Passenger Terminal** on the west side of Circular Quay. This was the place where most of the visitors from abroad once arrived, and some still do. Now and again you'll see a luxury cruise liner docked here and its passengers streaming down the gangplank, eager for their first glimpse of Sydney. Follow the quay past the **ferry terminals,** always the scene of much activity, and head up Circular Quay East. You'll come to **Bennelong Point,** the site of the Opera House. Go past and you reach **Farm Cove,** with the **Man o'War Jetty** at your feet, so called because the Royal Navy's three-masters used to take on supplies here back in the days of "wooden ships and iron men." Now strike out inland, across the 125-acre **Domain.** You walk past the sandstone keep and turrets of

Government House, over expanses of rolling lawn to what resembles a white fortress but is actually the **Conservatorium of Music.**

To your right, across a roaring traffic artery, runs **Macquarie Street,** named after the young colony's most enlightened governor and now one of the most stylish thoroughfares in Sydney. Here stand some beautiful Georgian-style buildings, the state's **Parliament House,** and at no. 145, the **Royal Australian College of Physicians,** one of the last veranda-fronted 18th-century town houses remaining in the city. Walking south on Macquarie Street you pass Shakespeare Place and the **State Library of New South Wales,** which recently acquired an impressive (and very necessary) 11-story extension. Pass the **Sydney Hospital,** a typical late-Victorian monstrosity, and you come to **Queen's Square.** To your right, at the corner of King Street, stands **St. James's Church,** another design by the convict-architect Francis Greenway, dating from 1819 and one more proof of how much better the Georgians built than the Victorians who followed them. You are now at **St. James Station,** with train and bus connection to any part of Sydney.

CITY WALK

This stroll is designed to take you through parts of Sydney's main shopping streets in the central business area. Start at **Martin Place,** most of which is a pedestrian mall. On your left stands the General Post Office. In the center you'll see the **Cenotaph,** a memorial to Australia's fallen servicemen. Every Thursday at 12:30pm soldiers stage a ceremony at the Cenotaph before marching off to the Anzac Memorial in Hyde Park.

The last street crossing Martin Place is **George Street.** Turn right here and walk two blocks to **Australia Square,** the source of endless confusion because it isn't a square but a circular cement-and-glass tower presently noted as the third-tallest building in the southern hemisphere. The plaza facing George Street is adorned with a massive Calder sculpture. Note the tapestries in the main entrance, which were woven at Aubusson in France from designs by Le Corbusier.

Continuing down George Street you pass the deluxe **Regent Hotel** on your left. If it's the right time and you don't mind spending $14 or so, you can take a very classy afternoon tea in the lobby café (the tea comes from silver samovars and the sandwiches *could* have come from London's Fortnum & Mason). A few steps farther is Circular Quay and the **Customs House.** The square in front features a sculpture of interlinked rings, symbolizing links between nations, a lofty ideal not quite in tune with the functions of Customs services.

Turn right, pass First Fleet Place, then right again onto **Pitt Street,** another main shopping area. At the corner of Spring Street stands the **Travel Centre of New South Wales,** a major source of maps, tour planning, brochures, and general information about the city and the state. Cross Martin Place and you walk into the heartland of Sydney's shopping region. This portion of Pitt Street has been turned into a pedestrian mall, no thing of beauty but very convenient. (You don't have to dodge cars, but watch out for bicycle riders; nobody seems to know what constitutes legal or illegal riding practices.) You pass the **Strand Arcade** on one side, the **Imperial Arcade** on the other, both chock-a-block with inviting specialty stores. Then, on the right, towers **Centrepoint,** with the famous sky needle stabbing upward from the corner of Pitt and Market streets, another maze of shops at its feet.

Go on past the **Piccadilly Arcade** (more shops) until you reach Park Street. There you turn right. At the corner of George and Druitt streets is the **Town Hall,** the building from which Sydney is governed—or partly so, considering the various institutions that participate in the governing process. The Town Hall is a classic Victorian extravaganza: stately, ugly, yet somehow impressive. Built during the boom period of the 1870s, it boasts an immense pipe organ in the main hall, which is used for occasional recitals. Outside the Town Hall there is an open area utilized by lunchers and elderly bench-sitters as well as by demonstrators on behalf of innumerable causes. For more organ recitals there is **St. Andrews Cathedral,** on Town Hall Square. This is a small, handsome church built in the style of the Gothic Revival period in the 1860s. It houses a unique organ with recently added computerized sections. Recitals are held every Thursday from 1 to 2pm. Town Hall Square has a train station and a major bus stop.

ELIZABETH BAY WALK

This is an exploration stroll through the surprisingly tranquil seafront neighbor of Kings Cross. It's mostly downhill, holds some quite unexpected vistas, but involves a certain amount of backtracking. Start in front of Kings Cross station and walk left on Darlinghurst Road, traffic-jammed and people-packed, day or night. You'll reach a pocket-size park called **Fitzroy Gardens,** graced with Sydney's prettiest water effect, the **El Alamein Fountain.** Erected to commemorate the World War II battle that stopped Rommel's advance in North Africa, the fountain resembles a waving, shimmering thistledown when it's playing, and a bunch of rusty copper tubes when it's not.

Cross the park and you're on Elizabeth Bay Road, where you turn left. You pass the elegant frontage of **Sebel's Town House** and continue downhill until you cross Greenknowe Avenue. On the other side starts Onslow Avenue, a street of charming walled homes crowned by **Elizabeth Bay House.** This gem of a mansion stands on a rise above a gem of a mini-park, winner of several landscaping prizes. The park—more correctly a garden—welcomes you like a serenely enchanting oasis, with flower beds, soft lawns, a hump-backed bridge across a pond flickering with goldfish, water lilies, and a tiny waterfall. And from the edge you get an overwhelming view of Elizabeth Bay below and the naval repair base of **Garden Island** in the distance.

The base, incidently, contains the **Captain Cook Graving Dock,** that can accommodate the largest battleships and aircraft carriers, and a gigantic, widely visible crane that can hoist an entire gun turret.

Onslow Avenue makes a dogleg turn into Billyard Avenue,

with more stately homes. The stateliest of them all is a Spanish-style villa, walled but with openings you can peer through, that seems to have materialized from the pages of *The Great Gatsby*. Actually the place was built by the inventor of the popular Boomerang harmonica and bears that simple Aussie name. Turn left and you come to **Bear Park,** a patch of green lapped by the waters of the bay, ringed by very stylish apartment blocks with penthouses on top. The park has a jetty with mooring facilities for sailing yachts and cabin cruisers, most of them belonging to the inhabitants of the surrounding apartments.

From the park you go uphill on Ithaca Road, cross Elizabeth Bay Road, and walk downhill until you come to the edge of another park. This is **Rushcutters Bay,** so called because in the bad old days convicts were chain-ganged and put to work down there to cut the rushes that covered the area. Today Rushcutters Bay is devoid of rushes and is one great recreation ground. On the left is the bayfront, and in the park are tennis, squash, and handball courts, interspersed with lawns dotted with topless sunbathers. At the eastern end lies the famous **Cruising Yacht Club.** You have to be a member or guest of a member in order to enter its portals, but you can admire the rows of superb white sailing craft bobbing at the club marinas. Adjoining it is the **Naval Reserve** with more marine craft, but for rather different purposes.

Beyond these buildings the park goes on, but changes its name to **Yarranabbe Park,** a slender and less trodden strip of greenery where boomerang throwing is practiced every Sunday morning by patrons of the Boomerang School (yes, there is such an establishment!). You can watch their attempts, but this is best done from behind a handy tree.

Cross Rushcutters Bay park to the south and you reach New South Head Road. The buses going right will take you back to Kings Cross and the center city. Those heading left will take you to the eastern suburbs.

5. A Drive-Yourself Tour

Once you rent a car, the touring possibilities become endless. I make this particular suggestion because it unfolds some of the scenic beauties of the North Shore (which is not tourist territory) and the Ku-ring-gai Chase National Park. Located 18 miles north of downtown, it can also be reached by train to Turramurra, then by connecting bus.

You start by crossing the Sydney Harbour Bridge. Then take the Manly overpass and turn right onto Military Road until you reach Spit Junction. Turn left at Spot Road and continue until you cross the Spit Bridge, which leads over one of the hundreds of harbor inlets. Drive up Spit Hill and turn right onto Sydney Road, which leads to Manly. But before going there take a very worthwhile detour to the right, up the hill and through the **Reserve** (part of which is military) to **North Head.** This is the northern portion of the entrance to Port Jackson, the official name of Sydney Harbour. It commands a fabulous view of the open Pacific on one side, the bay on the other, the city skyline to the south, and the string of surfing beaches to the north. On a clear day you can see Captain Cook. . . .

Now you backtrack into **Manly** and follow the **Ocean Road.** It's a magnificent drive along the cliffs, one beach resort following another like pearls on a string: Harbord, Curl Curl, Dee Why, Collaroy, Narrabeen. At the northern tip of this road lies **Palm Beach,** playground of the very well-heeled and site of some of the most sumptuous waterfront mansions in Australia, fronted by oceangoing yachts that seem to have escaped from the armada of an oil king. But you're not going to the end of the line.

Instead you turn onto Pittwater Road at **Mona Vale.** This takes you to the captivating bay of **Pittwater,** which the road skirts. Drive past Church Point and enter **Ku-ring-gai Chase National Park** by way of McCarr's Creek. You pay $4 admission per car. The national park is a wonderful area of hiking trails, picnic grounds, hidden coves, and patches of forest to provide shade. One of the prime spots here is the **Wildflower Garden,** at 420 Mona Vale Rd. "Garden" conveys the wrong impression for this extended bushland sanctuary, where a five-mile track winds down into the creek valleys and up again on the other side. You see some wildlife unique to this area and breathe the peace of a region where neither ballgames nor skateboards are permitted. There is a separate admission fee of $3 per car.

In case you fall in love with Ku-ring-gai, as many do, there are a couple of special hiking tours of the area taking place most days of the week. One is the **Wildlife Study Tour** (tel. 02/457-9753), which costs $40 and takes you to Aboriginal markings in the park and to the hidden dells where wildlife abounds, undisturbed by holiday crowds. Lunch is included in the price. These tours are guided by experienced naturalists who provide a fascinating commentary on the fauna and flora you encounter and *never* get lost, as hikers are apt to do on their own.

You can stay on West Head Road all the way to the tip of the peninsula at **Commodore Heights** and then turn back. Or you can take the Akuna Bay turnoff on your left and drive to the serenely beautiful **Coal and Candle Creek.** (Some decades ago local government officials decided to rename this spot after some Argentinian general, for "diplomatic reasons." Sydneysiders raised such a howl that the creek promptly became Coal and Candle again.) Drive along the creek and you come to **Akuna Bay.** This spectacular inlet boasts a superb marina, famous in yachting circles throughout the country, sheltering row upon row of luxury craft. This is the home base for the Skipper-a-Clipper charter cruisers (see Chapter XI) as well as scores of private vessels.

Overlooking the scene from a grandstand position ashore is one of Sydney's three-star restaurants, the **Akuna Bay Restaurant** (tel. 02/450-2660). The balcony tables with wonderful views of the creek always get filled first, but the fare is just as delicious indoors. The specialty is, of course, seafood—at least three kinds of fresh Hawkesbury fish daily, plus the famed lobster Akuna and the equally famous "Hawkesbury Platter," consisting of hot and chilled marine tidbits. During the summer the restaurant is open seven days for lunch and dinner. You'll pay around $20 for a main course, but the lobster dishes cost $23, and desserts, all homemade, around $5.50. The wine selection is quite lengthy and concentrates on Australian whites. Note that during winter this restaurant serves dinner only on Friday and Saturday.

From here, the drive back to town takes about 70 minutes, depending on traffic conditions. You turn right onto Mona Vale Road, stay on it as far as Gordon, then make a left onto the Pacific Highway, which leads to the Harbour Bridge and into the city.

VIII

THE ART SCENE

1. THE RISE OF AUSTRALIAN MOVIES
2. ART AND SCULPTURE

Only two facets of Australia's artistic achievements have so far gained anything like world recognition: literature and cinema. I would add music, except that while overseas audiences are familiar with Joan Sutherland and groups like the Bee Gees, Men At Work, and AC/DC, very few have ever heard an Australian non-pop composition. The literati gained international renown when Patrick White won the Nobel Prize for Literature and thus focused attention on his writing compatriots. Today the works of Australia's leading authors—people like Thomas Keneally, Christina Stead, Judith Wright, and Olga Masters—occupy what you might call global bookshelves. Robert Hughes's historical flashback, *The Fatal Shore,* topped U.S. and British best-seller lists for months.

1. The Rise of Australian Movies

But it is the meteoric rise of Australian moviemaking that receives the lion's share of world acclaim, so much so that a New York critic felt moved to ask rhetorically, "Is there such a thing as a bad film from Australia?" Yes, Virginia, there is and there were, but mercifully you'll never get to see them. For one of the benefits of the present adulation is that it makes people forget just how dismal the beginnings were. Throughout the 1950s and 1960s Australia produced films for which the term "turkeys" would have been complimentary. They were false and faded carbon copies of American and British formulas, staged by actors who didn't talk like Australians and seemed to inhabit some unknown cloud-cuckooland whose connection with Oz was purely coincidental.

In order to come alive, Australian films had to discover their national identity. They had to find the courage to portray *themselves*

—warts and all—instead of aping overseas formulas in speech and plot, performing what is known in Oz as the "cultural cringe." The search for an identity, for a soul you might say, took decades. But once completed it was as if a dam had broken, releasing a torrent of hitherto blocked talent and creativity.

Significantly, all the early Australian successes were attempts to come to terms with the country's past, especially the shadowy sides. Thus *The Chant of Jimmie Blacksmith* was a searing indictment of racism, *Breaker Morant* dealt with an Australian war crime, *Gallipoli* with an appalling military debacle, and *The Getting of Wisdom* with the tawdry snobbery of Victorian school education. Even a light-hearted story like *My Brilliant Career* had a strongly critical social undercurrent.

But it was with contemporary themes that Australian filmmakers sprung their biggest surprises. For this supposedly ultra-macho society produced movies that were not only sensitively poetic, but feminist, insofar as females activated the plot instead of being merely acted upon. If you've seen *High Tide, Careful He Might Hear You, Winter of Our Dreams,* or *Travelling North,* you will know what I mean. And having once established their identity, filmmakers could spoof it, as they did in *Crocodile Dundee,* which no Aussie regards as anything but a good-natured and pleasantly profitable joke.

2. Art and Sculpture

You'll hear a bit more about Australia's performing arts in Chapter XI, "Nightlife." Right now we'll deal with what is probably the least-known facet of the continent's cultural scene—the graphic arts. This is virgin soil for most visitors, but could be their most gratifying experience, because the same freshness and dynamic buoyancy found in Australian movies also exist in its paintings and sculptures.

THE ART SCENE

The advance guard of a distinctive Australian school of painting consisted of people like Sidney Nolan, William Dobell, Margaret Preston, Arthur Streeton, and to some extent, the Aboriginal bushcape artist Albert Namatjira. These and a dozen others are today considered the lodestars of Australian brushwork, and their pictures are priced accordingly. But there is a large group of young contemporaries following in their footsteps, some of them already overshadowing the pioneers. Look for the works of Brett Whiteley, Keith Looby, Ian Fairweather, and John Olsen if you want to see what moves and shakes the Australian art world today.

Versatility is the keynote of the youngest generation of Australian artists. They are the very opposite of specialists: they give you the feeling that one medium alone simply isn't enough for the torrent of creative energy that galvanizes them. This is also the chief characteristic of Sandy Bruch, who is currently carving her name on the Sydney art scene. Sandy's highly personalized creations branch into ceramics and virtually every facet of graphic art. To view some of Sandy Bruch's work you can contact her by calling 02/326-2110.

A Word on Prizes: You will constantly come across references to the Archibald Prize, the Wynne Prize, and the Sulman. These are the top awards Australian artists vie for, monetarily as well as for prestige value. One is given for portraiture, the second for landscape, and the third for genre painting. The bestowal of these awards creates considerable furor each time. At the end of the year you can see the competing works hanging in the Art Gallery of New South Wales and hear the debates raging about their respective worth—fair proof that Australians argue about things other than politics and yacht races.

THE GALLERIES

Sydney has only a few state-owned art museums, but an immense array of private galleries: some very large and beautiful, others modest little storefront affairs. Most of the galleries are concentrated in prosperous Paddington, north of Oxford Street, but you get some surprising treasure troves tucked away in drab industrial surroundings, where rents are cheap. In all of these establishments admission is free, visitors welcome, and browsers encouraged. In any picture gallery the world over, lookers outnumber buyers at least 50 to 1.

Art Gallery of New South Wales, Domain (tel. 02/225-1700). The official art showcase of the state consists of two wings, one built at the turn of the century and the other in 1970, both admirably suited to their contrasting exhibits. The traditionally skylit, wine-walled galleries of the old wing contain European and Australian art dating from the Renaissance to the early 20th century. The new wing, all angled white walls and harbor-framing glass, houses impressionist and modern works, including some striking paintings by the famed Australian trailblazers Sidney Nolan, William Dobell, and Russell Drysdale.

The first floor displays changing exhibitions from the permanent collection and a selection of Asian art. All loan exhibitions from overseas are shown in this museum, but when they involve a famous signature you may have to wait in a long line of enthusiasts to get in. The building also features a good licensed restaurant, an excellent shop selling books, prints, and souvenir catalogs, and a small auditorium screening films on art subjects. Admission is free and so are the conducted tours of the premises. Open seven days a week: Monday through Saturday 10am till 5pm, on Sunday from noon till 5pm.

Aboriginal Artists Gallery, 477 Kent St. (tel. 02/261-2929), displays traditional arts and crafts by the original Australians. Exhibits include bark paintings, weaponry, carved animals and religious symbols, musical instruments, mats, and ornaments—some crude, others remarkably sophisticated. The gallery also sells books on Aboriginal art, beautifully illustrated. Open Monday through Friday to 5pm and on Saturday from 10am to 1pm.

Holdsworth Galleries, 86 Holdsworth St., Woollahra (tel.

02/32-1364), is the largest private art gallery in the southern hemi-sphere and possibly the handsomest. One of the premier showcases for contemporary Australian artists, the building is so beautifully designed and laid out that it could pass as an artwork itself. The ex-hibitions change—sometimes three shows are displayed simultaneously in the vast hanging space available—but they invari-ably reflect the best efforts produced by native painters and sculptors. Names like Margaret Olley, Sidney Nolan, Sali Herman, and Arthur Boyd are regulars, with new unknowns occasionally get-ting their start here. Open seven days till 5pm.

Holdsworth Contemporary Gallery, 221 Liverpool St., East Sydney (tel. 02/331-7161), is a companion establishment of the above. It places a somewhat stronger accent on avant-garde and ab-stract art, includes photography in its showings, and tends to be rather more experimental. The last exhibits I saw there were by Terry Pyros, an abstract surrealist who works as a photographer and paint-er and derives his inspirations from his photographs. Open Tuesday through Saturday from 11am to 5pm.

Robin Gibson Gallery, 278 Liverpool St., Darlinghurst (tel. 02/331-6692). Hard to say which is more attractive about this place—the house or the contents. The superb 19th-century build-ing used to be the residence of Australia's first postmaster general, a gentleman, it seems, of impeccable taste. Now it is one of the most prestigious galleries in the country, representing, among others, Tim Storrier, Brett Whiteley, and Bryan Westwood. Exhibits change every three weeks. Open Tuesday through Saturday from 11am to 6pm.

Bloomfield Galleries, 118 Sutherland St., Paddington (tel. 02/326-2122). Although the mainstay of this gallery is the con-temporaries, it specializes in the work of a bygone controversial—Norman Lindsay. He was one of Sydney's original bohemians, whose voluptuous and highly provocative nudes outraged the Edwardians (who bought them eagerly). The major portion of Lindsay's work is on show in a museum in the Blue Mountains (which we shall visit), but Bloomfield always has some of his excel-lent pencil sketches and etchings on display. Open Tuesday through Saturday from 10:30am to 5:30pm.

New Guinea Primitive Art, Dymock's Building, 428 George St. (tel. 02/232-4737), looks at first glance like an anthropological museum, since it has an immense display of art, tools, and weaponry from New Guinea and Melanesia, some of it very impressive. You wander among decorated spears, elaborate carvings of wood and stone, hand-woven baskets, and fierce little totem statues that look amazingly at home on Californian coffee tables. Watch for the pow-erful primitives from the Trobriand Islands. Open Monday through Friday from 9am to 6pm.

The Hogarth Galleries, Walker Lane and Liverpool St., Pad-dington (tel. 02/357-6839), are two distinct showcases under one roof, forming an intriguing contrast. One displays Aboriginal art, including bark paintings and the strangely haunting rock carvings from Arnhem Land, the wildest and least explored portion of Northern Australia. The other exhibits contemporary (white) Australian art and features some prominent names. Open Tuesday through Saturday from 11am to 6pm.

Australian Centre for Photography, 257 Oxford St., Paddington (tel. 02/331-6253), as the name indicates, is a gallery for camera artists, though it also shows an array of art posters. The exhibitions change, as do the subjects of the photographers, but the standard remains very high indeed. Open five days a week 11am till 5pm; closed Monday and Tuesday.

Watters Gallery, 109 Riley St., East Sydney (tel. 02/331-2556). Perhaps the most widely publicized of the private galleries and therefore a magnet for modern painters who want to make it into the limelight, Watters has the largest collection of Australian contemporary painters in town, including some who have already achieved fame. Lots of hanging space and a very obliging staff who will show you the work of—and talk about—any of their legion of clients. Open Tuesday through Saturday 10am till 5pm.

Irving Sculpture Gallery, 144A St. Johns Rd., Glebe (tel. 02/692-0880), is the only gallery in town that concentrates solely on sculpture, some from overseas artists, the majority the work of local talent. It can be realistic or abstract, symbolic or representational, depending on the exhibitions (which change every month). Open Tuesday through Saturday from 11am to 6pm.

Australian Craftworks, 127 George St. (tel. 02/27-7156), probably has the most unusual setting of any showcase in the world. The premises were originally a colonial-era police station, and the old holding cells are now used to "hold" exhibits. It displays craftworks in the widest sense, but also has specialized exhibitions for particular categories. Materials used range from leather and straw to silk and stone, and every item you see is for sale. Open Monday through Saturday 9am till 6pm.

And More Galleries

The above are merely a few of the galleries flourishing in Sydney. If you amble through Paddington you'll come across another gallery every couple of blocks—or so it seems. Two of Sydney's leading department stores, Grace Bros. and David Jones, have small but distinguished galleries of their own. Still more galleries can be found in the University of Sydney, the Argyle Centre at the Rocks, and the City Art Institute.

Guided Art Tours

There are several conducted tours to guide you around Sydney's art world, which comparatively few overseas visitors get more than a glimpse of. Among the best are the **Helene Springer Tours** (tel. 02/231-4444), which take in as much of the scene as is possible in half-day jaunts. You visit some well-known artists in their studios, view a gallery, and get a look at Aboriginal artwork. The commentary is knowledgeable, but even more interesting are the comments made by the artists themselves. Tours operate every Thursday from 9:30am to 1pm. You get picked up from and returned to your hotel, and reservations are necessary.

Meeting the Artists

Australian artists are as "meetable" as their colleagues the world over—providing you know where to find them. The best place, of course, is the pub they drink in. Failing that, any gallery that is showing their work at the moment. A few—a very few—have combined studio-offices, keep business hours, and employ staff. One of these is Michel Santry, who could be called Australia's most successful sculptor. He lives and works in an enchanting Victorian cottage in Hunter's Hill, on the North shore, and has created some of the most eye-catching, and controversial, public artworks in the country. His best-known creation hangs in Melbourne and caused a middling uproar when first unveiled. It forms the main decoration of the Victorian Arts Centre (Melbourne's reply to Sydney's Opera House)—a gigantic three-ton golden sculpture for lighting, made of 4,000 pieces of polished brass and stainless steel, that hangs suspended through a six-story void in the foyer of the concert hall of the complex.

In Sydney you will undoubtedly notice Santry's contribution to the Centrepoint complex: three huge steel relief murals in polished colors. Other examples of Santry's art you will, hopefully, not encounter. He once accepted and delivered an order for 2,160 headstones.

SYDNEY SHOPPING

Let me preface this chapter by stating that Sydney is *not* a bargain basement. Prices for men's and women's clothing are about the same as in the U.S., except for beachwear, which is slightly cheaper. Books, toys, and any kind of gadgetry are more expensive, even if you take the favorable dollar exchange rate into account. You can utilize your tourist status by buying at the legion of duty-free stores all over town and at the airport, but you can use what you buy only after you leave the country.

A Note on Credit Cards and Shipping: The most widely accepted credit cards throughout Australia are American Express and VISA. And if you just can't carry home your prized purchases, most of the shops I've listed here will arrange for packing and shipping to the U.S. But since the policies differ from store to store, ask before you buy.

1. The Best Buys

What most visitors want are not utility bargains, but distinctly *Australian* objects, things that symbolize the continent. And here I'd like to sound a warning note. Sydney is inundated with stores selling "tourist souvenirs," frequently advertised in half a dozen languages. They offer row upon row of plastic boomerangs, tin Harbour Bridges, mulga-wood pipe stands, stuffed koalas, kangaroo-hide belts and wallets, Opera House paperweights, rubber crocodiles, etc., ad-almost-infinitum. Not only are most of these fabrications pure junk, but many aren't even made in Australia, as a quick look at the manufacturer's label will show.

FOR GENUINE AUSTRALIANA

For these items you should look to certain specific goods which, while not necessarily cheap, are excellent buys. On top of the list go the **wool products**—such as knitwear and scarves—the winners of every quality award the world can offer. The Rolls-Royce of Aussie knitwear (and correspondingly priced) is the Merino Gold sweater, made from the finest wool of 17 micron thinness (finer than cashmere) and rather scarce, since only 200 bales of this material are auctioned each year. Going price roughly $200.

The Australian Wool Corporation has devised a special swing ticket that is attached to products to ensure tourists can tell the real home-grown stuff from inferior imports. The ticket shows a—well, sheepishly smiling lamb against a navy background and carries explanatory texts in English, German, and Japanese.

In the same category you can get the wonderful **sheepskin coats** worn by outback riders in frosty weather, and sheepskin car-seat covers; **digger hats,** probably the most attractive military headgear ever devised, and equally so on men and women (the upturned brim, by the way, was for parade purposes only, enabling troops to shoulder arms; in action the diggers wore the brim down); and **Akubra hats,** their civilian derivations, guaranteed to give city slickers that sunburnt, crinkly-eyed country look.

For Australian **art prints and travel posters,** try to get hold of reproductions of some works by Russell Drysdale and Sir Sidney Nolan: no one has captured the essence of the great outback and its people like these two.

Australian **folk records** can be remarkably good. You might even discover one with the *original* version of "Waltzing Matilda" instead of the hackneyed derivation that's been thumped to death.

ABORIGINAL ARTS AND CRAFTS

These are not only uniquely Australian, but unique in their own right, a blending of forms and colors that seems to reflect the immense, haunting bushland that inspired them. They are primitive in the same way Haitian paintings can be called that, with an artistry that conveys moods and impressions rather than details. Their abstract ornamentation has a strikingly "modern" look, almost as if our contemporary taste had just caught up with their tradition. There are an awful lot of imitations floating around, but I'll give you some outlets that sell the genuine articles only. Here are some hints of what to look for:

Bark paintings are painted on sheets of prepared bark with a feather or twig brush. A red ground color is applied first, then rubbed over with orchid juice to provide a firm surface. Only recognized tribal artists may paint sacred subjects, like totems or rituals, but any person may render secular scenes.

Clap sticks are musical implements beaten against each other to provide rhythm backing for the ritual chanting at Corroborees.

Pointing bones are rather sinister devices made of kangaroo shin bones sharpened at one end. They are used by witch doctors and tribal elders to "point a curse" on members who have broken tribal laws or taboos.

Woomeras. One of the simplest yet most ingenious hunting and fighting implements, the woomera is attached to a spear as an extension of a man's throwing arm. Both are carefully balanced with each other and the woomera imparts additional thrust to the throw as well as a spin to the hurtling spear, making it fly farther and more accurately.

Bullroarers, used to summon men for sacred tribal ceremonies, are made of an oval length of wood with a hole at one end to which long strings of human hair are attached. When one is swung around rapidly it produces a roaring sound that can be heard for long distances in the silent bushland, and simultaneously scares off evil spirits.

Mook mooks are small carved amulets in the shape of spirit beings that are worn around the neck as lucky charms.

Didgeridoos. You may have heard their sounds in an Australian film or concert—an eerie melodious hum that seems to linger in the air. These musical instruments are made from small hollowed tree trunks, picked for resonance. They can be plain or richly painted, but the peculiar haunting drone they emit takes a lot of practice.

OPALS

These are Australia's national gemstones and nearly all the world's supply comes from here. They're on sale in special gem stores, and it's a good idea to stick to the specialists—one reason being that they won't try to sell you anything else. There is, for instance, no such thing as Australian jade (anyone trying to sell you any is attempting to palm off an inferior imported article). But opals come in an immense variety of shades and values. They range from the famous incandescent black stones to the flashing fire opals with a light-greenish base, from solid light crystal opals to rainbow-hued rocks that glow in different colors depending on where the light strikes them. You get opals worth a fortune, like the 1,560-carat Empress of Glengarry (a so-called black stone which is actually azure blue), and you also get very cheap, loose rough specimens you can polish up yourself. In between these extremes you find every gradation in price and size. There are also mounted stones called doublets and triplets, which possess some of the richness of the full gems but come considerably less expensive. Furthermore, overseas visitors pay no duty or purchase tax on opals destined for export.

Most opals are found at Lightning Ridge in New South Wales and Coober Pedy in South Australia, scorched and arid regions that seem to guard their treasures by sheer harshness of environment. You can go and try a bit of fossicking there yourself, if you don't mind back-breaking toil under a scorching sun. You might even recoup your trip expenses. Meanwhile, I'll give you the addresses of some excellent gem specialists in the more hospitable realm of Sydney.

2. The Major Outlets

The main attractions of a Sydney shopping spree are the locations and nature of the retailers. Few cities in the world offer such charming and/or unorthodox shopping environments. There are, of course, thousands of ordinary and mundane stores such as you'll find anywhere else. But I will concentrate on the more original aspects of the retail trade. Chief among them are the **shopping arcades,** which existed in Australia long before they were introduced to America (with suburban shopping centers and supermarkets, it happened the other way around). These arcades range from baroque Victorians to air-conditioned streamliners, but are all of them a joy to browse and amble through, sheltered from rain, wind, or summer sun.

The heart of Sydney's shopping world is a relatively small area stretching from Park to King streets and between Elizabeth and George streets. Crammed into these few blocks are an awesome number of retail stores—not to speak of hotels, restaurants, theaters, cafés, and offices. It contains the **Pitt Street Mall,** not as attractive as the mall in Martin Place, but boasting far more shops. Here you'll also find both of Sydney's main department stores, most of the shopping arcades, all of the central shopping centers, and some very snazzy fashion outlets. Practically speaking, you don't have to stir out of this region to buy whatever you wish. That, however, would be a pity because some of the most intriguing shopping temptations lie way beyond it, as you will see.

DEPARTMENT STORES

The two largest in town are **David Jones,** with two locations, at the corner of Elizabeth and Market streets and at the corner of Market and Castlereagh streets (tel. 02/266-5544), and **Grace Bros.,** 436 George St. (tel. 02/238-9111). Both of these giants have branches throughout the continent; both have art galleries, restaurants, ticket outlets, travel agencies, and beauty parlors; and both sell virtually every commodity you can think of. David Jones is somewhat more British in its choice of merchandise, in that it places the greater accent on luxury items. This is particularly noticeable in the famous food hall of the Market Street store.

SHOPPING CENTERS

Above the **Centrepoint,** at the corner of Market and Pitt streets, is a completely unmistakable sign—the sky-jutting Sydney Tower rising from the top (see Chapter VI). Down below it's a merry maze of 160 specialty shops (with the accent on the fashion trade) connected by means of walkways to the two department store biggies. You can choose among 60 or so retailers dealing in women's clothing that runs the gamut from haute couture to outrageous.

MLC Centre, at the corner of King and Castlereagh streets. It's best to come here outside the lunch hour to avoid the most hectic crush. The MLC has winding passages of luxury shops, such as Dunhill and Gucci, and at ground level an imposing selection of food stalls, cafés, and snack bars. Also on the block are the Theatre Royal and the Dendy Cinema, plus two first-class restaurants—so the crush starts all over again around 8pm.

There's more elbow space at the **Westpac Plaza,** located at the northern end of the central business district at the corner of George and Jamison streets. Smaller and newer, the Westpac provides an extremely wide range of goods and services, including Games World, which is entirely devoted to board games and covers the range from backgammon to Dungeons & Dragons. Lots in the food line, though catering mainly to a lunchtime clientele. But with 20 eating spots from brasserie to gelato bar, Westpac probably has the highest dining density in the city area.

SHOPPING ARCADES

Probably the most delightful features of Sydney's commercial scene, they are also an old established Australian tradition—some of them were built in the 1890s. Basically these are covered passages connecting one main street with another. But most of them also have side passages and split levels, so that a simple walk-through can

---

QVB

The most glamorous shopping complex in Australia is the **Queen Victoria Building,** on George Street between Town Hall and Market Street, the absolutely magnificent restoration/modernization of a grand edifice that had fallen on hard times. For several decades it housed the Municipal Library and the rumor went that the fumes from the wine cellars in the basement had been harnessed to drive the elevators. Now the venerable and ramshackle QVB has been transformed into something palatial, but with the original facade left intact. Inside, under a stained-glass dome, the building looks like a cathedral of commerce. Unlike most cathedrals, it's open 24 hours a day, seven days a week, and is air-conditioned. There is a grand central staircase with wrought-iron balustrades, wheel-arched stained-glass windows, timber shopfronts, and subtly lit gallery tiers. As a centerpiece the Royal Clock, 18 feet long and weighing over a ton, shows animated pageant scenes from history.

The QVB houses 200 shops, boutiques, restaurants, and cafés, mostly for what is known as the "executive market"—that is, expensive. You don't come in here hunting for bargains. You can, however, view replicas of the British crown jewels, a wax model of the young Queen Victoria, and a time capsule on display in the topmost gallery. The shops range from high-fashion lingerie to duty-free (stuffed) koalas; the bistros, from English afternoon tea to sushi.

turn into a voyage of exploration. Since arcade rents are high, the accent is usually on the glamour trade, though you'll find a sprinkling of bargain outlets if you explore long enough.

The **Royal Arcade**, beneath the towering Sydney Hilton, runs between Pitt and George streets opposite the Queen Victoria Building. It houses about 50 shops of the expensive breed, particularly in men's wear.

The **Strand Arcade**, also linking Pitt and George streets, is the oldest in Sydney and has a distinctly Victorian look, rather like an ultra-refined railroad station (the Strand opened for business in 1892 and retains the individualism of the period). The 82 shops are small, distinctive, and one-of-a-kind, a welcome throwback from today's overwhelming standardization. You can also sip a gracious afternoon tea and invest in a reading of the tarot cards.

The **Imperial Arcade**, 83 Castlereagh St. (connecting Pitt and Castlereagh streets), concentrates on fashions for both women and men. The 114 shops are small in size, big in taste, and include bridal wear, furs, shoes, sports outfits, and designer-label jeans.

Cosmopolitan Centre, Double Bay. Only a section of this outstanding shopping hub is actually an arcade. But the streets and alleys around it are so compactly grouped that the whole area must be regarded as one—very fashionable—unit. Focal point is the Cosmopolitan Hotel, with its chic café-restaurant, adjoining the actual arcade. Outside run Knox Street, Knox Lane, Cross Street, and half a dozen little lanes and yards housing some of the most glamorous shopping Sydney has to offer.

You get so-called collectibles that range from old prints to hand-loomed table linen, little fashion boutiques with one or two original (and untagged) items in the window, a Swiss deli in which even the floor covering looks edible, a restaurant specializing in venison, toys for kids who already have every conceivable toy, a duty-free store with designer jewelry, magnificent flower baskets, Scandinavian furniture, rare books, a French charcuterie . . . I'm sure you've grasped the general tenor of the region. Double Bay is an inner eastern suburb, a few bus stops past Kings Cross. Even if you purchase nothing but an espresso, you'll have a memorable shopping stroll.

MARKETS

Sydney has nowhere near enough of these outlets and for the same reason most Western cities don't—shopkeepers don't like them and *they* pay most of the taxes. The few Sydney can boast are so much fun and so popular that there would be customers for at least double the number.

Paddy's Market held a place in Sydney's history for over 150 years, and magnetized locals and tourists to equal degrees. Then this happy chunk of controlled chaos was arbitrarily evicted from its traditional home in the Haymarket downtown, and for a while it seemed as if Paddy's had joined the dodo in extinction. Luckily it has been resurrected, *almost* in its former glory. Paddy's now functions in two locales: Saturday and Sunday in the railway workshops at Redfern Station; Friday and Sunday along Parramatta Road, right at Flemington Station. The action goes from 9am to 4:30pm. It features more than 1,000 stalls at each location and requires a lot of footwork. You'll find almost everything there, mostly at bargain prices, but with no guarantees for either quality or longevity. Goods offered (loudly) run from food to footwear, from pottery to pets, from T-shirts to toys, from woollies to watches. Take your time browsing, because many of the stalls sell identical wares at wildly different prices and you can end up kicking yourself for buying an item at stall A, then find it being sold a buck cheaper at stall Y.

Paddington Village Bazaar, Village Church, Oxford St., Paddington, is a smaller and somewhat tamer affair, but highly original with a medieval European touch. It consists of about 200 stalls, many devoted to handcrafts and folk art, but you also find very smart clothing by upcoming young designers, beautiful Australian woven products, unusual toys, and jewelry and antiquarian books that may turn out to be treasures. Among the special attractions here are the street buskers—roving minstrels, jugglers, jazz musicians, folk guitarists, balladeers, and the like, who keep the market throngs entertained. The market is open only on Saturday from 8am to 5pm.

---

3. Duty-Free Shopping

A commodity Sydney has in overabundance. You'll find duty-free stores all over the city and in most of the inner suburbs, as well as at the airport. You can make your purchases long before your departure date, but you'll have to show your airline ticket and frequently your passport as well. It's a sensible idea not to leave your buying till the last moment but to give yourself time for some comparison-shopping. The listing below names only a few of the scores of retailers in this field.

Hardy Brothers, 74 Castlereagh St. (tel. 02/235-0083), has leather goods, watches, jewelry.

Angus & Coote, 496 George St. (tel. 02/267-1363), specializes in a wide range of jewelry, diamonds, and watches.

Le Classique, 33 Bligh St. (tel. 02/223-1455), is a new showroom displaying perfumes, camera gear, radios, hi-fi equipment, and video.

Downtown Duty Free, 20 Hunter St. and 84 Pitt St. (tel. 02/232-2566), has one of the largest selections of mixed merchandise, including liquor and leather.

Passport Duty Free, in the Kingsgate Shopping Centre, Kings Cross (tel. 02/356-2322), in the heart of tourist territory, has photographic supplies, tobacco, perfumes, audio equipment, and special Australian gifts.

Darrell James, 69 Pitt St. (tel. 02/278-084), combines three stores in one complex carrying such famous labels as Dior, Cartier, and Dunhill, as well as a wide range of Australian memorabilia.

Orbit Duty Free, 74 and 276 Pitt St. and 20 Elizabeth St. (tel. 02/233-8399), is a trio of stores at different locations but all in the same vein. Between them they stock almost anything a visitor could take back.

4. Specialty Stores

OPALS

There are two ways of looking at Australian opals: as one of the world's most beautiful and "alive" gemstones or as an excellent financial investment. The beauty of the stone lies in its individuality. The combination of colors and their intensity vary so greatly that no two gems are exactly alike. These hydrated silica (if you want to be scientific about them) consist of minute particles of closely packed spherical aggregates. The varying arrangements of these aggregates causes reflected light to be split into the full range of colors of the spectrum.

As an investment . . . well, world opal prices are governed entirely by supply and demand. Australia produces over 90% of the global supply, and the major gem fields in New South Wales, South Australia, and Queensland are slowly petering out. Therefore it stands to reason that international demand for opals will outstrip the supply and your stones rise in value. Providing, that is, you are prepared to invest at least $500 for a small stone and to hang on to it for a minimum of five years.

The kind of stone to buy for investment is a "solid" opal, which is also the most expensive. Doublets and triplets, which are artificially pieced together, look very attractive but aren't likely to increase in value.

Whatever your reason for buying, the main attribute to look for is color play—there should be no "dead" or colorless spots on a stone. As a general rule the so-called black opals are more precious than lighter ones, and the rarest show clear red or violet-purple hues. A really fine opal with a dark body, high transparency, and maximum color brilliance, including a large proportion of red, would sell at over $1,000 per carat.

George Olah, at the corner of Darlinghurst and Bayswater roads, adjoining the Hyatt Kingsgate, Kings Cross (tel. 02/358-6208), is a friendly family-owned operation with an enormous range of opals and other gemstones. The opals can be bought either as solids or in the form of doublets or triplets. The Olah family guarantees all the precious stones on their premises. They also have a branch store on Maui, Hawaii.

Gems of the Earth, Shop 11, Argyle Centre, The Rocks (tel. 02/27-7087). Another family business with close connections with opal miners in the fields, the shop is part of the historic Rocks scene and a tourist attraction in its own right. Open seven days from 9am to 5:30pm.

A Gem Show

The **Opal Skymine** (tel. 02/247-9912) may sound like a contradiction in terms, but this one happens to be on the sixth level of Australia Square (which isn't a square, but a circular 50-floor tower and the third-tallest building in the southern hemisphere) on George Street. Step into the combination shop/museum/theater and you walk into a cleverly simulated and animated opal mine (with the heat, grime, and claustrophobia left out). It does, however, give you an idea of the cramped conditions and precarious earth walls that make real fossicking such devilish toil.

Continuous color films show life in the Andamooka opal fields, and gem cutters and polishers at work, honing out the stones as *you* finally get to see them. It drives home the fact that you probably wouldn't recognize a high-grade gem if you found one. Long counters of opals are for sale, ranging from around $30 to upward of $50,000. Expert advice is given free of charge, and so is admission to the showroom and exhibition. Open six days from 9am to 5:30pm. Closed Sunday.

ABORIGINAL ARTIFACTS

You'll find outlets for them all over town, some as phony as three-dollar bills. In order to reach the source of the real stuff you'd have to go bush "until you see birds fly backward to keep the dust out of their eyes." Since this may not be practicable, I'll list a few places where the goods are guaranteed genuine.

Aboriginal and Oceanic Art Gallery, 98 Oxford St., Paddington (tel. 02/332-1544), is both a gallery and a shop for a vast range of native Australian and Melanesian artifacts, clothing, jewelry, ceramics, and weaponry as well as books and music tapes from the regions. Some of the carved animal figures and bark and sand paintings are gems of so-called primitive art. Joe Croft, a partner in this enterprise, is an "urban tribal elder" who retired from government service and now organizes Aboriginal art exhibitions, craft fairs, and dances.

Boomerang School, 138 and 200 William St., Kings Cross. A lot of nonsense has been talked and written about this deceptively simple aerodynamic marvel. Boomerangs, in fact, have different shapes for different purposes. The returning kind is made for sport or for hurling at flocks of birds. Hunting boomerangs do not return, nor do the fighting variety, which are hooked. Finally you have the footprint boomerangs, which aren't meant for throwing, but tell the story of a particular hunt by means of painted footprints and pawprints. The "school" sells boomerangs of all these types at $8 to $15 each. Included in the price are lessons in throwing them, given by expert teachers at a nearby park every Sunday morning.

Coo-ee Australian Emporium, on the first floor of the Strand Arcade (tel. 02/221-5616). The name is derived from the traditional Aussie bush cry, and fits nicely. The emporium stocks both Western and Aboriginal handmade goods, each unique in its own way, plus pottery, wooden utensils, and a range of scarves, sarongs, and covering fabrics with Australian designs. Closed Saturday afternoon and Sunday.

BOOKS AND RECORDS

The largest bookshop in Australia and among the biggest anywhere, **Dymock's Book Department Store,** 424 George St. (tel. 02/233-4111), has specialized sections on matters Australian, artistic, and audio, plus an outstanding map department, and features a computerized customer service system that gets very fast results. Open seven days a week (on Sunday from noon).

Clay's Bookstore, 103 Macleay St., Kings Cross, is a small store with a huge stock—half hardcover, half paperback. In operation since 1954, Clay's offers possibly the widest range of reading matter in town . . . and what they haven't got they can get. Open Monday to Saturday 9am to 5:30pm.

Folkways, 282 Oxford St., Paddington (tel. 02/33-3980). A record label as well as a music store of unusual quality, Folkways has international offerings from Berlioz to Buddhist chants, but with special emphasis on Australian music of every ilk: symphonic, ballet, bush, folk, political, jazz, and Aboriginal. Among the most intriguing buys are 19th-century convict songs and the musical scores of Australian films. Open seven days a week (on Sunday from 11am).

ART PRINTS

A cross between a store and an art gallery, except that it sells prints instead of originals, **Strokes,** 308 Oxford St., Paddington (tel. 02/360-4646), offers an outstanding selection of limited-edition etchings, woodcuts, lithographs, silkscreens, and prints by Australian artists. Also display posters that are worth taking home. Closed Sunday.

CLOTHING

On the second floor of the Strand Arcade, **Flamingo Park** (tel. 02/231-3027), is not a park and has no flamingos. The odd name hides the outlet of Australian fashion designer Jenny Kee. She has made an international reputation with her hand-knitted sweaters bearing koalas, kangaroos, parrots, and other Oz motifs. (I didn't see any with flamingos.)

Sydney Harbour Shop, 123 George St., The Rocks (tel. 02/27-2737). Chances are that you'll recognize the work of Ken Done even if you don't know the name. His explosively cheerful creations are now selling almost as fast in America as in Oz. Done paints designs that are both simple and evocative. His work appears on anything wearable or hangable, from T-shirts to tapestries. This is his shop (he has a studio somewhere else) and you get an idea of the amazing range of his materials. Prices go from around $30 for a sweatshirt and $25 for a poster to $4,000 for one of his joyful tapestries. In between are coasters, placemats, greeting cards, and bumper stickers. Open seven days (on Sunday from noon to 4pm).

Morrisons, 105 George St., The Rocks (tel. 02/27-1596), a decidedly masculine store, Aussie style, sells all the garments people associate with the outback male, except swagman's hats with corks dangling from the brim. You get the inimitable bush hats, moleskins, riding breeches, sheepskin coats, hacking jackets, and all other requisites of Oz male country fashion. The only thing you have to supply yourself is the suntan. Open seven days till 6pm.

R.M. Williams, 71 Castlereagh St. (tel. 02/233-1347), has more bushwear, but for both genders. This was the first company to sell jeans in Australia and has since diversified into other spheres of ruggedness. It has a big range of very smart-looking belts, the kind of oilskin rainslickers you wear in the outback "wet," elastic-sided boots, etc., all with its own company label. Closed Sunday.

THE THEATERS OF SYDNEY

1. THE LIVE THEATERS
2. THE OPERA HOUSE
3. MOVIE THEATERS

Australia in general, and Sydney in particular, has a Thespian tradition covering some 180 years, dating back to the performances of deported convicts—who included a good proportion of "actors, vagabonds, and other paupers." From these planks-over-rumbarrels stages emerged a large and vigorous crop of legitimate theaters and music halls, flourishing in every large town of the continent.

They were driven to the verge of extinction by the combined effects of the Depression, rampant wowserism, managerial myopia, and chains of cheap movie houses. After World War II, when Sydney had a population of 1½ million, it boasted exactly two regular theaters, both presenting bad imitations of English drawing-room farces and passé American musicals. The work of Australian playwrights was considered box-office poison. "The public," managers intoned, "will only pay for acclaimed overseas material." (Don't laugh . . . not so many years ago the moguls of Detroit declared with the same divine assurance that Americans didn't *want* small cars.)

The only lights on the greasepaint horizon were a troupe of North Shore players, led by a courageous female martinet named Doris Fitton, who dared to put on some mildly nonconformist pieces, and an even braver bunch of leftist radicals—all unpaid—who enacted "message plays" in drafty city halls.

The "cultural revolution" that swept Australia in the 1960s brought about an astonishing upsurge of live theater—doubly astonishing, because the same period also ushered in television, which pulverized flesh-and-blood shows in other countries. The reason behind this turnabout was the same as in the film industry: Australian theater had found its own voice, and people flocked to hear it. The cycle had started with a few locally written plays like *The One Day of the Year,* which dealt with a specifically Australian and contemporary theme. But it took the applause earned abroad by *Summer of the Seventeenth Doll* and the ballet *Corroboree* to convince managers at home that they wouldn't court bankruptcy by putting on their own country's products. Eventually a reasonable balance was achieved —the imports are still coming in, but now audiences have a choice of what they'd like to see, and in fact a much wider choice than is the case in most American cities.

Today Sydney has 23 live theaters, not counting the dozens of amateur stages functioning in church and community halls, schoolrooms, tents, and converted warehouses all over town. The city's professional companies put on more than 200 plays and musicals annually, and this doesn't include the revues performed in pubs and supper clubs as part of the nightlife scene. Contents and themes vary tremendously, but the general level of quality is very high, occasionally superlative.

Sydney, however, suffers from a geographical handicap: it has no "Broadway" and therefore no "off-Broadway" definition. (Actually, there *is* a Broadway, but theatrical it ain't.) All of the grand old playhouses stood in the path of some urban development or other and were consequently wrecked. The town, therefore, has no theater district, and the major showcases are scattered all over the place. It's even difficult to define the term "major" except in size. The best I can do is state that the big, lavishly equipped theaters charge between $20 and $38 per ticket and the smaller ones between $10 and $18. You can buy tickets at the box offices or through the **Mitchells Bass Agency** by calling 02/266-4800.

Performance times vary according to the programs, but it's usually around 8pm. You'll find the programs in the entertainment sections of the newspapers or in the excellent publication *This Week in Sydney,* available gratis in hotel lobbies. What these listings don't reveal is the *kind* of playhouses concerned, which is the purpose of the list below.

1. The Live Theaters

Opera House Drama Theatre, Bennelong Point (tel. 02/250-7111), the main nonoperatic auditorium of the Opera House, is given over in turns to the Sydney Theatre Company and the Sydney Dance Company. The range, therefore, is anything from classical ballet to very broad bedroom farces interspersed with occasional children's plays and avant-garde dance productions.

Theatre Royal, in the MLC Centre, King St. (tel. 02/231-6111). Large and lavish, the Royal is the top showcase for imported smash-hit musicals, staged splendiferously. A bar on the premises helps in keeping audiences happy.

Her Majesty's, 107 Quay St. (tel. 02/212-3411), another of the big traditionals (seats 1,500), offers grand-slam musicals and ballets, Christmas pantomimes, and historical epics. It has several bars and a café, and audiences that dress up for their night out.

State Theatre, Market St. (tel. 02/266-4030), is actually one of the old-time "picture palaces" of the 1930s. A cross between McDonald's and the Taj Mahal, and camp on the grandest scale, it has marble staircases, Moorish columns, artificial stars twinkling on the ceilings, and a "Butterfly Room" for ladies to powder in. Now features a mixed fare of movies and musicals, and is the home base of the Sydney Film Festival. But it's worth a visit just for the decor, regardless of what's being offered.

Ensemble Theatre, 78 McDougall St., Milsons Point (tel. 02/929-8877). Located on the North Shore harborfront, this charming playhouse operates in conjunction with a pier restaurant serving pre-curtain buffet-style meals—a highly practical combination.

Seymour Centre, at the corner of City Road and Cleveland Street, Chippendale (tel. 02/692-3511), is an entire Thespian complex, with three separate theaters under one roof. For good measure, the centre also features periodic chamber-music recitals, as well as modern-dance performances. The trio of stages makes for a fascinatingly mixed bag—you frequently get a choice of straight drama, offbeat comedy, and surrealistic experiments on the same evening.

Belvoir Street Theatre, 25 Belvoir St., Surry Hills (tel. 02/ 699-3273), one of the best, most original, and most variegated showcases in Australia, is actually two cases, because there's an upstairs and a downstairs stage. Housed in a distinctly drab portion of town, with decor badly in need of cosmetic surgery, this theater generates originality. It features Australian works on the widest scale—including Aboriginal themes—mixed with satire, topical revues, and children's shows. The Belvoir Street has a near-fanatical local following, but is also a magnet for overseas visitors with artistic curiosity.

Stables Theatre, 10 Nimrod St., Kings Cross (tel. 02/33-3817). Placed in a region largely known for a *different* brand of entertainment, this little theater holds its own against the surrounding jungle of strip shows. With a minute stage and minimal foyer space, the Stables has acquired a great reputation for quality performances of Australian works, famous or obscure, and for a pungent line of comedy. You sit on wooden tiers, but enjoy excellent bar service during intermissions.

Bay Street Theatre, 73 Bay St. (off Broadway), City (tel. 02/ 692-0977), is a converted church that now also houses a bar. The Bay concentrates on contemporary material, drama or comedy, interspersed with occasional one-man (or -woman) presentations that can range from pure mime to satire. Shows Tuesday through Saturday.

New Theatre, 542 King St., Newtown (tel. 02/519-3403). Not "new" at all, this was an offspring of the Great Depression, founded in 1932 as a platform for social protest and commentary. Originally housed above a wholesale grocery, it frequently changed premises in the course of a very stormy career, playing in private homes, on streetcorners, in union halls, and once even in the pit of a striking coal mine. Success has mellowed the troupe, but only to a degree. Its most famous production was Australia's first authentic musical, *Reedy River* in 1953, with a score woven around real and wonderfully catchy old bush ballads. It gets resurrected at intervals and if it's on, don't miss it. You'll come out humming "Click Go the Shears." Now comfortably settled in solid premises, the group still maintains its sharp cutting edge on social issues, but is somewhat more laid-back than in the old days.

Phillip Street Theatre, 169 Phillip St. (tel. 02/232-4900), originally made its reputation by staging Australia's sharpest and funniest topical revues. It still has them, all too infrequently, but now mainly concentrates on conventional comedies, presented with commendable polish.

Footbridge Theatre, Sydney University, Parramatta Rd. (tel. 02/692-9955), actually stands behind a footbridge spanning the road in front. As part of the university it naturally attracts a strong student clientele and caters to the tastes of young academia— meaning satirical, off-the-wall, and generally light-hearted fare, comfortably mocking the establishment.

Northside Theatre, 2 Marian St., Killara (tel. 02/498-3166), is a small modernistic playhouse on the North Shore, situated in a rather exclusive suburb. It has a restaurant and cocktail bar on the premises, with fixed-price meals timed nicely with the show times, and presents good standard theatrical mixture of drama and comedy, mostly well-tried and noncontroversial.

Genesian Theatre, 420 Kent St. (tel. 02/529-9190), is in interesting premises in an erstwhile church. The actors are members of a cooperative, but their offerings do not by any means reflect religious themes. They present English, Irish, and Australian plays, and occasionally very ribald Restoration comedies.

Q Theatre, Railway St., Penrith (tel. 047/21-5735), began life as a lunchtime theater on Circular Quay, but has graduated to being the only fully professional stage in the far western region of Sydney. It performs mostly Australian plays and does them brilliantly, with clever innovative touches. Audiences don't mind the hour's drive from Sydney to see them. For visitors, the ideal time to catch a performance there is when you're on your way to or from the Blue Mountains area (see Chapter XIII).

Rocks Theatre, 106 George St., The Rocks (tel. 02/241-1391). This enchanting stage is the headquarters of the Marionette Theatre of Australia, performing puppetry that's almost as great as the Italian original. It features wondrous lighting and stage effects for magical programs that range from the classic *Pinocchio* to specially adapted versions of Kipling's *Jungle Book.* Don't miss it, even if you haven't packed any kids.

2. The Opera House

Because this is an entire cultural complex, you get a large variety of offerings in the various auditoriums. Standard are the **Australian Opera,** the **Australian Ballet,** the **Sydney Dance Company,** the **Sydney Symphony Orchestra,** and **Musica Viva.**

Other groups divide their appearances between the Opera House and their own (more modest) premises. One of them is the

Sydney Theatre Company. This outstanding ensemble uses its own **Wharf Theatre,** Pier 4, Hickson Rd., Walsh Bay (tel. 02/250-1700), for intimate or esoteric fare and the Opera House for broadly popular big-stage shows. This group has a splendid reputation for its handling of Australian dramatic themes. Half of their theater is actually on a wharf above the water.

---

3. Movie Theaters

Called cinemas in Australia (or "the pictures" by the older generation), movie theaters have gone the way of the celluloid castles in other countries—there are a third as many as there used to be, and those that remain are three times as expensive. Ticket prices are roughly the same as in the U.S., and so is the theater's configuration. They tend to be grouped into complexes housing half a dozen screens each, with a few individual houses scattered here and there. You can divide them roughly into "popular" and "art" theaters, though the distinguishing line gets shadowy at times.

A number of theaters specialize in certain types of films, and here is some help in locating them:

Chauvel Cinema, at the corner of Oatley Road and Oxford Street, Paddington (tel. 02/332-2111), is run by the Australian Film Institute and shows old classics, including some of the deplorable early efforts by Australian producers.

Village Cinema Complex, 377 New South Head Rd., Double Bay (tel. 02/327-1003), presents the more sophisticated and/or artistic international efforts.

Roma Cinema, 628 George St. (tel. 02/264-3321), shows movies from around the globe not intended for mass audiences.

Academy Twin Cinema, 3A Oxford St., Paddington (tel. 02/33-4453), has new releases, both Australian and foreign, that could be classed as artistic in a loose sense.

Opera Playhouse, Sydney Opera House, Bennelong Point (tel. 02/250-7111), shows films in between stage productions, concentrating on second releases for movies that didn't quite make it in the big commercial houses when first screened. These often become cult perennials with the more specialized audiences the Opera House attracts.

For program details and reviews, see the special entertainment section of the *Sydney Morning Herald* on Friday and Saturday.

NIGHTLIFE

Sydney's nocturnal scene has to be divided into two broad sections: the first is an actual night "scene," a special environment in which you can drift along, dropping into one spot or another, but mostly taking in the sights and sounds until you get tired enough to head home. The second consists of individual entertainments where you go to spend an entire evening—the traditional "night out." In this chapter I'll take each in turn.

1. Kings Cross

Sydney's night scene is Kings Cross, the Down Under version of Times Square, North Beach, and Montmartre, with touches of Hamburg, Amsterdam, and Singapore thrown in. The Cross is a blatantly frank red-light district (though the lights are predominantly pink) of a breed that is almost extinct in America. It keeps the kind of hours that once prevailed on the Broadway of Damon Runyon's era—the action doesn't really get under way till 10pm and the streets are thronged around 3 in the morning. The milling crowds in the main thoroughfares make it a safe area, though the little dark alleys are somewhat less so (but watch your purse and hip pocket).

The odd thing about the Cross is that, technically, it doesn't exist. The region is merely a vague geographical definition, the area where Darlinghurst, Potts Point, and Elizabeth Bay meet and join hands in a bit of heel-kicking before going their separate ways. But the meeting is pretty hectic and produces more after-dark whoopee than you'll find anywhere else south of the equator. Within one square mile the Cross generates every conceivable type of night action, from super-svelte to ultra-sleazy, with all gradations in between.

All this is a relatively recent development. Until the Vietnam War, Kings Cross was a pleasantly cosmopolitan, mildly bohemian neighborhood of continental restaurants, late-closing coffee bars, and low rents, where all the disrobing was done by artists' models. "R&R" changed the scene, almost overnight. For tens of thousands of GIs, who flocked here from the hell among the rice paddies, the Cross became a patch of sulfurous paradise to be dreamt about when you were back among the bullets. The locals swiftly added a third "R"—remuneration—to the other two, and Kings Cross changed to its present state. The GIs have been replaced by overseas and interstate tourists, by sailors on shore leave, businessmen on convention, and suburbanites on a spree, but their reasons for coming have remained much the same. The Cross is still collecting remuneration.

The main thoroughfares, **Darlinghurst Road** and **Macleay Street,** and the adjacent alleys, are chockablock with eateries, nightclubs, strip joints, indoor and outdoor cafés, peep shows, sex shops, massage parlors, discos, cocktail bars, and porno stores beside, underneath, and on top of each other. At the corners and on parade wait and saunter battalions of pale strung-out teenage hookers of both genders, supporting their dope habits by turning tricks. In the pocket-size park, slightly away from the glaring neons, lurk the traders of capsuled happiness, selling everything from coke to crack.

The pink-light establishments are disarmingly frank about their business, spurning discreet doorways and furtive knocks. They have "hostesses" yoohooing from the balconies and shills inviting you to "Step inside and look at the ladies. Looking is free." One of these establishments bears a sign proclaiming "Australia's Largest Bed" and offers printed "menus."

But in between and sometimes alongside them you'll find many of Sydney's finest hotels, restaurants, and supper clubs, outstanding bookstores and delis, and cozy little cafés. They are all part of the same scene and keep the same late hours. And at the arterial hub of the Cross, the exquisite **El Alamein Fountain** shimmers in the floodlights like a giant thistledown, dispensing delicate beauty in all directions, free of charge.

It's useless to try to list the entertainments hereabouts; they are too many and they change names too often. You'll see a number of the more permanent ones among the classified sections that follow. Here, I'll merely pick out a few raisins and assure you that there are many others in the pie:

The **Texas Tavern Hotel,** 44 Macleay St., houses an entire amusement complex. In the basement, the **Civic Club** features long rows of slot machines. The **San Antonio Bar,** one floor up, has live jazz and a dance floor. The **Air Crew Club,** on the fifth floor, has little to do with aviation, but boasts an excellent bar, fine views, a dance floor, disc jockey, and periodic live and romantic band ($4 cover). The **Lan Club,** on the same floor, is almost—not quite—Japanese territory, charges near-Tokyo prices, and offers exceedingly smart Aussie geishas.

The Oz Rock, at the corner of Victoria and Darlinghurst roads, is variously called a "hotel" or a "café," but could be neither or both, according to how you define the term. At the moment it's Sydney's premier entertainment beehive—five floors of fun—ranging from raucous to refined. Outside, a Walk of Fame bears the imprints of local and international celebrities. Inside, the three lower floors are crammed with rock debris and vibrate with funk, acid, disco, and pop. Here drinks and good standard pub grub go at economy prices, first-rate DJs take turns with live bands, and the action is young, noisy, and oriented toward singles wishing to become doubles. Upstairs the scene turns svelte and middling expensive. Hartes Nightclub and Jimmy's Roof Top Bar enforce dress codes, charge door prices, cultivate murmuring intimacy, and present low-decibel background music that allows you to hear the ice tinkling in your glass and what your partner is talking about. The whole place keeps going "until late" six nights a week; till 10pm Sundays. Cover charges run from $3 to $10, depending on the night and on who's performing.

The **Pink Pussy Cat,** Darlinghurst Rd., has leather-lunged barkers outside, relays of long-stemmed ladies dressed in demure smiles on the inside. Somehow Aussie peelers always give an impression of wholesomeness because of their suntans.

But just down the road there's a different kind of enterprise. The **Wayside Chapel,** 29 Hughes St. (tel. 02/358-6577), was built with voluntary labor by a freewheeling Methodist minister named Ted Noffs in 1964. Open "to all faiths and none," the chapel has since married more people than any other church in Australia, and probably helps more desperate souls as well. This is where you go when you're in trouble (it functions as a 24-hour crisis center), if you want to locate any group or association in Sydney (straight, gay, or otherwise), if you need a crash pad or a solo bed for the night, if you're sick in body or spirit, suicidal, lonely, or broke. You'll get whatever help human goodwill and know-how can bestow, and you'll get *no* hassles. Instead of normal services, the tiny chapel holds "Celebrations" every Sunday, featuring jazz, folk, and rock music, occasionally Buddhist chants. Sunday evening there are lectures rather than sermons, on anything from drugs to AIDS. Upstairs is a coffeehouse selling "cuppas" for 50¢, meals from $1. The theater in the rear puts on stage shows, films, and debates. You can call to learn what's going on that evening. Better still, drop in and put something in the donation box. It'll be money well spent.

2. Theater Restaurants

These are having a renaissance in contemporary Sydney. The food is mostly standard and uninspiring, the theater anything from slapstick farce and "mellerdrammer" to straight plays or music-hall variety. These amusements tend to be on the pricey side, but usually highly satisfying.

The most famous of them is the **Argyle Tavern,** 12 Argyle St., The Rocks (tel. 02/27-7782). Decidedly tourist-oriented and filled with coachloads of visitors, the Argyle is nevertheless wonderful fun, and often the happiest memory patrons take home with them. Occupying the basement of a restored warehouse, the tavern has a huge, table-filled auditorium and exudes early-Aussie atmosphere, complete with convict-hewn rock walls. Waitresses in calico gowns hand out souvenir menus with the texts of the Oz ballads to be sung printed on them, so at least you'll get to know the lyrics of "Tie Me Kangaroo Down" and "Waltzing Matilda," complete with explanatory footnotes. The courses start arriving at 8pm, good, solid fare like rcast lamb, roast pork, roast beef, meat pies, and strawberries with whipped cream. At 9:30pm the band strikes up and leads the assembled guests in a sing-along. Then comes the *Jolly Swagman Show,* a musical cavalcade that crams huge chunks of popularized Australiana into a couple of colorful hours. It's all there—the convict and the bushranger, the swagman and the barmaid, the trooper, the Aborigine playing the didgeridoo, the campfire poet, the squatter, and "Crocodile Cooee" complete with a rubber croc. The songs are jaunty, sentimental, melancholy, and defiant in turn, wildly funny in parts, climaxed with a rendering of "Click Go the Shears" during which a live sheep is shorn on stage—the last curl falls with the last "click." The whole treat costs $49.50 and you'll be glad you went.

Dirty Dick's, 313 Pacific Hwy., Crows Nest (tel. 02/929-8888), purports to be a vaguely Elizabethan banquet, with lords, ladies, jesters, merry pranksters, serving wenches, and bards. Actually it's a freestyle romp with much improvisation and audience participation. The banquet is heavy on the beef-and-pudding side, the jesting pretty broad, the musical insertions contemporary Oz. (You get neither roast swan nor "pleasing roundelets.") Feasting is

---

A Different Drummer

The other end of the scale from the Argyle Tavern is **Les Girls,** South's Leagues Club, 265 Chalmers St., Redfern (tel. 02/358-2333). This decidedly offbeat program features young and less-so female impersonators, highly talented and stunningly attired. They romp through a middling Rabelaisian variety show abrim with campy humor and awash with double entendres. All the singing is (superbly) mimed to pretaped voices, but the dancing and stripping is done in person. It has a sumptuous setting, done out in scarlet and glitz, with velvet wherever you look. All slightly hysterical and deliberately overdone, it's a tremendous drawing card for visitors who've never witnessed such gyrations. Show times are 9:15 and 11:15pm Tuesday through Sunday. Dinner and show cost $26.

from 7pm to midnight, and the cost is $28 during the week, $30 on Saturday. Closed Sunday.

Bluey's Down Under, Merlin Centre, at the corner of Allen and Pyrmont streets, Darling Harbour (tel. 02/692-9273). Presents a semi-ethnic but most entertaining cavalcade of singing, dancing, and comedy acts, plus items like rope-spinning, artistic whipcracking, live reptiles, and an in-house art gallery. The acts run from Aboriginal dances (with didgeridoo accompaniment) to alleged bush numbers showing much bare leg. Tickets include a three-course dinner flavored by genuine fruits and berries from the bush, a tutu-shaking contest, and dancing on the part of the audience. Costs $40 on weeknights, $45 Friday, $49.50 Saturday and Sunday.

Blue Gum Theatre, 220 Railway Parade, Kogarah (tel. 02/588-6266). Located in a southern suburb, this showcase-restaurant puts on original Oz productions, mostly short plays, delightfully accompanied by a master of ceremonies who has the right audience touch. The humor is broad ranging to midraunchy, but not so "in" that it can't be comprehended by benighted foreigners. The drinks start flowing at 7pm, the show starts at 8pm, and you pay $35 to $38 for the works, including a three-course repast.

Harbourside Brasserie, Pier 1, Hickson Rd., Millers Point (tel. 02/278-222). Situated exactly as the name indicates, this plush venue presents a happy mixture of theater, cabaret, and dance club, combined with excellent supper fare. New shows every week; comical, musical, or both. After the show (around midnight) you dance to live bands until after 3am. The panoramic harbor view adds to the atmosphere. The fun runs from Tuesday to Saturday and costs $38 to $40 per diner/dancer.

---

3. Nightclubs and Discos

Juliana's, in the Hilton Hotel, Pitt St. (tel. 02/266-0610), is definitely a place for dressing up and "being seen," whatever that means. It caters to the smart younger set (those who can afford it), and puts on excellent floor shows earlier in the evening, often featuring international celebrities. It becomes a disco in the late hours and goes on until around 3am. Cover is $12 to $20.

The Cauldron, 207 Darlinghurst Rd., Kings Cross (tel. 02/331-1523), is another mingling maze for "beautiful people," and there's something distinctly mazelike about the intertwining passages, patios, and secluded rooms. Frequented by a lot of corporate talent and their gorgeously attired escorts, on warm summer evenings the focal point is the open courtyard—a feature rare among nightspots. Goes till 3am or later. The cover charge on weekends is $10.

Williams, Boulevard House, William St. (tel. 02/356-2222), one of the plushest nightspots in town, is furnished with genuine antiques and inviting couches, and frequented by a fashionable crowd dressed to kill (don't attempt entry without a tie, gentlemen). The dance floor has a spectacular yet subtle light show, far superior to the usual disco pyrotechnics. There's softly romantic piano music earlier in the evening, disco strains later on until the very wee hours.

Hip Hop Club, 11 Oxford St., Paddington (tel. 02/332-2568), is very trendy and one of the "in-est" spots on the continent —at the moment. It has a very amusing floor show, consisting of a mixture of comedy and dance acts—sharp on the ears and easy on the eyes. After the show there's disco dancing, then a late show, followed by more disco until 3am.

Players, 209 Oxford St., Bondi Junction (tel. 02/389-5051), is an astonishing complex, consisting of three floors with a disco at the top. You start in the restaurant portion downstairs, enjoy a good and not too expensive meal (main courses around $13), then climb up to the disco and boogie off the calories. This is very nearly an around-the-clock operation, serving breakfast at 7am and swinging till 3am.

The **Cuckoo's Nest,** corner of Market and York streets (tel. 02/29-2055), a real underground venue, has stairs leading into a basement that branches out into a restaurant, lounge, and disco, all neon-lit and dreamlike. It caters to a very young, very hip crowd for whom the latest tracks are automatically the best. Usual nightclub hours, but lower-than-usual prices.

Don Burrows Supper Club, 199 George St. (tel. 02/238-0000), is truly elegant and caters to a well-heeled, well-dressed, well-mannered clientele. The changing lineup of jazz combos are all smooth and ideal to dance to, the floor large and never overcrowded. An ideal night out for Mr. and Ms. Executive who value polite service and don't mind paying for it. Entry is $8 to $14, depending on the performer, and the party goes till 2 or 3am.

More splendid harbor views are at **Bobby McGees,** South Pavilion, Darling Harbour (tel. 02/281-3944), plus highly imaginative service. The wait*persons* are costumed actors of all genders, playing roles like Charlie Chaplin, Maid Marian, Dracula, or Lucrezia Borgia. The various rooms of the establishment have different themes: nautical, horticultural, and vintage Hollywood, for instance, and the drinking glasses are impolite conversation pieces. Swings Monday to Saturday till 3am and charges $8 to $10 cover.

Round Midnight, 2 Roslyn St., Kings Cross (tel. 02/356-4045), subtitled Latin Quarter, is a suave and dressy nightspot catering to a distinctly adult clientele. The music starts a little before midnight and features live groups delivering the smoothest bossa, tango, salsa, blues, and soul. The decor is as polished as the bands, including lacquered tables and marble bars. Goes till 3 or 5am every night and has a cover charge hovering around $10.

Café Royale, 36 Bayswater Rd., Kings Cross (tel. 02/358-4528), is the mingling ground of the *jeunesse d'orée,* mixed with equal numbers of young executives. Festooned with video screens, picture windows, and decorative art, the Royale serves outstanding cocktails at outstanding prices, has a sleek dance floor, and music to flirt by. Open seven days a week till 3am.

---

4. Cabarets and Comedy

There are flocks of these in Sydney—birthing, dying, and virtually impossible to keep abreast of. They function in pubs, in basements, in tents, or in fairly elaborate premises. Humor is their stock in trade, but the brand of comedy they dispense depends on their audiences. These fall into two main categories, "ockers" and "trendoids," distinguished not only by what they wear but also by what they laugh about. For the ockers of both genders, comedians rely on endless series of "poofter" jokes and sketches, on beery misadventures, and on a very broad brand of hetero humor. For the trendoids they'll produce political satire with a left-wing slant, skits on TV programs and pop stars, and jokes about ockers.

One additional point: The humor retailed in these establishments can be either extremely raunchy or very "in." In the first instance you run a risk of being offended; in the second, of not understanding the jokes.

Tilbury's Cabaret Room, in the Tilbury Hotel, at the corner of Forbes and Nicholson streets, Woolloomooloo (tel. 02/358-1295), is open Thursday, Friday, and Saturday nights in the backroom of a very popular pub in the Loo. Excellent middle-brow entertainment. Drinks come at pub prices and there's a $5 admission charge.

Trade Union Club, 111 Foveaux St., Surry Hills (tel. 02/212-1188), is home of the Gap theater as well as numerous slot machines and pool tables. Admission is $2 to $5 for sharp, politically flavored satire—very funny if you know what it's all about.

Kirribilli Pub Theatre, Broughton St., Kirribilli (tel. 02/92-7071), is a small tavern stage that puts on light-hearted cabarets. Show tickets cost $7.50, and you can get a very good and rather extensive three-course meal for about $13 in the pub, but that's entirely optional.

Comedy Store, 278 Cleveland St., Surry Hills (tel. 02/699-5731), has a wonderfully assorted bag of professional comedians, promising amateurs, and semi-vaudevillian entertainers. Thursday night it's an all-female show—frequently the sharpest and funniest of the week. You can come for dinner and the show or for the show only, which starts at 9pm Wednesday through Saturday. Show tickets cost from $6 to $20.

Harold Park Hotel, 15 Wigram Rd., Glebe (tel. 02/692-0564). A very unpretentious pub that hides one of Sydney's best entertainment venues. The offerings resemble a smörgåsbord catering to every palate in turn. On Monday nights you get comedy. On Tuesday it's literature, with readings by contemporary Australian authors. Wednesday is theatrical—two short plays that can be comic, dramatic, or both. And on weekends come the rock bands. Tickets cost from $6 to $8, depending on the night.

5. Jazz, Folk, and Rock

The Basement, 29 Reiby Pl., Circular Quay (tel. 02/27-9727), Sydney's oldest established jazz cellar and a wonderful place for syncopation fans, has a resident combo as well as visiting bands from interstate and overseas. There's also a good, cheap restaurant on the premises. Goes six days a week till the early hours; closed Sunday. Admission is $4 to $10, depending on the performers.

Soup Plus, 383 George St. (tel. 02/29-7728), is a jazz restaurant where the fare is cheap (dinner starts at $10) and some of the best musicians in town play—if you're lucky. Music starts at 7:30pm every night except Sunday. But you'd better reserve a table, just in case a jazz great is on that evening.

Benny's Bar, 12 Challis Ave., Potts Point (tel. 02/358-2454), a rock/pop mixer that enjoys tremendous popularity with a young crowd not suffering from sensitive eardrums, has a spacious dance floor and a good Sino-Japanese food department (about $8.50 for a main course). You gain entry by pressing a buzzer and passing scrutiny, but the scrutineers are mainly concerned about your age bracket. In action seven nights till 3am.

Rose, Shamrock and Thistle, 193 Evans St., Rozelle (tel. 02/810-3424). The name, of course, refers to the English, Irish, and Scottish folk music played and sung here on Friday, Saturday, and Sunday. (Local folkies have dubbed it the Three Weeds.) An old pub by origin, the place is unpretentiously cozy and one of the friendliest anywhere. You get a nice mix of folk and blues music, occasionally a celebrity band or vocalist. No door charge, an inexpensive menu (main courses around $9), and drinks at pub prices (about $2). Open till 11pm.

Jazz on the Water

Not a riverboat, but a harbor cruiser, the **Richmond Riverboat** combines great New Orleans–style jazz with dancing, drinking, and dining. The jazz is sometimes varied with blues and reggae, but the food served is unvariedly fine, the vibes great (helped along by an excellent bar). You pay $15 for the four-hour cruise, extra for whatever you eat and imbibe. Cruises depart at 7:30pm on Friday, at noon and 6pm on Sunday, from Pier 4 Pontoon, Walsh Bay (next to the Rocks). Call 02/27-2979 for reservations.

Springfields, 15 Springfield Ave., Kings Cross (tel. 02/358-1785), is a haunt for night owls as well as people in the music industry (often interchangeable). A renowned rock band plays from 11pm to 5am seven nights a week. Admission runs $4 to $6, depending on the night.

The Craig Brewery, Harbourside Marketplace, Darling Harbour (tel. 02/281-3922). Immense beer selection reinforced by cocktails and special house spirits. On Fridays and Saturdays the place becomes a disco with resident DJ; on Sundays you get live bands. No cover charges.

Real Ale Café, 66 King St., City (tel. 02/262-3277). Another beer palace, bearing no resemblance to a café. Serves solid meals at gentle prices and boasts an early-evening piano bar. Wednesday through Saturday nights it's live jazz and dancing "until late," and the (weekend only) door charge is $2.

Site, 171 Victoria St., Kings Cross (tel. 02/358-4221), looks like an oversize Lego set and features some of the most strident rock in town. The music is mostly recorded, with periodic live band interludes. It's disco dancing at its wildest as the album groupies let fly, to funk, acid, techno, soul, rap, and other insurrections. Goes till 2am Monday to Saturday.

Space, 383 Bourke St., Darlinghurst (tel. 02/331-6200). Believe it or not, this place was once a funeral parlor, then became a comedy club before acquiring its current split identity. Now it has a restaurant and cocktail bar downstairs, Space upstairs. Programs and entertainers change every night and run the scale from gay events to innovative dance, guest DJs, and soul music. Call ahead to find out what's in store any given night till 3am.

---

6. Leagues and Other Clubs

The term "club" in Sydney can denote something quite different from what it means anywhere else. Here it signifies certain private premises that are permitted to operate slot machines—or one-armed bandits, or "pokies," as the locals call them. And in order to lure customers to these contraptions, the clubs put on lavish entertainment, supply cheap liquor, and serve very good, inexpensive meals (around $7). All of which can be legally enjoyed without going near a gambling device.

The word "private" may daunt visitors, but the label is pleasantly stretchable. The majority of clubs simply look at your passport, identifying you as a bona fide tourist. Then you sign a book and—hey, presto—you're a "temporary member" for the evening. With the big-timers, the Leagues Clubs, proceedings are a little more elaborate. You call them first, stating who you are, where you're from, and that you'd like to see their show. Your name will be left with the doorman, you will be smilingly admitted, and you become an honorary member for the rest of your Sydney stay. The Leagues Clubs are athletic associations, but also vast casinos with rows of slot machines, plus stages, bars, restaurants, and lounges.

Australia's largest club, with 55,000 members, is the **South Sydney Junior Rugby League Club,** 558 Anzac Parade, Kingsford (tel. 02/349-7555). Here the shows are staged in a 1,000-seat auditorium and the casts include top-level entertainers—all for free! Call for current programs or consult the "What's On in Your Club" column in the Sunday papers.

The most lavish revues in the city are staged in the **St. George League Club,** 124 Princes Hwy. (tel. 02/587-1022), with 36,000 members, whose glittering suburban edifice is known as the "Taj Mahal." Name artists appear; call for program and reservations (required). Shows are at 8:30pm on Friday and Saturday, jazz on Sunday afternoons.

Going on to the smaller outfits, we have the—

Taxi Club, 40 Flinders St., Darlinghurst (tel. 02/331-4256). Actually hidden inside the Grosvenor Club, this place attracts "night people" of all kinds, from cab drivers and waiters to showgirls and shift workers. The premises are plain, but the atmosphere is rich. You get occasional impromptu floor acts that can be startling. There are also rows of pokeys a-clatter, a bar selling economy-priced drinks, and a small disco of sorts. Nothing much doing here until around 10pm, but the activity goes till 6 in the morning.

Mandarin Club, 396 Pitt St. (tel. 02/211-3866). Huge and glittering, this Asian-Aussie melting pot operates on three levels, boasting half a dozen bars, a dance floor, and a restaurant. Shows have Chinese or local vocalists, bands, and dance acts, as well as disco dancing and slot machines. It's like three nights out rolled into one, and at pleasingly moderate prices. Goes till morning seven nights.

Teacher's Club, 73 Bathurst St. (tel. 02/267-7199). Despite the label, there's nothing schoolteacherish about this place. Big and brassy, with bands, bar, bistro, and bandits (one-armed), the club has a young and very lively clientele and a weekend bash on Friday and Saturday when the action goes on till 4am.

7. Wine, Cocktail, and Piano Bars

Centrepoint Tavern, Pitt St., Centrepoint (tel. 02/233-1622). Located in the Pitt Street pedestrian mall, this isn't so much a tavern as a complex that tries to be all things to city workers. There is a restaurant section serving counter meals, a café-pâtisserie, and no fewer than three bars. Main courses run $9 to $13; drinks, $3 to $6. One of the bars, the Pompadour Room, becomes a piano bar after dark, complete with pink lighting, romantic seating, and a wonderfully versatile pianist specializing in romance on the ivories. Patrons here are mainly well-dressed, well-behaved office staffers, frequently from the same office, enjoying an evening out. Closed on Sunday.

Tavern Bar, is the Inter-Continental Hotel, 117 Macquarie St. (tel. 02/230-0200), is on the ground level of one of Sydney's deluxe hotels, paneled in red cedar wood with a white checkered floor underfoot. "Smooth and polished" are the words to describe both the staff and the clientele, mostly young and designer-dressed, interspersed with visiting business execs. Open till 11pm weekdays; closed Sunday.

Old Sydney Bar, in the Sheraton-Wentworth Hotel, 61 Phillip St. (tel. 02/230-0700), is a vast, laid-back, and friendly establishment with a dance floor and free helpings of popcorn. The music is pleasantly low key, but there's a cover charge on Friday and Saturday nights. Otherwise drinks go at pub prices ($3 to $6). It gets a youngish business crowd who enjoy the informality of the atmosphere. Very few tourists. Open weekdays till 10pm, on Friday and Saturday till 2am; closed Sunday.

The **Sydney Hilton Hotel,** 259 Pitt St. (tel. 02/266-0610), has a trio of bars forming an intriguing study in contrasts. The first and most famous is the **Marble Bar,** in the basement, which was saved from destruction by the refusal of building laborers to wreck it—or to let anyone else do so. It's a real Victorian nostalgia nook, dating from the time when bars were retreats for gentlemen wearing mustaches, watch chains, and bowler hats, and women were barred from the premises. The bar boasts huge marble columns and a ceiling of colored glass. Decorations include buxom music-hall beauties, lovingly painted in gowns that may as well not be there at all. Despite its ornate splendor, the Marble Bar is quite casual, attracting a broad cross-section of clients—so broad that it's hard to get in at night. Entertainment includes guitarists and occasional rock bands. Open till midnight during the week, till 2am on Friday and Saturday; closed Sunday.

On the second floor, the **America's Cup Bar** has the reputation of being *the* elite rendezvous in town. Cocktail prices are steep ($5 to $15), service is impeccable, and the decor vaguely nautical, with colored pennants and stately yachts as the dominant motif. The bartenders periodically invent new cocktail mixtures, which are presented with due flourishes. Patrons are mostly upper-echelon executives. Open seven days till midnight or 1am, and on weekends a singer provides nonintrusive background entertainment.

Henry the 9th is on the ground floor, but has only a few slight Tudor touches despite its name. It's a place for after-work drinks with a convivial atmosphere and a high decibel level. Everybody seems to know each other, or pretend they do. The selection of beers is unusually large, and later in the evening you get a variety of live bands—from rock to folk—to add a few more decibels. Open seven days a week till midnight.

Boulevard Cocktail Bar, Boulevard Hotel, 90 William St. Perched way up on the 25th floor of this swank hotel, the cocktail bar (no other name) offers panoramic vistas along with the liquor. The elevator shoots up like a silent rocket, and then there's all of Sydney unfolding below. This is also the site of a very plush restaurant with tabs tailored for expense accounts. The view, night or day, adds a magic ingredient to the drinks. Open till midnight Monday through Saturday, till 3pm on Sundays.

Habit Wine Bar, 185 Glebe Point Rd., Glebe (tel. 02/660-

Powerful Liquids

The **Pumphouse Brewery,** 17 Little Pier St., Darling Harbour, is the only such establishment I know of that was built around an old water-pumping station. The original pumphouse rose in 1891 to provide high water pressure to power Sydney's elevators—electricity was not considered reliable enough. Nowadays all the hydraulic power goes into the brewing and tapping process. The immense cast-iron water tank of the old pumphouse is still there, but alongside it today is a very pleasant roomy beer garden with upstairs balcony. As I sat with my beer I mused on the peculiar Sydney habit of wedging taverns and restaurants into sites like incinerators, funeral parlors, and pumphouses. In this case the result was a charmer, which—aside from a vast array of potables—also serves tasty and economical meals. Open seven days till 10pm and located behind the Entertainment Centre.

2498). I have no idea what the "habit" signifies, unless it's the habit of gathering here, which the patrons do with a regularity akin to addiction. This is a genuine wine bar, serving only the noble grape juice, plus tasty food at modest prices. It's one of the coziest and most comfortable imbibing spots in town, with subdued lighting, wood paneling, and a spiral staircase winding up to the restaurant above. The clientele is soft-spoken and slightly arty (definitely not the audience for which to stage dwarf-throwing contests). Instead they appreciate the solo guitarists providing jazz or blues background notes. Open seven days a week till midnight.

Talking Two-Up

If you're a male traveler on your own, you may be invited to join a two-up game, or "school." Don't do it—because if the organizers have failed to grease the right palms you're liable to get arrested. Two-up is Australia's national game, but it happens to be illegal *anywhere* outside licensed casinos. Only it's illegal the way whisky was during Prohibition. If you fly over Sydney at night, you'll see hundreds of lighted rectangles where some suburbanites play night tennis. In the dark patches in between, the rest of the population allegedly plays two-up.

Aussies call two-up *swy* (from the German *Zwei,* meaning two), and consider it as much part of their military tradition as the famous digger hat. It was said that you could spot Australian trenches in both world wars by the two coins perpetually whirling in the air above them. It's a fast game and an honest one. It's fast because all you do is bet on whether two pennies tossed from a board (or "kip") will land heads or tails. And it's honest because it's safer that way. Some decades ago a game organizer tried using a two-headed penny. He was last seen locked in his car in the process of being rolled off Port Melbourne pier. There hasn't been a double-header around since.

Honest, yes. But, as stated earlier, strictly illegal.

SPORTS AND SPECIAL EVENTS

1. SPORTS
2. SPECIAL EVENTS

To call sports an Australian passion would be an understatement—"obsession" is more accurate. Those who can't play it, watch. Those who can't watch, listen. And all of them argue about it.

In this chapter I'll cover both the spectator and participation sports available around Sydney. Then, at the end of the chapter, I'll mention some of the major special events Sydney offers each year, to residents and visitors alike.

1. Sports

By and large the sports mania is evenly spread throughout the continent, except for Australian-rules football which, for mysterious reasons, inspires fervor only in Victoria (but there with an unholy vengeance). Sydney is representative of Oz sporting tastes in general, and has both the climate and the playing room to indulge in all of them.

Although overseas the Aussies are mainly known as tennis players, tennis is an also-ran when it comes to drawing crowds. The great spectator sports are horseracing, cricket, and various forms of football. Horseracing has the double attraction of simultaneously appealing to the Aussies' love of horseflesh and of **gambling.** They each spend $170 a year on *legalized* gambling (compared to $100 a head in the U.S.), and if you include the illegal kinds, it probably works out to four times that figure for every man, woman, and child annually. You can bet with licensed bookies at the racetracks or at official off-track bureaus called **TAB**. On Saturday it's virtually impossible to escape from the sound effects of the "rices" (native enunciation) emanating from hundreds of transistor radios, car radios, and pub radios. It's astonishing to hear the usually cool radio commentators breaking into hysterical shrieks because Fufflebum is streaking half a length ahead of Nincompoop.

HORSERACING

Sydney has four racecourses, open year round: **Randwick** (tel. 02/663-8400), **Rosehill** (tel. 02/637-2123), **Canterbury** (tel. 02/799-8000), and **Warwick Farm** (tel. 02/602-6199). Admission to any of them costs $5 or $6. The premier course is on Allison Road, Randwick, which also happens to be the handiest—only three miles from downtown and easily reached by special bus services going from Circular Quay and Central Railway. Randwick is a pretty plush affair, carries the prefix "Royal," and is the home of the venerable Australian Jockey Club. The Queen Elizabeth Stand has a panoramic vista room and offers a choice between smörgåsbord or formal dining while enjoying a spectacular view of the track.

CRICKET

Racing rules are universal, but those of cricket present as much mystery to the uninitiated as does, say, baseball. Cricket has certain similarities with baseball, but is a much more leisurely game, as players wear formal whites and decisions come—well, any hour. To anyone not familiar with the fine technical nuances, watching a game can be an experience akin to a tone-deaf person's attending a symphony. The mystery of the sport is the incredible devotion it inspires in those brought up with it. This embraces the entire fifth of the globe that was once the British Empire. Cricket is the eternal heritage Britain left to people who have long severed all other ties with her. Today nations as diverse as Jamaica and Nigeria, Pakistan and South Africa, Malaysia, India, Sudan, and New Zealand continue the cricket tradition with unabated zeal. Cricket's crowning glory, the "Ashes," are taken even more seriously than Americans take the World Series. The closest Australia ever came to leaving the British Commonwealth was during the historic "bodyline" cricket bowling row of the 1930s. (Bodyline was the nefarious trick of aiming balls at the batsman instead of the wicket, thus knocking over the players instead of the stumps.)

The cricket season runs from October to March. For information about the games, call the **New South Wales Cricket Association** (tel. 02/27-4053).

AUSTRALIAN FOOTBALL

Football, on the other hand, is a winter game, played from April to August or thereabouts, and frequently on the same fields devoted to cricket in summer. "Footy," as it's called, comes in three main varieties: rugby league, rugby union, and soccer. League and union are fairly similar, but soccer differs sharply insofar as the players don't carry the ball and use only their feet and heads to propel the leather. All three draw immense crowds of partisan fans (known as "barrackers"), wearing club scarfs, munching hot meat pies, and yelling their lungs out. While crowd demeanor isn't quite as homicidal as in European matches, it can be bad enough to necessitate large contingents of police and first-aid staff.

Sydney's newest and costliest sporting arena is the $60 million **Football Stadium,** located next to the Sydney Cricket Ground in Moore Park. Apart from league, union, and soccer matches, the stadium, which comfortably seats 40,000 people, also presents rock concerts and kindred crowd feasts. Take the Clovelly, Coogee, Maroubra, or La Perouse bus from Circular Quay or Central Railway.

SAILING

In Australia sailing can hardly be described as a spectator sport —not with an estimated 200,000 canvas craft out on the water on any given weekend. In Sydney every third kid seems to have a rigged nutshell of some kind bobbing in the bay. The real yachting set, of course, has its clubs—the **Royal Sydney Yacht Squadron** at Kirribilli and the **Cruising Yacht Club** at Rushcutters Bay— surrounded by a halo of exclusivity. But one sailing event is a true spectators' spectacle: the Sydney–Hobart Yacht Race, which takes place on December 26 of every year. This is the grandest marine shindig of the season. The sight of this yachting armada streaming out through The Heads en route to Tasmania is a sight you'll never forget. If you can't be out on a boat to witness the start, pack a picnic and find a position at Lady Macquarie's Chair in the Botanic Gardens—it's the next-best vantage point.

The big yachts may dominate the open sea, but Sydney Harbour belongs to the 18-footers, perhaps the most exciting sailing boats in the world. For sheer speed and exhilaration they are rivaled only by the ice-yachts of North America. The sailing season runs from September through March, and during that period 18-footer races are held every Saturday and Sunday. The competitors are semi-professionals and the races fought out like miniature Americas Cups. Spectator ferries follow the boats from Circular Quay, departing at 2pm both days. You're not supposed to bet on these events, but just about everybody does. However, it's wise to learn something about the craft and their crews before wagering any money.

If you want to do a bit of sailing yourself, you can rent dinghies at the **Balmoral Sailing Club,** The Esplanade, Balmoral Beach (tel. 02/969-8782). At the **Rose Bay Windsurfer School,** 55 O'Sullivan Rd., Rose Bay (tel. 02/371-7036), you can rent windsurfers at $12 an hour.

For a more luxurious canvas cruise, try **Aristocat Charters,** Akuna Bay (tel. 018/22-4310). This is a white, elaborately equipped 60-foot catamaran sailing the beautiful Pittwater region, serving buffet lunches (included in the price) and drinks from a well-stocked bar on board. The *Aristocat* sails from Newport Inn wharf at 11am every Tuesday, Thursday, Saturday, and Sunday. They send a courtesy minibus to pick up passengers at the Manly Ferry terminal and return them at around 4pm (depending on wind conditions). Prices start at $35 per cruise and advance reservations are essential.

BOATING

This is also big in Sydney, and "messing around in boats" ranks as one of the favorite occupations of the locals. For the best boat-rental services (as distinct from cruises) you should go to the region of **Ku-ring-gai Chase National Park,** a 40-minute bus ride or drive from downtown. The national park is a peninsula between the estuaries of the Hawkesbury River and Pittwater, dotted all around with tranquil coves, beaches, lagoons, and waterfalls. The water here is still and deep blue, sheltered from gales, alive with fish, and considered one of the finest cruising grounds in the world. The hundreds of square miles of waterway constitute an inland sea, protected on all sides by the steep forested hills of the Ku-ring-gai. It's absolutely ideal boating territory, made more so by the vicinity of some excellent shoreline restaurants. The craft for hire here range from simple little aluminum boats to deluxe cabin cruisers, with corresponding price ranges. You don't need a boat license for any of them, though with the larger ones you get a short briefing lesson before hoisting anchor.

The most luxurious outfit is **Skipper a Clipper,** Coal and Candle Creek, Akuna Bay (tel. 02/450-1888). You get a choice of three types of cruisers, all capable of carrying eight to ten people in various degrees of comfort. All come with fully equipped galleys (kitchens, to you landlubbers), refrigerators, electric anchor winches, ship-to-shore radios, fresh linen and towels, life jackets, and first-aid kits. Also unlimited diesel fuel, a dinghy, fresh water, gas stoves, and bags of crushed ice. Rates depend on what you rent, when you rent, and for how long—between $30 and $99 per person per day. A refundable deposit of $100 is required before you depart.

Halvorsen Boats, P.O. Box 21, Turramurra (tel. 02/457-9011), has motor cruisers on the Hawkesbury River capable of accommodating eight people. The ideal number is four, and a weekend of cruising for such a group would cost around $500 (prices depend on the time of year).

For something smaller, simpler, and intended mainly for fishing, try **Bait 'n' Boats,** 83 Brooklyn Rd., Brooklyn (tel. 02/455-1206). This company has handy little aluminum craft, light yet sturdy, that rent for around $45 a day. These boats are open and you'd be well advised to pay a bit extra for a protective canopy.

For a wonderfully lazy and relaxing day on the Hawkesbury, you can also rent a mobile houseboat—as distinct from the permanently moored breed. **Fenwick's River Houseboats,** P.O. Box 55, Brooklyn (tel. 02/455-1633), has these floating homes suitable for up to six people. They cruise slowly, are child's play to handle, and make ideal tanning, fishing, and just plain loafing bases. Prices on request.

TENNIS

Tennis is the game that has earned the Aussies their international sporting fame and the one you see them practice most often, from dawn till long after dusk (Sydney is dotted with lighted night tennis courts on which the locals are lobbing balls till the witching hour). Boys and girls start playing tennis in school and stay more or less wedded to their rackets thereafter. All of which makes renting court space easy, but winning a game rather more difficult. The major tournaments are held at White City in Rushcutters Bay, and at the Entertainment Centre, Darling Harbour. These top-money events are usually scheduled between October and February, and attract top-class tennis stars, male and female.

Court rentals cost somewhere between $5 and $17 an hour, depending on where and when you want to play. While you can always get a public court, renting tennis gear may prove elusive. Not all the courts have rackets for rent at all times, so it's best to inquire beforehand. Night courts take a bit of getting used to, at least until your eyes grow accustomed to the tricks played by the lighting effects.

Some of the handy inner-suburb courts are: **Trumper Park,** Quarry St., Paddington (tel. 02/32-4055); **Tennis Factory,** Prince Alfred Park, Chalmers St., Surry Hills (tel. 02/698-9451); **Moore Park Tennis,** Anzac Parade, Paddington (tel. 02/662-7002); and **Lyne Park Tennis Centre,** New South Head Road, Rose Bay (tel. 02/371-6048).

GOLF

Although Sydney is well supplied with public golf courses, the game is not as popular as in the U.S. The top Sydney golfing event is the New South Wales Open. You can contact the **N.S.W. Golf Association** (tel. 02/264-8433) for details.

Public golf courses charge around $9 for 18 holes. Some of the closest are **Moore Park Golf Course,** Anzac Parade, Moore Park (tel. 02/633-3960), and **Bondi Golf Links,** Military Road, North Bondi (tel. 02/30-1981).

Golfers Overseas Australia (tel. 02/440-8449) arranges golf tours tailored for visiting American and Japanese business executives. Run by Qantas airline captain David Skinner, a top-grade golfer, this venture has acquired a big reputation in Japan. Skinner not only arranges the tours, but also helps players on the links.

AND OTHERS

A latecomer on the local sports scene, **grass skiing** is now collecting a large and enthusiastic throng of fans. The advantages of this variation are obvious: you don't have to depend on snow and you don't need skis—sturdy legs and an old pair of socks do nicely.

You can grass-ski all year round, though the peak season is from April through September, the Australian winter months. There are public grass-skiing slopes at the corner of South Dowling and Cleveland streets in Moore Park, complete with ski lifts. You pay $10 per hour, and this includes the (very) basic equipment you require.

Boomerang-throwing is definitely not a national sport. In fact, few Aussies have ever handled one. But Duncan MacLennan, the man who runs the **Boomerang School,** 138 William St., Kings Cross, gives free lessons in the art to anyone who buys a boomerang from him. They proceed every Sunday morning from 10am to noon at Yarranabbe Park, since no such place as a public boomerang range exists as yet. Apart from being an expert thrower (it's all in the wrist), MacLennan is a drawling encyclopedia on the subject of these throwing sticks.

According to him, the Aborigines invented the boomerang to hurl at the legs of the animals they hunted. (Everywhere else game runs on four legs, so the prey could escape even with one leg out of commission. But in Australia, kangaroos and emus are two-legged, and hunters could stop them by hitting just one leg.) Returning boomerangs, he maintains, were an accidental discovery, developed from the much smaller and lighter types that were thrown high into the air at ducks. Throwing the three-foot-long regular hunting boomerang is extremely difficult. The smaller, returning kind takes somewhat less practice. Factory-produced boomerangs go for as little as $5 and can provide good sport—as long as you don't practice near breakable windows. But the high-quality, handcrafted types sell for $100 to $300, and the antique ones are considered collectors' items.

Australians call bicycles "push bikes" to distinguish them from the other kind, motorbikes. Sydney is fairly well equipped with **bicycling** paths, mostly around park areas, though not as well as other Australian cities. I'd suggest you stick to these paths for your pedal-pushing. Biking among downtown traffic—on the left—can be rather hazardous (Sydney's motorists are not known for their consideration toward the pedalers). One of the prime central cycling regions is Centennial Park (which was opened to celebrate the country's first centenary in 1888), along Oxford Street, Paddington. You can rent the metal steeds from **Centennial Park Cycles,** 50 Clovelly Rd., Randwick (tel. 02/398-5027). They rent half a dozen types of bikes, including tandems, at rates starting at $4 per hour.

The park also has **horseriding** trails, and you can rent a live steed for around $12 an hour from **Centennial Park Horse Hire,** RAS Showground, Driver Ave., Moore Park (tel. 02/332-2770).

2. Special Events

The longest and most varied "special event" on the continent is also the most difficult to capsulate. This is the **Festival of Sydney,** which runs right through January and features a slightly zany, extremely confusing, and totally joyous hodgepodge of popular entertainments, cultural events, and ethnic presentations, with outdoor markets, crafts fairs, and sporting competitions thrown in, plus a score of happenings that defy rational classification. The only way to summarize this civic cacophony is to say it's fun.

The fun spreads over most of central Sydney and well beyond. The harbor erupts in a frenzy of aquatic sports, including races by ancient ferry boats, a regatta in which all craft are made from Pepsi-Cola cans, and bathing-beauty contests with century-old costumes. Hyde Park is turned into a kiddieland with puppet shows and balloon flights. The Opera House stages a series of special performances, outdoors and in. The beaches put on surf carnivals and sandcastle competitions. Roadways feature bicycle races and antique car rallies, with drivers dressed in correct Edwardian garb. A Highland Gathering blasts off with a thousand pipes and drums, strolling minstrels and jugglers in medieval attire wander through the crowds, a dozen national groups display their folk dances and music, and at night the sky lights up with bursting fireworks. The final weekend, which incorporates **Australia Day,** sees a grand military tattoo and a reenactment of the landing of the First Fleet, with its uniformed soldiers and (involuntary) first settlers.

The **Royal Easter Show** is briefer, but even more spectacular because the action is concentrated. This is Australia's top agricultural event, staged annually since 1824, which has acquired a lot of extra trimmings over the years. The show is held over Easter week at the 72-acre Moore Park Showground and boasts an attendance record of 1½ million spectators! The 12-day display of agrarian wealth and achievement is the most important segment of the city's social calendar and the perennial zenith in the lives of country folks.

The show displays the best the rural countryside can offer: the finest cattle, sheep, dogs, wool, and wine. In return the city exhibits what it can offer the country: agricultural machinery, motor vehicles, household gadgets, and farm implements. This is the basic backbone event, but woven around this is a kaleidoscopic wreath of specials designed to fascinate even those who haven't the slightest interest in matters rural. There is a fun park with all the latest rides, slides, and whirls designed to test human stamina. The exhibition of paintings and sculptures seeks out the top artistic talent on the continent—being "hung" at the Royal Easter Show carries prestige as well as monetary rewards. Spectators see fashion shows presented by Sydney's leading models; ten different flower shows in the horticultural section; a carnival with trapeze acts, clowns, children's theater, magicians, and acrobats; and military marching bands. The contests with a true rural flavor are probably the most exciting of the lot: sheepdog trials, in which the little canine shepherds have to pen their obstreperous charges within a given time; woodchopping races with international competitors; rodeo riders, steer and bareback; and buckjumping, tent pegging, bulldogging, and whipcracking contests. At night there are some very stylish polo matches followed by fireworks. In all, the show features around 34,000 entries competing for prize money exceeding $200,000 each year.

Overseas visitors can go to the Information Centre, show their passports, and receive a special lapel ribbon together with all the help and guidance they need. For advance information, write or call the **Royal Agricultural Society of N.S.W.,** Box 4317, GPO Sydney, 2001 (tel. 02/331-9111).

EXCURSIONS FROM SYDNEY

Sydney is so large, diverse, and engrossing that it's easy to forget it's also the capital of a very big state—the "premier state" of Australia, in fact. **New South Wales** measures a third of a million square miles and has over five million people. Since 3.5 million of them live in the Greater Sydney area, you can imagine how much elbow room there is for the rest.

The state boasts a greater variety of beauty spots than any other on the continent. It has four distinct geographical regions, each with its own special characteristics. First there's the 1,000-mile coastal strip, offering some of the finest surfing and swimming beaches on the globe. Then there are the inland mountain ranges and plateaus, with snowy peaks rising to over 7,000 feet, forming a winter playground with ski lifts and alpine chalets. Third, there's the golden-green lushness of the western slopes, a region of warm lazy rivers and rich wheatfields, ideal for fishing and waterskiing. And finally there is the great western plains, the "woolbelt" of the state, presenting the real "outback" with immense flocks of sheep, little gray-black shepherd dogs, and flat horizons that stretch into eternity.

All I can do here is to give you a quick tour of the highlights, and only a few of those, worse luck. But you'll miss a lot if you copy those Sydneysiders who only leave their city to go abroad. They think that the Sahara Desert starts just beyond the Blue Mountains.

---

1. The Blue Mountains

Just 50 miles west of Sydney, these mountains rise from the coastal plain to form a background almost as spectacular as the harbor entrance. For these rolling, cliff-toothed ranges really *are* of a deep, dreamlike blue, a natural phenomenon produced by countless oil-bearing eucalypti. The trees constantly release fine droplets of oil into the surrounding atmosphere, reflecting the blue rays of the sun and wrapping the whole landscape in a vivid azure haze.

The Blue Mountains National Park is fringed with resort towns, ribboned with magnificent waterfalls, and crisscrossed by hiking trails. When Sydney is steaming below, the mountains are cool and fresh. And each of the resorts has its own bag of scenic delights and attractions.

Heart and capital of the region is **Katoomba,** which offers a considerable amount of resort bustle. There you'll find the **Scenic Skyway** and **Scenic Railways.** The former is an aerial cable car, suspended over a breathtaking chasm, costing $2.70 for adults, $1.20 for children. The latter is *allegedly* the steepest rail track in the world —at least that's what it feels like when you're riding it. Adults pay $2.70; children, $1.20. The **Megalong Valley Farm** is a charming mélange of working farm and showcase. You can go for tractor rides or pet baby donkeys, piglets, and foals. Then watch the cattle show, the sheep-shearing, and the heavy-horse show—in which you watch a draft horse jump a hurdle. The farm is open Wednesday through Sunday from 9:30am to 5:30pm. Admission for adults is $6, $3 for children.

From Echo Point at Katoomba you can see one of the most intriguing natural attractions of the region, the **Three Sisters.** These are a trio of towering stone pillars, looking uncannily like three upright female figures, particularly under floodlighting at night. According to an ancient Aboriginal legend they were once the three daughters of a mountain witch doctor. When a bunyip (mythical monster) tried to carry them off, the distraught father turned them to stone and himself into a lyrebird, since he lacked the power to turn the bunyip into anything. At midnight, the legend goes, you can still hear the lyrebird plaintively calling out to his stone children.

Adjoining the old courthouse in Katoomba is the **Renaissance Centre** (tel. 047/82-1044). This is a very attractive cluster of galleries, workshops, restaurants, museums, exhibitions, and performance space, housed on four levels of a rambling structure that encloses a whole cultural complex scaled down to resort proportions. There are 21 glass-fronted specialty shops selling books, pottery, antiques, handmade glass, and fashions. There are working craft studios where you can watch glassblowers, woodcarvers, hat-

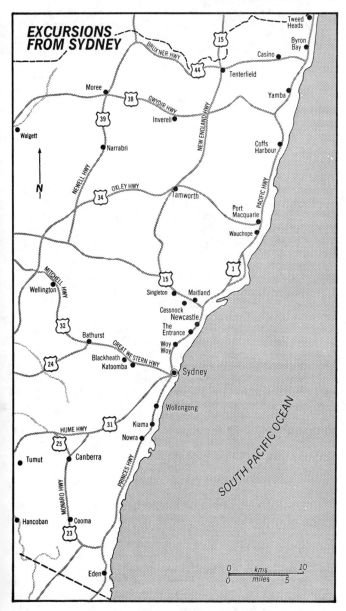

EXCURSIONS FROM SYDNEY

ters, and potters in action. There is a photographic museum with memorable mountainscapes on display, a fitness center, a brasserie, and periodic stage performances, making this structure an amazing all-rounder.

The neighboring town of **Leura** has a shopping mall and the magnificent mansion called **Leuralia.** This was the residence of H. V. Evatt, the Australian statesman who became secretary general of the United Nations. The house stands surrounded by glorious gardens and is furnished in art deco opulence. There is a small museum inside, dedicated to the life and work of Evatt, one of Australia's all-time political "greats." Admission is $2 for adults, 50¢ for children, and the house is open Friday through Sunday from 10 am to 5 pm.

Just west of Katoomba, at **Medlow Bath,** is the **Hydro Majestic Hotel,** Great Western Hwy., Medlow Bath, N.S.W. 2780 (tel. 047/88-1002). Aptly described as an "Edwardian Folly," the place opened in 1904 and became the epitome of utter and slightly wicked elegance to a generation of Sydneysiders for whom it was *the* weekend retreat. Today the Hydro is a National Trust edifice, and its glory has faded somewhat, but it remains a fun place to either wander through or stay in. The 55 bedrooms and cocktail bar have period decor but all modern facilities, the garden views are stunning, the swimming pool is a period piece, and the little picture gallery, a slice of shadowy nostalgia. The weekend rate here includes breakfast and dinner and is $208 double.

Falconbridge has the **Norman Lindsay Gallery,** a large stone cottage in which the celebrated artist lived and worked for 57 years. The house and surrounding landscaped garden are filled with his paintings, sculptures, and memorabilia. It's hard to convey today just how much Lindsay's joyous nudes shocked his generation (which didn't stop anyone from buying them, nor from perusing his "scandalous" books). But let's remember that his illustrations for the classic *Lysistrata* were banned in New York as well. The gallery is open Friday through Sunday from 11am to 5pm.

Wentworth Falls is the most spectacular waterfall in a region full of rushing water. The white cascade shoots down a rugged escarpment, then plummets some 500 feet into the Jamieson Valley. There is a lookout directly opposite the falls that gives a wide panoramic view of the drop. Just above Wentworth Falls, hidden away in a bush and parkland setting, stands **Yester Grange,** a Victorian country mansion that was once the home of a state premier. You can inspect the Victorian interiors and the garden Wednesday through Sunday from 10am to 5pm. Admission for adults is $3; for children, $1.50.

Farther to the west lies the **Jenolan Caves Resort,** a nature reserve and tourist site based around a labyrinth of world-famous limestone caves. Accommodations, wilderness walks, waterfalls, and swimming sites all abound, but the real magnet is the caves themselves. These are divided into three groups, conveniently labeled "strenuous" and "mildly strenuous." This refers mainly to the number of steps you have to climb in order to view their marvels —ranging from a mere 288 steps for the "Temple of Baal" to an athletic 1,332 steps for the "River." The caves offer grand adventure with an eerie beauty of their own. There are underground rivers and bleached bones, still, dark pools, and fluorescent rock walls that are sinister and eerie. You can choose from three tours, taking two hours each. They cost either $5 or $7 for adults, $3 or $4 for children. The third tour has a uniform price of $10 per person and is not recommended for kids. The caves are open daily, and you can get additional information by calling 063/59-3304.

GETTING THERE

You can get to the Blue Mountains from Sydney by either train, bus, or car. The **State Railways** operates a special Blue Mountains jaunt Monday through Friday, with trains leaving Sydney Central Station for Katoomba at 8:12am. Tickets for adults are $26; for children, $14. For further information, call 02/954-4422.

All the coach-tour companies mentioned in Chapter VII run excursions to the Blue Mountains as well. But if you prefer a touch of mild adventure go with **Wild Escapes,** GPO Box 4799, Sydney, N.S.W. 2001 (tel. 02/660-2584). This outfit provides knowledgeable guides and suitable equipment for several kinds of mountain jaunts. Transport is by four-wheel-drive vehicles fitted with CB radios and capable of traveling anywhere in rugged territory.

The Grand Canyon Adventure is a day of bushwalking and mountain climbing (with ropes), followed by a scenic hike along a meandering stream. The cost is $90 per person and the tour operates Tuesday, Thursday, and Saturday. For the same price you can participate in Blue Mountains Cycling. Good 10-speed mountain bikes are used along little-known paths to explore parts of the region not usually trodden by tourists' feet. Goes Monday, Thursday, and Saturday. At the opposite end of the strain scale is Canyon Liloing, a wonderfully lazy day spent drifting on inflated mattresses along the crystal-clear stream that flows through the towering Wollangambe Canyon, as well as some leisurely bushwalking and a picnic lunch. The outing costs $80 and takes place Thursday and Sunday.

Wild Escapes also runs white-water rafting on the Upper Schoalhaven River ($90), and a kayak-paddling tour around the calm waters of Sydney Harbour, with lunch on Clarke Island ($90).

---

2. The Snowy Mountains

More peaks, but much higher this time, and covered from about June to September in superbly skiable snow, the Snowy Mountains start their climb some 300 miles southwest of Sydney, and their tallest peak, **Mount Kosciusko** (7,314 feet), is the highest point in Australia. Mount Kozzie, as the natives call it, forms part of a vast winter playground that embraces all 2,100 square miles of the **Kosciusko National Park** and looks like a portion of Switzerland transported to the southern hemisphere. The skiing capital is a new, all-modern-conveniences-included resort village.

THREDBO

The brainchild of former Czechoslovakian ski champion Tony Sponar, **Thredbo Alpine Village** was built in the image of famous European winter sports resorts. In similar style, it offers outdoor and indoor fun in roughly equal quantities, but at less than European prices. You can share a room in an "economy lodge" or rent a holiday flat; all-inclusive six-day snow-holidays packages start as low as $500 to $600. In season (that is, *out* of season for Sydney) the whole village merges into one big party, scattered between the thumping disco of the Keller and half a dozen more intimate—but just as swinging—restaurants, bars, and bistros. Maybe it's the marvelously bracing mountain air, but most of the swingers manage to stumble onto a 2,000-foot chair lift next morning to zoom down 25 miles of ski trails, jet-turning and paralleling as if they hadn't rocked through the night.

Off season, the attractions include glorious views—a 1½ mile chair lift operates the year round to the top of **Mount Crackenback** (6,350 feet)—and such relaxing diversions as fishing, swimming, hiking, barbecuing, campfire nights, and dinner dances. Prices relax too, slipping well below the winter rates. You reach Thredbo by bus, train, car, or plane to Cooma, which is 56 miles away. Coaches then take you to the ski fields.

SNOWY MOUNTAINS HYDROELECTRIC SCHEME

Formerly a drowsy little mountain hamlet, **Cooma,** about an hour by air from Sydney, burst into cosmopolitan life when it became the scheme's launching pad and headquarters. Today the village proudly flies the flags of 27 nations, one for each country whose citizens took part in this titanic project. To see it you must cross the border of New South Wales into the neighboring Australian Capital Territory (ACT). This is a kind of federal enclave (not a state) drawn around the Commonwealth capital of Canberra, like the District of Columbia.

The "Snowy Scheme," as the Aussies call it, was named by the American Society of Civil Engineers as one of the "Seven Wonders of the Engineering World." It is the mightiest technological task ever accomplished in Australia and has become an almost mystical focal point of national pride. For sheer magnitude the "Snowy" can only be compared with America's Tennessee Valley Authority water scheme.

The significance of the SMA (Snowy Mountain Authority) stems from the fact that Australia is the driest of all continents, mainly because it has few massive mountain ranges to precipitate rain and give rise to rivers. The basic idea of the scheme was to divert the Snowy River from its original path into three new rivers that would flow west into water-needy country, and in so doing provide not only irrigation and thus fertility, but also a colossal amount of water-generated electricity for power and lights for homes, industry, and transport in the plains below. If you've seen the movie *The Man from Snowy River* you'll have an inkling—no more—of what kind of tiger country the project was tackling.

Begun in 1949, the project took 25 years to complete and cost $800 million, the labor of 6,000 men, and the lives of 54 killed by rockfalls and misfired tunnel blasts. This was the price paid for the astonishing speed of the tunneling operations, which frequently reached a rate of 541 feet per week. (The previous world record, set by the Swiss, was 362 feet of tunneling a week.)

The SMA boasts a mass of dazzling statistics: 90 miles of tunnels hewn through the mountains, 80 miles of aqueducts constructed, 1,000 miles of road laid down, seven power stations in operation, producing 4 million kilowatts of electricity! The entire scheme embraces an area of over 2,000 square miles and has created a chain of huge artificial lakes, the largest of them, Lake Eucumbene, containing nine times the volume of water in Sydney Harbour!

But better than all these figures is the loving care with which the whole undertaking has been blended into the scenery. Far from marring the beauty of the mountain ranges, the Snowy Scheme has enhanced them. Many of the power plants are underground and invisible until you reach the entrance. The immense silvery-white dams blend with the snow-capped peaks like natural waterfalls. The lakes—cold, blue, and crystal clear—have been stocked with rainbow trout and provide some of the best game fishing in the country. And somehow even the masses of sightseers attracted by the project are absorbed with a minimum of blatantly commercial tourism.

Tours of the project, lasting one to three days, leave Canberra and Cooma several times a week. There is, for instance, a one-day guided trip operated by **Pioneer,** 150 Northbourne Ave., Canberra, ACT (tel. 062/415-066), that includes a fascinating film show of the SMA and costs $30 for adults, $21 for children.

Khancoban, lying west of Cooma and halfway between Sydney and Melbourne, is the Cooma story in reverse. During the building of the hydroelectric project this was a beaver-busy work camp and boomtown housing around 4,000 people, nearly all construction workers. Then, when the scheme was completed, Khancoban became a restful little mountain retreat catering solely to holidaymakers. The village nestles in the foothills of the Great Dividing Range that marks the border of New South Wales and Victoria. All around rise the forested alpine peaks crisscrossed by foaming rivers and placid lakes and teeming with wildlife (no hunting in this nature reserve, but the trout fishing is superb).

The next valley over contains the gigantic lake created by the Snowy Scheme. On the slope stands the **Alpine Hideaway Village** (tel. 060/76-9498), one of the finest resorts of the region. The Hideaway is the creation of an Austrian couple, the Winterbergs, and bears unmistakable touches of similar resorts in the Tyrol, but with lots of Australian elbow room thrown in: it stands on 500 acres of private wilderness, offering panoramic views in all directions. Guests are housed in individual cabins more or less self-contained. Hartmut Winterberg, a former ski instructor, acts as guide on fishing, camping, horseriding, bushwalking, and canoeing ventures; his wife does the cooking. Full board (meaning dinner, bed, and breakfast) costs around $40 a day.

3. The Hunter Valley

Lying northwest of Sydney in a wonderfully lush landscape is Australia's oldest wine region. Although the bulk of the continent's wines today come from South Australia, the Hunter had an operating winery as early as 1828—long before California. Today the region has over 40 wineries, including some of the most famous brand names in the country: Wyndham Estate, Saxonvale, Lakes Folly, Rothbury Estate, Hermitage, Lindemans, Tuloch, McWilliams—music to a wine-lover's ears.

A visit to the Hunter Valley naturally turns into a wine-tasting tour. Since about half a million people come with the same idea, you can do yourself a *big* favor by timing your visit for midweek, when the restaurants have spare tables and the tasting sessions of the wineries can focus on individual visitors. During weekends they're packed. Another point—if at all possible, don't drive yourself. The Hunter highway police keep a sharp eye on motorists, and prolonged tasting tours do have certain side effects. Better to join one of the coach trips where the driver has to stay stone cold sober, which will make it all the easier to enjoy the Hunter's unofficial motto, "Say G'Day to a Chardonnay."

NEWCASTLE

Gateway and springboard to the valley is Newcastle, second-largest city in New South Wales (pop. 300,000) and a heavily industrialized steel and coal producer. But Newcastle also has great surfing beaches right near the city center, a fine art gallery, and just to the north, Port Stephens, one of the most magnificent and unspoiled waterways found anywhere in Australia.

Newcastle is certainly industrialized—among other things it has BHP, Australia's biggest steel producer. But all the plants are contained in one specific area, separated from the other districts by the broad Hunter River. The commercial center of the city is a wide, tree-lined pedestrian plaza, the **Hunter Mall,** a lively colorful market square with an amazing variety of department stores, boutiques, restaurants, and specialty shops. Just south of the city stretches **Lake Macquarie,** the largest saltwater lake on the continent. This is a mecca for thousands of lake sailors, yachtsmen, and fishermen or for folks who just enjoy lazing about in the sun. The spectacle of hundreds of bright sails on the sparkling (and unpolluted) water gives the area the appearance of a vacation resort.

North of the city lies the "Blue Water Wonderland" of **Port Stephens.** This is the name of a large peninsula blessed with an exceptionally agreeable climate that acts as the weekend playground for Newcastle's population. Port Stephens offers everything you'd expect from a resort region, including two sizable peaks for climbing. Below them lie patrolled surfing beaches, secluded little fishing coves, commercial centers with restaurants and shops, and any number of motels and holiday units.

One of the best features of the region is the fishing fleet, which brings large catches of fish, prawns, and local lobsters to the restaurants, guaranteeing the supply of fresh seafood. Port Stephens's claim to national fame is **oyster farming.** The young oysters are grown in the Salamander and Soldiers Point waters, then gathered and moved to quieter waters to mature and grow fat. A plate of local oysters in a shoreline restaurant is a treat well worth the short trip from Newcastle. And at **Moffat's Oyster Barn,** Swan Bay (tel. 049/97-5433), you not only learn how oysters are raised but also get to eat them, seven days a week, for lunch.

CESSNOCK

The center of the Lower Hunter region is Maitland, a rural trading township dating from the 1830s. But the most important town is Cessnock, a place unique among urban centers the world over. Cessnock is the only city on the globe that lives simultaneously by coal mining and wine growing, two activities usually regarded as mutually exclusive. This was the region of the mining empire run by the legendary John Brown, with the largest shaft mine in the southern hemisphere, which set world records for coal production.

But just outside the town lies **Pokolbin,** where the first commercially successful vineyards of the young colony were established by the pioneer vignerons from 1830 onward. Today the area embraces more than 30 wineries, thriving literally next door to the "black diamonds" that feed coal furnaces. The contrast makes visitors shake their heads in disbelief, although the locals take it for granted.

DUNGOG

For yet another contrast there is Dungog, the gateway to the magnificent **Barrington Tops National Park.** This is an unspoiled bushland reserve, a land of rugged timbered ridges, deep-green rain forests, and rushing streams. The animals are quite tame—you can actually feed the wild rosella parrots, possums, scrub turkeys, and kangaroos. If you'd like to linger for a day, there's the **Barrington Guest House,** Nature Reserve no. 81 (tel. 049/95-3212), a beautiful homestead-style lodge built in 1930, serving rustic meals cooked on wood-burning stoves. Guests are picked up at Dungog station, and pay around $125 per person at the special midweek rate.

THE WINERIES

The Hunter Valley stretches northwest of Newcastle and is divided into the Lower and Upper Hunter. It doesn't really matter which one you visit as both abound in wineries, in restaurants serving excellent food (and wine, of course), and in Tourist Information Centres supplying invaluable guidance.

The wineries vary greatly in size and reputation, but most of them have tasting rooms, several give conducted tours of their premises, and all want you to stock up on as many bottles of their product as possible. The examples below will give you a general idea.

Note: The wines are cheaper when bought in lots of a dozen, but rough prices for single bottles are as follow: $10 for cabernet shiraz, $11 for sauvignon, $12 for chardonnay, $7 to $18 for port, and $5 to $10 for rieslings.

Hunter Valley Wine Society, Wollombi Rd., Cessnock (tel. 049/90-6699), is a coordinated enterprise that lets you taste (and buy) the products of 36 Hunter wineries, and also serves a charcoal-grilled lunch seven days a week. It's a good on-the-spot comparison opportunity—providing your palate holds out.

McWilliams, Mount Pleasant, Pokolbin (tel. 049/98-7505), offers guided tours Monday through Friday four times daily, and also cellar-door sales of "limited release" wines, which really *are* limited.

Wyndham Estate, Branxton (tel. 049/38-1135), is reputedly the oldest winery on the continent. Beautifully situated on the banks of the Hunter River at Dalwood, via Branxton, five miles off the New England Highway, it has four restaurants on the grounds, cellar-door sales, and tastings seven days a week till 5pm.

Hungerford Hill Wine Village, Broke Rd., Pokolbin (tel. 049/ 98-7666), in the proclaimed "Heart of the Hunter Valley," has a motor inn, farmers' market, swimming pool, restaurant, and gift store, as well as wine-tasting and sales rooms. Open seven days till 5pm.

Marsh Estate, Deasys Rd., Pokolbin (tel. 049/98-7587), is a family property known for growing only classic varieties: traminer, hermitage, pinot noir, chardonnay, and cabernet sauvignon. Small, friendly, and more personalized than most wineries, with an exceptionally comfortable tasting room, it's open all week: till 4pm Monday through Friday, till 5pm on Saturday and Sunday.

In the Upper Hunter region, on the banks of the Hunter River, lies **Arrowfield,** Hwy. 213, Jerrys Plain (tel. 065/76-4041). Huge, modern, but scenic, this winery has barbecue facilities and is open for tasting and single-bottle sales seven days a week (on Sunday from noon).

Rosemount Estate, Denman (tel. 065/47-2467), the largest winery in the area, has an international reputation for high-quality chardonnay, sauvignon blanc, and semillons. Tastings and sales seven days a week.

Horderns, Yarraman Rd., Wybong (tel. 065/47-8127), is small, with limited output, but both historic and charming. Some of the buildings were constructed with stone taken from the ruins of nearby Bengala prison. The winery is famous for its wood-matured semillon whites. Open all week till 5pm (on Sunday till 4pm).

Wine Tours

For an inexpensive and nicely varied tour, pick the Hunter Valley Winetaster, operated by **AAT King's** (tel. 02/252-2788). The tour coaches leave Circular Quay at 8:45am on Thursday, Saturday, and Sunday, returning at 7:30pm. You visit the Hungerford Hill estate for a tasting and a steak lunch, and get a browse through the Farmers Market and a scenic return journey. Adults pay $59; children, $39.50.

If you prefer touring with a touch of style, you can travel with the exclusive day tours run by **Christopher Buring** (tel. 02/875-4720), a celebrated wine maker and consultant. He'll pick you up at your Sydney hotel at 8am and deliver you back around 6pm. En route you'll learn more about the Australian wines in general and Hunter Valley in particular than you'll need to impress any number of grape experts back home. The trip includes a gourmet lunch in the valley. Call for reservations and prices.

4. Illawarra

The region stretching inland from the Pacific shore about 50 miles south of Sydney takes its name from Lake Illawarra, but its oceanfront is known as the "Leisure Coast." It's not a strictly accurate label because the entry points, **Wollongong** and **Port Kembla**, are highly industrialized and far from leisurely. Port Kembla, in fact, boasts the largest steel mill in Australia. Wollongong, however, is undergoing an interesting transformation, adding strings of tourist attractions to its industrial backbone. The central part of the main street was rebuilt as a splendid pedestrian plaza with soaring steel arches, hanging gardens, and glittering water displays. The Wollongong North Beach Hotel is a three-star, international-style establishment.

At Helensburgh, just before you reach Wollongong, lies the **Symbio Koala Garden,** on Lawrence Hargrave Drive. Nestling in a large bushland setting, this nature park houses dozens of koalas as well as other grazing, nibbling, and flying Oz critters. There is a special nocturnal house for observing the night denizens. The garden is open daily from 9:30am till dusk.

Located five miles west of Wollongong is the **Mount Kembla Historic Village.** Not colonial this time, but early industrial, this is a preserved mining community from the turn of the century. It has a group of arts and crafts workshops, including a working smithy, and a monument to a pit disaster that occurred in 1902.

Along the South Coast the scene becomes a true leisureland, with small villages facing the blue ocean where main pastimes consist of swimming, waterskiing, hang-gliding, bushwalking, and horseback riding. At Kiama the top attraction is a natural phenomenon known as the **Blowhole.** This is a tunnel running through solid rock inland from the oceanfront. As heavy seas crash into the tunnel entrance, they force huge sprays of water up the tunnel opening at the other end—sending geysers into the air as high as 80 feet. The Blowhole was first discovered in 1797, but nobody has yet explained how and why the water hollowed out this narrow pipe through the stone.

Wilton has quite another kind of attraction in the **Macarthur Winery,** Mount Keira Rd. (tel. 046/30-9269). A large estate winery, this place has country music and bush dancing on Saturday nights, and serves sumptuous lunches on Sunday. Wine tastings daily from 10am to 6pm.

Southwest of Wollongong, on the Hume Highway, lies **Berrima,** the oldest village of its type in Australia. Founded in 1829 by the colony's surveyor general, the place still has 40 historic buildings constructed from local sandstone during the convict days. And you can still down a middy at the **Surveyor-General's Inn,** the oldest continuously licensed pub on the continent. It was a brutal place in those early days—the ancient Berrima Gaol was built by chained convicts driven by the lash. Laggards were habitually chained up in cells measuring three by six feet, heated to the temperature of bake ovens by the sun. There was a solemn Royal Commission instituted to look into these cruelties, but the honorable commissioners of the time preferred to disregard all such claims made by the convicts.

Today Berrima is a placid little country hamlet, proud of its antique Court House, which now houses a video display of early Berrima, and Australia's first trial by jury, which was held there (as distinct from the usual administrative courts-martial, which were held everywhere). You can wander into the quaint general store, with signs for century-old newspapers costing one penny, faded calendars dated 1880, and yellowing posters advertising Beechams Pills (for your liver) and Parsons Infant Powder (for another place).

Joadja, just off the Hume Highway on Wombeyan Caves Road, is a ghost town with a resident—and quite benevolent—ghost. The whole town actually belongs to an American woman, Pat Lee, who bought it for a song when she migrated here from her native Georgia more than 30 years ago. The ghost's name is Robert McGregor and he allegedly wears hobnailed boots you can hear at night. Joadja is open for visitors till 4pm on weekends only, but it's best to call ahead and make sure (tel. 048/71-2888). A row of miners' cottages, the old schoolhouse, and some ancient kilns are still standing. And after dark there's Mr. McGregor . . .

GETTING THERE

Wollongong is only an hour by road from Sydney, but if at all possible, do the trip by train. The track follows one of the most scenic routes on the continent, skirting the edge of the Royal National Park, then winding along the Escarpment, where the mountains seem to push into the sea with only the narrow track in between. The New South Wales Railway operates the **South Coast Spectacular,** the first and third Tuesday of every month. Trains leave Sydney Station at 8am and return at 4:15pm. At Wollongong you transfer to coaches and ride to Mount Kembla, then on to the Blowhole at Kiama. The tour costs $35 for adults, $31 for children.

5. The Holiday Coast

The stretch of New South Wales coastline that runs from Port Macquarie, north of Newcastle, to Tweed Heads on the Queensland border has been voted the most pleasant part of Australia to live in. It has a live-cheap climate, towns large enough to provide entertainment but not so big as to create urban problems, endless beaches, and a subtropical background to add color. It's a region where the taxis come fitted with surfboard racks, where protesters actually *won* their fight to save the rain forests, and where the fish bite so eagerly that the locals say you have to hide behind a rock in order to bait your hook.

It's so easygoing that the influx of practitioners of "alternative life-styles" didn't raise an eyebrow among the natives. They simply incorporated the newcomers as part of the scenery—beards, headbands, hip-hugging babies, hash pipes, reed flutes, and all.

TIMBERTOWN

Some 15 miles inland from Port Macquarie, on the Oxley Highway near Wauchope, stands Timbertown. This is an enthralling re-creation of a 19th-century logging village, complete to the trailing skirts and pinned hats worn by the female inhabitants. The houses are made of sawn slab and shingle roofs, creaking bullock teams haul giant logs to the working sawmill, and you can ride a puffing open-car steam train over a spectacular trestle bridge.

The village store sells licorice by the yard and the blacksmith hammers out horseshoes and iron tires for wagon wheels, exactly as his forebears did a century ago. The woodturner makes carved chairlegs from rosewood, the steam mill operates a dragsaw, and open wagons, drawn by mighty Clydesdales, rumble over bush tracks. Timbertown is open for visitors seven days a week from 10am to 5pm.

COFFS HARBOUR

An unusual combination of resort and deep-water port, Coffs Harbour started out as a harbor for the timber trade, then gradually drew in more and more tourists until it achieved its present dual existence. The big ocean freighters still dock almost in the town center, while the other end of the foreshore belongs to the swimmers. On Orlando Street is a famous **Porpoise Pool,** where the porpoises are so tame they stick their heads out to be patted and respond with friendly puffs from their blowholes. Open daily from 10:30am to 5pm, with porpoise and trained-seal performances.

At Micalo Island, east of Yamba, lies an attraction you'll find hard to believe—a **prawn stud farm.** This is no joke, but a serious and gratifyingly lucrative business. The "farm" consists of huge saltwater ponds where millions of succulent prawns are bred from specially selected stud prawns. The offspring are exported to Sydney and Tokyo restaurants, but the studs stay on to breed further exports. You can pick out those prawny Casanovas by their sheer size (like small lobsters) and aquatic arrogance.

And just north of Coffs Harbour there is another unlikely show —**Merino Mac's Agradrome,** on Pacific Highway (tel. 066/49-4405). This is a sheep show to beat all others, where the sheep act both as passive objects—being shorn, displayed, and herded by sheep dogs—and as star performers. Sheep are supposedly not stage material, but at least two of these performing rams have obvious theatrical personalities. You also learn a lot about Australia's wool in-dustry while admiring those splendid merinos romping around the stage. An indoor, all-weather attraction, open seven days in shearing season.

NIMBIN AND BYRON BAY

In the area around Nimbin and Byron Bay you become aware of the influence of the so-called counterculture. Only here it doesn't run counter to anything—it's just part of the scene. The "straight" farmers, fishermen, and tourists mingle easily with saffron-robed Hare Krishnas, long-bearded and maned fiddlers, and couples with babies, all wearing homespun sacking, or what looks like it.

Seaside pubs stand next to shops painted with transcendental designs, community centers blaze in atmospheric murals, and half the cafés advertise vegetarian or Hunza fare. At the aptly named **Friendly Bar** in Byron Bay there are usually bearded musicians strumming, fiddling, and fluting bush ballads, rebel songs, and blues. The town is bursting with artisans and craftspeople in a doz-en different branches, and some of their top-quality work in pottery, leatherware, sculpture, glassware, weaving, and painting is dis-played at the **Cape Byron Gallery.**

Market days here are an old-fashioned delight. You can get some real bargains (and equal amounts of junk) at the crafts stalls, especially in the jewelry line, although some of the homemade clothing defies description. But you'll find it hard to resist the local fruit on display, representing the riches of the subtropics: avocados, mangoes, lychees, sugar bananas, pawpaws, macadamia and pecan nuts, nectarines, and the most luscious peaches you've ever tasted.

At Casino, a few miles inland, there is a **Platypus Pool** below the bridge on Summerland Way, where you can watch that incredi-ble little beast in its natural surroundings. The platypus has a duckbill but is covered in fur, lays eggs but then suckles its young, and spends all its time in the water but is an air-breathing mammal. When the early explorers brought back descriptions of this critter, the Royal Zoological Society flatly refused to believe its existence.

TWEED HEADS

The northern tip of the Holiday Coast is Tweed Heads, which straddles the Queensland border (the borderline runs right down the main road, Boundary Street). One side is Tweed Heads, New South Wales; the other is Coolangatta, Queensland. Quite apart from the fact that in summer there is a one-hour time difference be-tween the two places, the borderline has other than academic distinction. In fact, the distinction is something from which Tweed Heads makes an annual bundle.

The Tweed Heads bonanza stems from the legal technicality that Queensland does not permit poker machines, whereas New South Wales does. On the N.S.W. side there's a cluster of luxur-ious clubs whose revenues depend on the one-armed bandits. They happily subsidize meals, transportation, drink, and lavish en-tertainment to entice tourists over from Queensland to feed those insatiable slots. Whole caravans of "pokey buses" come all the way from Brisbane and points in between, loaded with visitors who make straight for the clubs. Ostensibly these institutions are "private"—that is, for the use of members only. But in practice they admit "bona fide" visitors. Either you or any Queenslander simply has to show some proof of identity (driver's license or passport) to the doorman and the gates fly open. You're welcome to partake of some of the best—and cheapest—victuals on the coast, and watch first-class floor shows at no extra cost. And nobody forces anybody to gamble.

The **Twin Towns Services Club** (tel. 075/36-2277; for show reservations, 075/36-1977) puts on a galaxy of Australian and overseas stars every afternoon and evening. The lineup changes, but the plush cocktail bar, smörgåsbord bistro, sports room, and air-conditioned lounges are permanent fixtures. Dinner will cost you from $5 up.

Terranora Lakes Country Club (tel. 075/90-9223) features a show band plus selected solo performers. In the bistro dining room, roast beef, pork, or chicken go for very little.

Tweed Heads Bowls Club (tel. 075/36-3800) does indeed offer bowling, but also a revue show, famous stage and television comedians, a French restaurant, and six bars, plus 300 slot machines. There's a $2 cover charge, and bistro meals hover around the $5.50 mark.

Seagulls Rugby League Club (tel. 075/36-3433) has the Stardust Room, the most modern extensive auditorium on the national club scene, with elbow room for 2,000 people to enjoy the spectacular stage presentations. There is also a range of luxury bars and a row of dining spots, as well as gymnasiums and play and training fields for those actually practicing rugby.

In fairness it must be stated that Tweed Heads offers considerably more than a dazzling club scene. This little fishing village, which has grown into a sprawling resort, still retains its local fishing fleet and processing plant, but has added a huge shopping mall and residential complex. Most of the funds for these developments came from the $73 million spent annually by Queenslanders crossing the border for you-know-what.

The **Minjungbal Aboriginal Museum,** Kirkwood Rd., South Tweed Heads (tel. 075/54-2275), has displays on Arnhem Land and Central Australian Aborigines. Open Tuesday through Friday from 10am to 3pm.

Natureland Zoo, Binya Ave., has one of the largest private animal collections in Australia, including lions. Open daily from 9am to 4pm. Admission $4.

There are large numbers of hotels and motels for overnight stays. One of them is the modernistic **Nicabela's Beach Resort,** corner of Coast Rd. and Pandanus Parade, Tweed Heads, N.S.W. 2488 (tel. 066/761-555), which has a pool and spa and 27 units with ocean views. The daily rate is around $36 per person.

GETTING THERE

You can reach the Holiday Coast by direct rail connection from Sydney, and also by direct coach service daily from Sydney to Port

Macquarie. If you're driving, head for Newcastle first, then take the Pacific Highway (National Rte. 1) all the way.

---

6. New England

Forget all about the New England *you* know. This region, inland from the Holiday Coast, looks nothing like it. It's lushly green countryside, dotted with large, prosperous sheep and cattle holdings, waving with silver birches, elms, oaks, and willows, and moistened by tumbling waterfalls. It does, however, share a certain academic flavor, stemming from an almost British-style university town.

The entrance, so to speak, is the Oxley Highway running from Port Macquarie over the Great Divide through the grandiose **Apsley Gorge National Park.** This is highland country with awe-inspiring scenery, where the roaring waters of Apsley Falls drown out conversation.

At **Uralla** you come into "Thunderbolt Country," so called after the legendary Captain Thunderbolt, one of the most famous of Australia's bushrangers. Thunderbolt, whose real name was Frederick Ward, plundered travelers on the roads between Newcastle and the Queensland border for six years from 1864 onward. He was not an ordinary thief and his courtesy toward the mail-coach passengers he held up became legendary. When one of his victims complained of nervousness and wanted to smoke, Thunderbolt not only gave him a cigar but lit it for him.

In May 1870 Thunderbolt was surprised during a robbery by two mounted troopers. During a furious gun battle, the polite bushranger received a bullet through the heart. He lies buried in Uralla Cemetery, and the locals regularly place flowers on his grave. In 1970 they even held a Thunderbolt Centenary Celebration at which he was honored by a plaque in the Uralla Shire Council Chambers.

ARMIDALE

Some 352 miles north of Sydney on the New England Highway, Armidale is the heart of the region, seat of the **University of New England** and a miniature Down Under version of Oxford. Of the town's 18,000 inhabitants, over 2,000 are students and staff of the university. True, inside the campus park deer mingle with kangaroos in a most un-Oxonian fashion, but the collegians make up for it by having officials called yeoman bedells and talking in terms of "Town and Gown," just like in the Old Country. And the town is sprinkled with cathedrals with dreaming spires and excellent and numerous pubs, and enjoys the crispest, most multicolored autumn in the state. For visitors interested in educational facilities, there is also Australia's first country teachers' college.

The college houses a remarkable art collection, including a Rembrandt etching, given to the institution by a shipping tycoon who wound up being worth about $50 because he spent all his fortune on paintings that he gave away to galleries.

The **Armidale Folk Museum,** at the corner of Rusden and Faulkner streets (tel. 067/72-8666), has interesting displays of Victoriana, including room settings, kitchens, lighting fixtures, and 19th-century transport vehicles. Open daily from 1 to 4pm; free.

The **New England Regional Art Museum,** Kentucky St. (tel. 067/72-5255), housed in an impressive building set in beautiful grounds, features a large collection of Australian art spanning more than a century. Open seven days till 5pm.

Other museums in Armidale specialize in antiquities, zoology, and one dealing in rural life and industry.

On the New England Highway going toward the airport lies the **Berry Patch,** which is actually the largest hydroponic berry farm in Australia. Try the pies and strudels filled with berries every day from 8:30am to 6pm.

For accommodations, try the **Cattleman's Motor Inn,** 31 Marsh St., Armidale, N.S.W. 2350 (tel. 067/72-7788), which has air conditioning, a spa, pool, sauna, and video movies, and no holiday surcharges. Rooms begin around $50.

You can reach Armidale from Sydney by express train every Monday, Wednesday, and Friday. The trip takes eight hours.

INVERELL

About an hour's drive northwest of Armidale, Inverell has the **Pioneer Village,** one of the best of its kind in Australia. The historic buildings were transported here, intact, from their original sites, which were scattered all over the place. Now they form a compact and authentic outdoor museum, spanning the period from roughly 1840 to 1930. There's a tiny church, an equally tiny school (complete with battered and carved-up desks). The village store still has some of its archaic merchandise on the shelves. Paddy's Pub, with a bark roof, was once a stopover for the Cobb & Co. stagecoaches regularly held up by Captain Thunderbolt. There's *The Times* printing office with its old flatbed presses, and the Aberfoyle Telephone Exchange, about the size of a dog kennel, and a couple of dozen other buildings and homesteads. Call 067/22-1725 for information.

At the Serpentine River on the New England National Park Road, about 50 miles from Armidale, is the **L. P. Dutton Trout Hatchery.** This is a series of huge tanks containing the region's famous trout varieties in various stages, from fingerlings a couple of inches long to sleek, fat, and hefty beauties. The hatchery is open every day from 9am to 4pm, and conducted tours of the breeding ponds take place every half hour. Admission free.

TENTERFIELD

Tenterfield, north of Armidale on the New England Highway, was founded by Sir Stuart Donaldson, who later became premier of New South Wales and the last man in Australia to fight a duel. This happened in 1851 and had an unbloody conclusion—one of the pistol balls passed through Donaldson's hat, so the seconds wisely called it a draw.

One of the town's attractions is the **Hillview Doll Museum,** Palham St. (tel. 067/36-1491), displaying over 1,000 dolls from all parts of the world, including the locally made "Appleheads." Open daily from 9am to 5pm. Admission: $2.

About 25 miles north of Tenterfield stretches **Bald Rock National Park,** a vast bushland reserve, full of flora and wildlife, which harbors one of the state's most spectacular—and least known— natural wonders. Bald Rock, the focal point of the landscape, is the largest exposed granite monolith in Australia and (after Ayers Rock) the second-biggest rock in the world. It's an awesome sight—sheer gray granite rising 170 feet above the surrounding bushland. You can climb up a marked walking track—it's hard going at first, but easier in the later stages. From the peak the view is breathtaking— you can see all the way across the Queensland border and to the ocean.

---

7. Lightning Ridge

A real Australian "outback" town, sunbaked and flat, but with a tourist lure few others possess—you just *might* leave it richer than you came—Lightning Ridge, 480 miles northwest of Sydney, is the only place in the world where the most beautiful and valuable type of opal is found, the so-called "black" opal which actually blazes in a rainbow of colors, and which some connoisseurs consider the finest gem on earth. The first black opal was discovered here in 1907, but production peaked in 1914 and has been declining ever since—hence the rising value of the stones. The local population of around 1,500 sift through the old mullock, the residue excavated by the pioneer miners, by means of a "puddler," a type of metal sieve. "Puddlers" are for rent and visitors are invited to fossick on the heaps or dig down in any "unoccupied" holes. Do they find anything? Many don't, but some gather enough rough opal pebbles (called "nobbies") to pay for their vacation. A few—a very few— strike it rich, such as the schoolboy who picked up a nobby worth $3,000.

But even if you leave with no souvenir other than the dirt under your nails, you'll be richer for the experience. For this is the frontier Australia so many of us come seeking. At least half of the residents here came to find opals and stayed on because they liked the vibes. The place is easygoing friendliness personified. It's taut, hot (broiling for five months of the year) countryside where you can sip an ice-cold Fosters in a grand old pub called Diggers Rest beside men called Crank Joe, Shameless, and Spider Brown. For your creature comforts there are several motels, a spa pool, and a caravan park with on-site vans for overnighting. You can browse through two museums with gemstones on display, and the quietly amiable townsfolk are only too willing to talk prospecting lore with anyone who'll listen. It's a long, long way to the rat race.

The nearest town of any size to Lightning Ridge is **Walgett,** with all of 2,700 people. It has an airfield, the railroad terminal for the trains from Sydney, and several cabs that will take you the 46 miles to the Ridge. **Air N.S.W.** (tel. 02/268-1262) runs three flights a week from Sydney to Walgett. For organized tours to Lightning Ridge, contact the **Travel Centre of N.S.W.,** at the corner of Pitt and Spring streets, Sydney (tel. 02/231-4444).

Lightning Ridge lies at the center of what is known as the **North West Country,** a very large and extremely varied region. It changes from scenic mountain ranges in the east to vast flat plains in the west, from rich agricultural land to semi-desert. The North West includes the little town of Bourke, and "back o' Bourke" in Oz phraseology is where the Outback starts.

A unique feature of the country is the artesian basin that provides a constant flow of *heated* subterranean water, in contrast to normal artesian bores that run icy cold. This basin feeds the spa baths in the country towns (including Lightning Ridge), and you can see the thick jet of hot water gushing out of the **Dunumbral Bore,** one of the attractions of the North West.

At **Moree** stands one of Australia's four OTC Satellite Earth Stations, operated by the Overseas Telecommunications Commission, which provide telephone, telegraph, telex, and TV service between Australia and the rest of the world. Moree also boasts the most luxurious of the artesian spa baths, with two Fiberglass hot pools and every modern spa facility.

The largest town of the region is **Tamworth,** on the Peel River at the junction of the New England and Oxley highways. Tamworth, with a population of 35,000, was actually the first city in the southern hemisphere to have its streets lit by electricity (1888). Today its fame is derived from being the "Country Music Capital" with an annual country music festival held every January. Tamworth also has the **Gallery of Stars Wax Museum,** a must for country music fans from everywhere.

---

8. The Outback

The term "outback" is more of a mental image than a geographical definition. It means the bush, the remote countryside, the land "beyond the black stump," and a different area in every state. In New South Wales it refers to the extreme western portion up to the border of South Australia. It's not quite the "great Australian loneliness," but close enough to give you the flavor.

It's a dramatic landscape of brown and green, furrowed with dry riverbeds, studded with gnarled ghost gums—endless plains extending to the far horizon, with an immeasurable pale blue sky hanging above, blurred with heat mirages that trick your eyes into believing that a giant body of water lies only a few miles off. There are sprinklings of isolated homesteads, white-walled with rust-brown corrugated iron roofs, a windmill pumping artesian water on the side. Where the Darling and Murray rivers run, their banks burst into dark-green tangles, and here and there the rocks are engraved with ancient Aboriginal markings, telling of hunts and ceremonies staged long before the white man came. You see occasional groups of kangaroos and strutting emus, and up in the crystal-clear sky the wedge-tailed eagles float on hot air currents. The suburbs of Sydney seem as distant as Mars.

BROKEN HILL

Yet it is here that you'll find the place that transformed Australia from a pastoral nation to the industrial hub of the South Pacific. This is Broken Hill, the town sitting among an immense chain of hills that hold the most valuable lead, zinc, and silver deposits in the world. The 130 million tons of ore that were mined here acted as the propellant that shot the continent from the agricultural to the factory age. The first thing you notice in Broken Hill is the huge machinery atop the pits, producing the annual 5.5 million tons that keep Australia's smelters roaring.

Broken Hill was made by the mining industry, and the mining industry made modern Australia. You can visit some of the mines in operation and get a glimpse of what the industry is all about. **Delprat's Mine** (tel. 080/88-1604) takes you on underground tours 90 feet below the surface and shows you the initial stages of ore extraction. Tours start at 10:30am Monday through Friday and at 2pm on Saturday. Cameras are permitted. **North Mine** (tel. 080/97-325) has a surface tour starting at 2pm Monday through Friday; no cameras allowed.

Beyond the mines, Broken Hill is quaint in some parts, ultramodern in others, fascinating everywhere, and completely *different* from anything you might have expected. It has wonderful old country pubs, a huge civic-center complex staging top theatrical performances and symphony concerts, Victorian buildings that look like birthday cakes baked from bricks, stone cottages with wide verandas, and an astonishing number of art galleries and museums.

These galleries owe their existence to the "Brushmen of the Bush," a world-famous group of artists like Jack Absalom, Pro Hart, Eric Minchin, and Hugh Schulz, who epitomize Australian contemporary painting. Their work, and that of their less renowned contemporaries, can be seen in more than a dozen galleries. To mention a few, the **Ant Hill Gallery** (tel. 080/2441) features the cream of the local artists as well as local crafts like pottery and china (open daily till 5pm); the **Pro Hart Gallery** (tel. 080/2441) houses the work of the artist and is one of the largest private collections in Australia (open daily till 5pm); the **Absalom Gallery** (tel. 080/5881) has works by Jack Absalom, plus a large collection of opals (open daily till 5pm); and the **J. C. Art Gallery** (tel. 080/3415) displays paintings by a range of local artists as well as craft works (open weekdays, except Wednesday).

The **Gladstone Mining Museum,** at the corner of South and Morish streets, South Broken Hill (tel. 080/6277), is a replica of a working mine built into an old hotel, showing past and current mining procedures by means of life-size models. Open daily from 2 to 5pm. The **Daydream Mine,** on the other hand, is not a replica but the real thing, circa 1880. Visitors can walk down the underlays to the workings. For open hours, call 080/2441.

Broken Hill has a great many other attractions, unrelated to mining. There is a **Muslim mosque** (tel. 080/6060) dating back to the earliest days of the town. It was built as a place of worship by the Afghan camel drivers on the site of the former camel camp. Camels handled most of the land transport in the region before the advent of railroads and automobiles. Later the camels ran wild, and proliferated, in the saltbush deserts, the Afghans scattered to other towns, and the mosque lay abandoned until it was restored by the local historical society. Open for visits every Sunday afternoon from 2 to 3pm.

A few miles out of town, beside the Barrier Highway, lies the base of the **Royal Flying Doctor Service.** Made famous (and fictionalized) by films and TV, this remarkable organization maintains radio contact with over 400 outposts, providing medical assistance by way of long-range diagnosis and advice on treatment, dispatching doctors and removing patients by air. For thousands of bush dwellers this is the sole medical help available. The annals of the Flying Doctor Service are full of landings and takeoffs under the most appalling conditions imaginable, the little mercy planes staggering in and out of grazing paddocks and half-cleared scrubland, undeterred by floods, tropical thunderstorms, or bushfires. Inspections of the base are conducted at 10am and 4pm Monday through Friday and at 10am on Saturday. All reservations must be made at **Silver City Travel,** 35 Sulphide St. (tel. 080/2564).

Almost equally famous is the **School of the Air,** headquartered at Broken Hill. This unique school conducts lessons via two-way radio for the children of isolated homesteads scattered over hundreds of square miles of bush. At the receiving end the radio sets are often powered by foot pedals, but the educational standards are equal to, if not better than, those of normal classrooms. You can visit the facilities during school terms at 8:40am Monday through Friday. Arrangements must be made in advance at the **Tourist Information Centre,** corner of Blende and Bromide streets, Broken Hill (tel. 080/6077).

Broken Hill has about 20 tourist hotels, motels, and guesthouses, plus a couple of caravan parks. One of the most modern is the **Overlander Motor Inn,** 142 Iodide St., Broken Hill (tel. 080/88-2566). Small and centrally located, the Overlander provides a sauna and spa, laundry, and free in-house movies. Also a courtesy car to and from the airport and bus depot. Rates begin around $45 per person.

Air New South Wales has flights from Sydney to Broken Hill every Monday, Wednesday, Friday, and Sunday. By rail it's a comfortable but long 18-hour trip from Sydney, on air-conditioned sleeping cars departing three times a week.

SILVERTON

Some 18 miles northwest of Broken Hill lies Silverton, a semighost town that has become a kind of outback Hollywood. Originally Silverton was a rip-roaring mining community of about 3,000 people, digging for valuable ore in the 1870s. But the ore petered out and the people drifted away, leaving the place nearly deserted.

Then, about a century later, movie producers discovered some magic in the quality of the light at Silverton, as well as the cinematic charisma of its antique buildings. So the town began its second career as a backdrop for any script requiring a romantically dramatic bush setting. A score of films, such as *A Town Like Alice, Mad Max, Hostage,* and *Wake in Fright* were shot here, as well as TV shorts and countless commercials. The native population stays at around 100, but film crews, actors, tourists, and visitors from Broken Hill swell it to several times that number.

Sooner or later they all drift into the wondrous old **Silverton Hotel,** whose staff has grown somewhat blasé about serving beers to screen deities. They're more concerned about Misty the movie horse, who trots up to the bar to get a hot scone with jam, followed by tea (Misty despises beer).

The **Silverton Gaol,** the restored old hoosegow of the town, is one of the grizzled structures camera crews love for picturesque backgrounds. Instead of imprisoned drunks it now houses a collection of relics from the town's past.

Camels no longer transport much in the region, except a great many tourists. For a ride around the area on a swaying hump, contact **Camel Treks** (tel. 080/91-1682).

MENINDEE

For a complete change of environment you only have to go to Menindee, about an hour's drive southeast of Broken Hill. This is a gigantic lake region with a water area eight times that of Sydney Harbour. There you can fish from the shore, ride in speedboats, or swim and generally wallow in this tranquil green oasis that makes it hard to recall the stark dryness you've just left. But there is a reminder. In the township of Menindee is the camping ground of the tragic explorers Burke and Wills. Here they rested and fished and swam before setting out on their last journey into the deserts in the north, where both perished.

AND AFTER
SYDNEY . . .

Sydney is not Australia, just as New York isn't America. It is, however, the transportation hub of the country, the logical launching pad from which to take off in all directions. This chapter will give you an idea of the tremendous variety and amazing contrasts the rest of Australia has to offer . . . a very large rest. For Australia is a continent as well as a country (the only one on earth that is both) measuring nearly three million square miles, extending from cool Tasmania in the south to broiling tropical Arnhem Land in the far north. Most of the places mentioned here are a long way off (it's 885 miles from Sydney to Adelaide, 2,717 miles to Perth), so for the sake of convenience, I'll start with those closer at hand.

1. Canberra

Capital of the commonwealth and seat of the federal government, Canberra—like Washington, D.C.—is an "artificial" city created for the purpose of housing bureaucrats in conditions of maximum comfort. Unlike other such creations, Canberra turned out a complete success. The capital was placed almost exactly midway between Sydney and Melbourne to stop the perpetual squabbling of the two rivals for national supremacy.

Like the Sydney Opera House, the design of the "model capital" was the result of an international competition, won by a Chicago landscape architect named Walter Burley Griffin. The capital didn't really go into action until 1927, when Parliament moved there from Melbourne. Canberra then boasted about 7,000 inhabitants. Today the figure is a quarter of a million, but the original design was so far-sighted that Canberra suffers from none of the urban woes that afflict other fast-growing centers. It has no slums, no air pollution, no traffic jams, and all the parking facilities others only dream about. In fact, Canberra motorists are so pampered that they become virtually unfit for driving anywhere else. Instead of shopping streets, Canberra has malls and plazas. Instead of a river, the city has a huge artificial lake right in the center, brimming with pure water and stocked with trout.

Focal point of interest is **Parliament House,** which opened in 1988 as part of Australia's bicentennial celebrations. This is the executive heart of the commonwealth, created at a cost of $349 million to replace the old "temporary" structure from which the country had been governed for more than 60 years. Set on Capital Hill, the symbolic center of Canberra, the white, majestically colonnaded edifice was designed to blend with rather than dominate its surroundings. The interior is palatial, but again in a subdued style that welcomes visitors without dwarfing them. The main public area, white-pillared and marble-floored, contains a restaurant, an exhibition space, a theater, and an open veranda offering panoramic vistas of the city.

The actual engines of government, so to speak, are housed in two halls: the **House of Representatives** and the **Senate Chamber.** Tours take place when only one chamber is in session—then the other one allows visitors. The only day of the year Parliament closes is Christmas Day.

Canberra's top tourist attraction, however, is the **Australian War Memorial,** at the corner of Limestone and Fairbairn avenues. This is an absolutely splendid edifice in honor and memory of the 100,000 men and women who died for the commonwealth in two world wars. It is filled with vast and superbly detailed dioramas of combat and the mechanical relics of it. You see the strutted biplanes, sleek Spitfires, and huge bombers flown by Aussie airmen in both wars; the guns, tanks, and landing barges they manned; the colossal German Amiens gun of World War I and the toylike Japanese midget submarine that attacked Sydney Harbour in World War II. The memorial is open to visitors every day from 9am to 4:45pm. Admission is free.

Canberra is definitely a city of "sights," so many that I can only give a brief summation. There is the **Australian National University,** covering an area of 320 beautifully landscaped acres and an

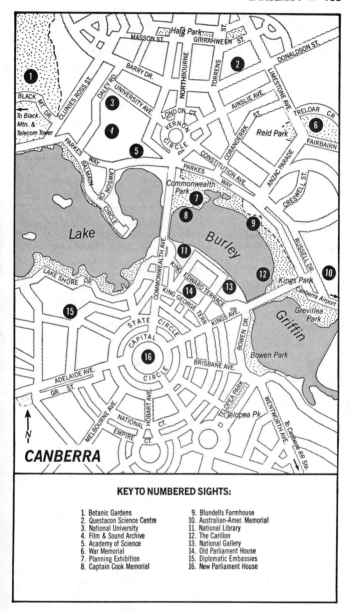

KEY TO NUMBERED SIGHTS:

1. Botanic Gardens
2. Questacon Science Centre
3. National University
4. Film & Sound Archive
5. Academy of Science
6. War Memorial
7. Planning Exhibition
8. Captain Cook Memorial
9. Blundells Farmhouse
10. Australian-Amer. Memorial
11. National Library
12. The Carillon
13. National Gallery
14. Old Parliament House
15. Diplomatic Embassies
16. New Parliament House

enrollment of more than 6,000 students. The **Australian National Gallery,** on the shores of Lake Burley Griffin, houses permanent exhibitions of some of the world's greatest artists, including America's Jackson Pollock and France's Claude Monet, plus a wide range of Australians. The **embassies** of over 50 countries stand in the suburbs of Red Hill, Forrest, and Yarralumla. Their architectural styles range from tasteful to terrible. You might be glad to know that the U.S. embassy, housed in a Virginia mansion, is one of the most charming.

The **Royal Australian Mint** is where they make the filthy lucre. You can watch the operation of the production floor through plate-glass windows. They don't hand out free samples, but the machines can be seen in action Monday through Friday from 9am to 4pm. The **National Library** on Parkes Place is the newest and handsomest of Canberra's public buildings. It houses two million books (including several by yours truly), 300,000 maps, 440,000 sound recordings, and 65,000 films, several dozen of which date back to the very earliest days of cinematography in the southern hemisphere. It's open from 9am to 10pm Monday through Thursday and 9am to 4:45pm Friday through Sunday. The **Canberra Carillon,** one of the largest musical instruments in the world, is a tall white pillar containing 53 bells—the biggest weighs six tons; the smallest, only 15 pounds. It is played from an organlike keyboard in regular Sunday and Wednesday recitals.

GETTING THERE

Canberra lies within a 934-square-mile area known as the **Australian Capital territory** (ACT), roughly equivalent to the D.C. that surrounds Washington. The city is 150 miles southwest of Sydney, and is very accessible. By train the journey costs $20.50. The bus trip (Pioneer or Greyhound) takes 4¼ hours and costs $18. By air (Australian Airlines or Ansett) it's a 30-minute hop costing $107.

---

2. Melbourne

The capital of Victoria, Melbourne is Sydney's great rival to the south, the butt of endless and tasteless jibes by its stand-up comics. With three million people, Melbourne is slightly smaller than Sydney, but considerably richer—the stronghold of high finance, stately homes, Australian-rules football, and reputedly the best restaurants on the continent. Melbourne is cooler, more conservative, cleaner, and vastly better run than Sydney, but lacks its magnificent harbor setting and much of its joie de vivre.

In contrast to Sydney's chaotic street tangle, Melbourne is laid out in precise checkerboard fashion. The main shopping thoroughfare, Collins Street, is probably the smartest in Australia, and St. Kilda Road one of the most impressive boulevards in the world. It's a city of superbly kept parks and gardens, of chic little fashion boutiques, ivy-wreathed colleges, and the Melbourne Cup, the horse race for which the entire country stops once a year.

Melbourne's answer to Sydney's Opera House is the **Victorian**

Arts Centre, a huge and palatial complex housing the National Gallery, three theaters, and the Concert Hall, which is unsurpassed in the excellence of its acoustics. The complex is crowned by an abbreviated version of the Eiffel Tower, transformed into a silvery beacon at night. Even if you don't attend a performance in the Concert Hall, don't miss touring the building. The foyer blazes with 100 frames of a mammoth creation by Sir Sidney Nolan titled *Paradise Garden,* depicting Australian flora from its organic beginnings, pushing through the earth, and following seasonal cycles. You can spend a wonderfully variegated day in this complex, visiting the gallery first, dining in one of the restaurants, and finishing off with an evening concert, play, or ballet. Guided tours of the Concert Hall, daily between 10am and 5pm, cost $2.50 for adults, $1.25 for children. The art gallery is open six days a week (closed Monday) with admission of 80¢ for adults, 40¢ for children.

Other city attractions include the **Old Melbourne Gaol,** appropriately situated opposite the Russell Street police headquarters. This is an old bluestone prison built in 1841. It contains relics of the wildest pages of Australian history. The prize exhibit is the bullet-dented homemade armor worn by Ned Kelly—the Australian Jesse James—during his last fight with police troopers at Glenrowan in June 1880. Kelly was the undisputed king of Australia's bushrangers, and for five years his gang ran the colonial authorities ragged. But finally even his armor couldn't save him. The troopers brought him down by firing at his unprotected legs, and he lived to be hanged in this jail. Open six days a week (closed Sunday) from 10am to 5pm; adults pay $3.50 for admission; children, $1.75.

The **Royal Botanic Gardens** are unreservedly the most beautiful in Australia and among the world's finest examples of classical landscaping. They comprise three lakes, 43 acres of flowerbeds, and 35 acres of lawns. The King's Domain, between the botanic gardens and downtown, displays a floral clock containing 10,000 plants.

Melbourne boasts a wonderful restaurant region in the inner suburb of **Carlton.** Once a largely Italian blue-collar district, it has drastically changed its appearance while retaining its ethnic backbone. Now the main thoroughfares, Lygon and Faraday streets, consist primarily of swank, middling, and budget restaurants and street cafés, offering some of the finest fare found anywhere in the country. Since Carlton is also the home ground of Melbourne's university, you get a lavish layer of college clientele adding to the attractions of the smaller and cheaper cafés.

I mentioned Melbourne as the stronghold of **Australian-rules football,** but that's putting matters mildly. Melburnians are absolutely fanatical about the game, a remarkable mélange of rugby, soccer, Gaelic football, and guerrilla warfare, in which players wear no protective gear, which accounts for the staggering casualty rate. What's difficult to explain is why this native version of football became popular *only* in Victoria, but there to a degree that borders on religious frenzy. Begun in 1858, Australian football now has 14 clubs (the Victorian Football League) battling for the annual championship. Between April and September each year the Melbourne media is saturated with football coverage (six matches are held each

Sunday) climaxing with the six finals. For comprehension of the rules, get the special brochure published by the VFL (write to GPO Box 1449N, Melbourne 3001)—it's complimentary.

PHILLIP ISLAND

Located at the entrance of Westernport Bay, about 90 miles southeast of Melbourne, Phillip Island is linked to the mainland by a concrete bridge. Apart from having a famous car-racing circuit, the island is the most fascinating nature reserve in Victoria. There is a colony of fur seals that can be watched at close range as they bask in the sun. There are amazing mutton birds, looking deceptively small when standing but displaying an enormous wing span as soon as they take off. During November the sky is black with them as they return from their migratory flights to Japan.

The top attraction, though, is the **Penguin Parade.** This proceeds every evening at dusk, so regularly that the starting time is posted outside the car-racing circuit. The performers are waves of penguins splashing ashore at Summerland Beach after hunting fish all day. They head back to their burrows in the sand dunes, waddling ceremoniously and oblivious of the spotlights turned on them. If you sit quietly, they'll march past within arm's reach like so many fat little men in dinner jackets filing out of a banquet. The parade lasts up to an hour and as many as 2,000 penguins have been known to participate.

BALLARAT

Lying 70 miles west of Melbourne, Ballarat is a prosperous town with a turbulent past written in gold and gunpowder. The past comes to life on **Sovereign Hill,** a re-created gold-rush village, complete with armed stagecoach, a gold office, Chinese joss house, blacksmith shop, livery stable, and the office of the *Ballarat Times,* whose editor was publicly horsewhipped by the notorious Lola Montez for writing that she "danced like a hussy."

Here also stands the **Eureka Stockade,** the site of the only battle ever fought on Australian soil. It happened on December 3, 1854. The Ballarat gold diggers, fed up with being bullied and browbeaten by the colonial administration, built a stockade on Eureka Hill, raised a rebel flag with the Southern Cross, and elected a fiery young Irishman named Peter Lalor as their commander. The governor's reply was to send a regiment of redcoats to crush the diggers. The fight was brief and bloody—the stockade was stormed, 34 men killed, hundreds wounded, and Peter Lalor was a hunted fugitive with a reward on his head.

The cause of the diggers seemed lost, but the colonial government had learned quite a bit since the experience of the American Revolution. Instead of making a martyr out of Lalor, they pardoned him. Less than a year after being outlawed he was elected to the Victoria parliament and most of his followers' demands were granted.

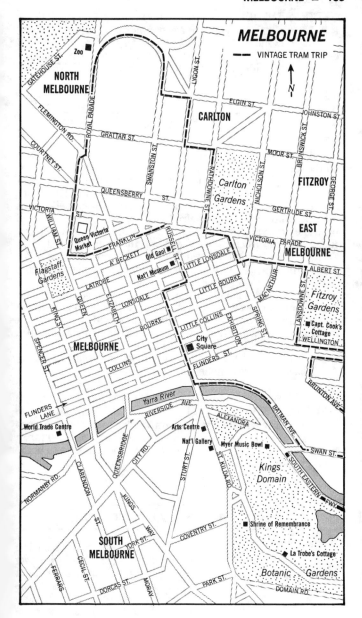

MELBOURNE

- - - VINTAGE TRAM TRIP

GATEHOUSE ST.

Zoo

NORTH MELBOURNE

FLEMINGTON RD.

COURTNEY ST.

ROYAL PARADE

LYGON ST.

ELGIN ST.

CARLTON

JOHNSTON ST.

GRATTAN ST.

BRUNSWICK ST.

SWANSTON ST.

QUEENSBERRY ST.

RATHDOWNE ST.

Carlton Gardens

MOOR ST.

NICHOLSON ST.

GEORGE ST.

FITZROY

GERTRUDE ST.

EAST

VICTORIA ST.

WILLIAM ST.

Queen Victoria Market

FRANKLIN

A'BECKETT

Old Gaol

Nat'l Museum

RUSSELL ST.

LITTLE LONSDALE

VICTORIA PARADE

MELBOURNE

ALBERT ST.

Flagstaff Gardens

LATROBE

QUEEN ST.

ELIZABETH

LONSDALE

BOURKE

LITTLE BOURKE

LITTLE COLLINS

EXHIBITION ST.

SPRING ST.

MACARTHUR

LANSDOWNE ST.

Fitzroy Gardens

Capt. Cook's Cottage

WELLINGTON

KING'S ST.

SPENCER ST.

MELBOURNE

City Square

COLLINS

FLINDERS ST.

Yarra River

FLINDERS LANE

World Trade Centre

RIVERSIDE

AVE.

CITY RD.

Arts Centre

Nat'l Gallery

STURT ST.

ALEXANDRA

Myer Music Bowl

ST. KILDA RD.

BATMAN AVE.

BRUNTON AVE.

SWAN ST.

SOUTH EASTERN

NORMANBY RD.

CLARENDON ST.

QUEENSBRIDGE

KINGS WAY

SOUTH MELBOURNE

YORK ST.

CECIL ST.

FERRARS

COVENTRY ST.

Kings Domain

FWY.

Shrine of Remembrance

La Trobe's Cottage

Botanic Gardens

DORCAS ST.

MORAY

PARK ST.

DOMAIN RD.

They had lost the battle but won their war. Ever since then, the word "digger" has been the generic label for Australia's fighting men. And the Southern Cross, first raised as the rebel symbol at Eureka, is today's Australian flag.

GETTING THERE

The flight from Sydney to Melbourne takes only an hour and costs $194. One of Australia's crack trains, the *Southern Aurora,* does the trip overnight in sleeping-car comfort and lounge-car conviviality. By bus it's a lengthy haul of 14½ hours costing $75.

---

3. Tasmania

Australia's smallest state is an island that hangs like a pendant off the southern tip of the continent. Affectionately known as Tassie, the island lies 150 miles from the mainland across the turbulent Bass Strait. Because of its handy size, only 26,383 square miles, it's easy to make a circuit tour of the entire place by bus or car. Tasmania looks astonishingly un-Australian, rather as if it had been towed from the northern hemisphere and left anchored here by mistake. But its role in early colonial history was the grimmest of all. Van Diemen's Land, as it was called then, held the most dreaded of the penal settlements, **Port Arthur,** and even today the preserved relics of the place cast a chill on visitors.

Most of Tassie is a smiling, lushly green landscape of apple orchards, winding rivers, and densely forested mountain ranges. But the western portions are wild territory, thinly settled and not yet fully explored, the last retreat of the savage little carnivores dubbed Tasmanian devils. The capital, **Hobart,** is a quaint little harbor town whose landmark, rather incongruously, is the ivory-hued tower of Australia's first legal gambling casino.

GETTING THERE

You can fly directly from Sydney to Hobart, but the best way to reach Tasmania is by ship from Melbourne. The *Abel Tasman,* a handsome passenger liner, runs three times a week, taking 14 hours for the crossing. The cost is $78 per bunk in a four-berth cabin.

---

4. Brisbane and the Gold Coast

Some 630 miles north of Sydney lies Brisbane, the capital of Queensland, Australia's number-one tourist state. The city has over a million people and was the proud host of World Expo '88, but retains a pleasant out-of-the-rat-race air that charms overseas visitors and drives high-powered executives from the south nuts. You can feel the influence of the tropics in Brisbane's slower pace, more languid speech, and haphazardly regulated traffic. The sun shines with patriotic persistence, and the air is balmy when it isn't hot.

Brisbane is the only capital that lies 25 miles inland, linked to

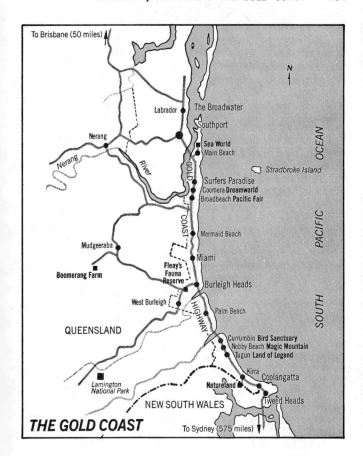

To Brisbane (50 miles)

N

Labrador
The Broadwater
Southport
Nerang
Sea World
Main Beach
Nerang River
GOLD
Stradbroke Island
Surfers Paradise
Coomera Dreamworld
Broadbeach Pacific Fair
COAST
Mermaid Beach
Mudgeeraba
Miami
Fleay's
Fauna
Reserve
Boomerang Farm
Burleigh Heads
West Burleigh
HIGHWAY
Palm Beach
QUEENSLAND
Currumbin Bird Sanctuary
Nobby Beach Magic Mountain
Tugun Land of Legend
Kirra
Coolangatta
Lamington
National Park
Natureland
Tweed Heads
NEW SOUTH WALES
THE GOLD COAST
To Sydney (575 miles)

OCEAN

PACIFIC

SOUTH

the ocean by the winding Brisbane River. Its top attraction is **Lone Pine Sanctuary,** a short drive to the west, the first and best koala reserve established in the country. But from the tourist angle, Brisbane's main role is as the gateway to the Gold Coast, which starts at its southeastern doorstep.

THE GOLD COAST

The Gold Coast is Australia's premier tourist playground, a 20-mile chain of resort towns and surf-crested beaches along the warm Pacific. Beginning at Southport and running all the way to the New South Wales border at Coolangatta, the Gold Coast is one vast play, sport, and recreation area, with hotels and motels wall-to-wall, restaurants, galore, interspersed with amusement parks, gambling casinos, nightclubs, and shopping centers. When darkness descends the entire coastal strip becomes a dazzling neon necklace. If you like Miami Beach you'll *love* the Gold Coast. And it's topless to boot.

Technically the entire stretch of Gold Coast is one town, with one mayor, but in practice it consists of a dozen or so small townships, with **Surfers Paradise** as unofficial capital. The native population is only around 250,000, but during holiday seasons this swells to well over two million and "natives" become as hard to find as the proverbial needles in haystacks.

The Gold Coast offers a huge number of attractions on virtually every taste and price level. There is **Sea World,** which ranks among the greatest aquatic showplaces found anywhere on earth. It's a miniature Disneyland covering 50 acres, packed with land, sea, and sky rides, viewing pools, fun parlors, bars, restaurants, and gift shops. Admission costs $25 for adults, $16 for children.

Pacific Fair, at Broadbeach, is Australia's most unusual shopping center. Built around a central lake, the complex is divided into half a dozen distinct national and period styles selling appropriate merchandise. They range from an English Tudor village to a colonial frontier boardwalk, through an Indian village to "Basin Street, New Orleans," from the Place de la Concorde to the Lindenstrasse. It makes shopping great fun, even if you don't buy a thing.

Land of Legend, at Tugun, behind a fairytale castle front, is a series of miniature to life-size displays. They present a happy mix of history and legendry: King Arthur and his knights and a scene from pioneer Australia, Cinderella's ballroom and a model railroad landscape. Admission is $6.

GETTING THERE

From Sydney you fly to Brisbane in 1¼ hours, and the trip costs $201. From Brisbane it's a two-hour bus ride ($9.70) or car drive to the Gold Coast.

5. The Great Barrier Reef

Stretching for 1,250 miles along the northeastern coast of Queensland is one of the great natural wonders of the earth. The living creatures are corals and here they created a breathtaking environment of reefs, cays, islands, and tiny islets covering a total area of 80,000 square miles and lying between 10 and 200 miles offshore. The term "Barrier Reef" conjures up a false picture of what is actually a marine labyrinth of lagoons, pools, and rocky outcrops extending all the way into the region of New Guinea. As an oceanic wonderland there is nothing to match it on the globe. The shallow sea bed is rarely more than 100 feet deep, the water warm and of a marvelous greenish-blue, so transparent that you can see its denizens as on a TV screen. They include 1,400 varieties of fish as well as giant sea turtles, sharks, huge rays, jellyfish, starfish, octopi, and some 900 species of shells and clams. You can observe them through a scuba mask or the hulls of glass-bottomed boats; they'll leave you in awe either way.

Because of the length of the reef there are a dozen ways to approach it. The most convenient entry point is **Cairns,** the northernmost city in Queensland. A thriving little tropical port, Cairns is famous among big-game fishermen as the world's marlin-fishing capital. In Cairns you can join a tour, rent a boat, or take an aircraft to explore the reef or make for one of the scores of island hotels that dot the paradisiacal coral patches just off shore.

Some 12 miles north of Cairns lies a fascinating showplace called **Wild World.** This is a combination reptile and animal park, containing about 150 Queensland crocodiles. They range from babies looking like clockwork toys with needle teeth to monsters 16 feet long and a century old. The park also shows Australia's deadliest snakes, the taipans, plus birds, kangaroos, and giant pythons. You can watch the crocs being hand-fed, the snakes being "milked" of their venom. Admission is $12 for adults, $5 for children. Open every day till 5pm.

Many of the Great Barrier Reef islands are tourist resorts, ranging from economy-priced to four-star luxury. The choice is vast.

The most popular island, offering the most fun facilities and drawing the biggest crowds, is **Green Island,** a small coral cay, densely wooded and only two feet above sea level. Anchored on the seabed offshore stands the **Underwater Coral Observatory,** where you actually walk on the ocean bed and gaze at the submarine scenery through viewing windows. For a view from above you can take a ride in a glass-bottomed boat, among the island's top attractions. On shore there's **Marineland Melanesia,** a sunlit arcade of tanks displaying fabulous fish, sea snakes, living corals, and possibly the most spectacular collection of crocodiles on view anywhere—up to 18 feet in length. Next door stands the **Castaway Theatre,** showing color movies of underwater reef scenes.

Dunk Island is a rather plain name for a dazzling patch developed into a luxury resort. Dunk has everything you'd expect from a tropical paradise, including delicate reef fish and gourmet chefs to prepare them, cool cabana units stocked with imported wines, and a hectic nightscene that breaks loose when the sun dips below the horizon.

The central section of the Great Barrier Reef comprises the Whitsunday Group of islands lying between the coastal towns of **Townsville** and **Mackay.** Townsville, with a population of 100,000, is Australia's largest tropical city as well as the southern gateway to the Great Barrier Reef. Five miles offshore (35 minutes by ferry) lies **Magnetic Island.** This is perhaps the most idyllic of these coral dots, with tall stands of pines, rugged headlands, a sealife aquarium, and several very velvety resorts.

Brampton Island looks exactly like one of those South Sea Edens they used to create specially for Hollywood sarong epics. The island has forest-shrouded hills with kangaroos that are nearly tame, groves of coconut palms, ribbons of dazzling white beaches, some

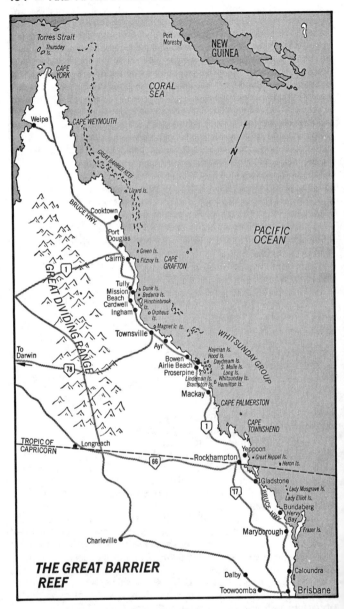

THE GREAT BARRIER REEF

of the finest fishing on the reef, and clouds of rainbow lorikeets that will peck from your hand.

Great Keppel Island is a tiny fun-filled dot lying in the blue Pacific about four hours by seaplane from Sydney. The island has 17 superb beaches, all fringed by jungle vegetation, some thronged with tourists, others wonderfully secluded. It also boasts a disco with a resident band, a bar, café, restaurant, and a young and lively clientele. Aside from deluxe accommodation in air-conditioned holiday units, it also has a camping ground and caravan park for the budget-conscious.

The above represent merely a small slice of the island world of the Barrier Reef . . . there are dozens more along the same lines. And the living corals, of which the reef has more than 350 varieties, built the reef with infinite slowness over millions of years and are still at it, still building. Recently the coral polyps seemed in danger of extermination. There was a sudden mass incursion of their worst enemy, the crown-of-thorns starfish, which wiped out entire colonies of them. But government skindivers fought back and destroyed about half a million of the starfish. And—as far as the eye can see—the starfish haven't made much of a dent in the reef.

GETTING THERE

The best way to reach Cairns is from Brisbane, and you can do it by plane, train, or bus. The air trip (Australian Airlines or Ansett) takes 2½ hours and costs $265. The bus (Greyhound or Pioneer) costs $95. From Cairns, and also from Townsville, Mackay, and Rockhampton, you can select the kind of Great Barrier Reef excursion that best suits your timetable and pocketbook. Transportation to the offshore islands ranges from little ferryboats to twin-hulled double-decker catamarans and seaplanes.

Other possibilities are the various package deals, direct from Sydney, offered by airlines and travel agents. One example: Australian Airlines operates a holiday package to Dunk Island, comprising seven days there, plus transportation and all meals, for a total price of $1,343.

---

6. Adelaide

The capital of South Australia stands 885 miles west of Sydney, as the crow flies or the jet zooms. It is birthplace and showcase for the biennial Adelaide Arts Festival, the oldest, finest, and most prestigious cultural carnival on the continent. Beautifully laid out, and filled with trees and greenery, Adelaide also features some rather odd paradoxes. On the one hand it has more churches per capita than any other state capital. Simultaneously it boasts a huge and very plush gambling casino inside the main railroad station. Adelaide leads the field in the number of missionary societies, but also opened the first nude beach in Australia. The city has the strongest temperance movement in the land, yet dispenses more wine than Sydney, which is three times as big.

The reason for that, of course, is the closeness of the **Barossa Valley,** Australia's largest and most productive wine region. The valley lies 40 miles to the northeast and the vineyards were planted by German immigrants in the 1840s. Even today the architecture of the villages, their names, and the brands they produce read like inscriptions straight from the Rhineland—happily mingled with a mélange of Anglo-Saxon and Aboriginal labels. If you're lucky enough to get there the week after Easter—Australia's autumn— you can join the Vintage Festival, when the entire valley goes into a whirl of parades, dancing, singing, and partying to the sound of clinking glasses.

Some of the contrasts found within the state of South Australia boggle the mind. After the wine-moistened lushness of the Barossa Valley, take a look at **Coober Pedy.** The name is Aboriginal and means "white man live underground." Which is precisely how they live. Coober Pedy lies in a lunar landscape of flat-topped sandstone ridges 590 miles northwest of Adelaide, where daytime temperatures soar to 130° Fahrenheit and nights are often freezing. By burrowing like moles, the locals escape these drastic extremes and achieve conditions approaching comfort.

In this town of over 2,000 people the only structures above ground are the post office, police station, school, stores, and (air-conditioned) motels. Everybody else lives in underground caverns, some amazingly well furnished with carpets, liquor cabinets, record players, and landscapes on the walls. You might ask, "Why should anyone live there at all?" The answer is simple: Coober Pedy sits on the largest opal deposits in South Australia. Every morning the citizens emerge from their cozy burrows to dig out about 80% of all the opals produced in the world!

GETTING THERE

You can travel from Sydney to Adelaide by jet in two hours, by bus in 23½ hours, and by train in 25¼ hours.

---

7. Perth

Perth is the capital of Western Australia, the "Far West," and *far* is the right word. In terms of distance, Perth lies closer to Singapore than to Sydney, and is the only state capital facing the Indian Ocean instead of the Pacific. Western Australia is a gigantic state—with its million square miles it could swallow up Texas four times over. Most of it is completely empty, as you'll see when you fly over. Then you land in Perth and find yourself in one of the prettiest towns on earth, and probably the most charming metropolis in Australia.

Perth is isolated, but the distance separating it from other centers has worked in its favor. Aided by an ideal Mediterranean climate and the immense mineral wealth of the state, Perth achieves a remarkable standard of comfort, beauty, and liveliness for its one million inhabitants. It has broad, tree-lined boulevards, wonder-

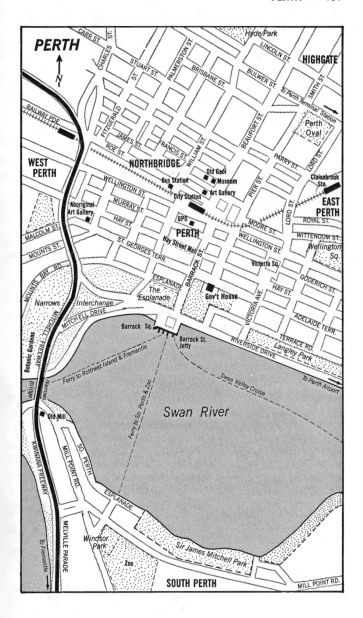

ful parklands along the Swan River, superb beaches within easy reach, and an amazingly exuberant night scene. And all this while avoiding most of the grime, crime, and drug problems usually associated with big-city life.

Perth's harbor town of **Fremantle** briefly leaped into world prominence when the America's Cup races were held there. The cup has gone, but the cosmopolitan veneer it spread over Fremantle has remained. The Royal Perth Yacht Club is still a mecca for canvas sailors around the globe.

Perth has a wonderful shopping street, the **Hay Street Mall,** linked with the **London Court,** a real museum arcade built in mock-Tudor style, complete with "dungeon towers" and moving clockworks of tilting knights. It also has a surprising nightlife strip along and around William Street, a glittering ribbon of bars, cafés, restaurants, and cabarets, thronged with pedestrians well past the witching hour.

The port of Fremantle, 12 miles from downtown, is an engaging mix of mushrooming shops and chic "in" eateries and brooding old-world streets and wharf structures dating back to the windjammer days. The **Fremantle Museum,** on Finnerty Street, is one of the most intriguing showcases in Australia. To make matters perfect, it's free. The place is crammed with a mass of memorabilia ranging from century-old front pages to the harpoons used by Fremantle whalers, from a raised cannon that armed a sunken 17th-century Dutch East India trader to the jewelry worn by fashionable colonial ladies.

Some 12 miles offshore from Fremantle lies **Rottnest Island.** A patch of tranquil beauty in the deep blue Indian Ocean, the island shelters a unique species of marsupials called quokkas, cute, pint-size furry beasties that hop around in bunches. "Rotto," as the locals nicknamed it, is a solidified tonic for frayed city nerves—a resort with no cars or engine noises. The only means of transport are bicycles whirring softly over smooth roads.

GETTING THERE

The Sydney-Perth flight takes 5¼ hours and costs $502. But if you're a real railroad buff you can take the *Indian-Pacific* train that rolls across the continent in three days. Two of these days are spent on the "Long Straight," the tabletop-flat, treeless **Nullarbor Plain,** the longest straight line of track in the world. When you finally get off at Perth's central station you'll have gained a true appreciation of the meaning of the word "distance."

8. Alice Springs

Known as **the Alice,** this town sits at almost the exact geographical center of Australia . . . a long way from anywhere. Although it lies in the misnamed Northern Territory (not a state), the territorial capital of Darwin stands 954 miles to the north. Alice Springs exists in a kind of luxurious vacuum, surrounded by endless, empty, reddish-brown desert but filled with air-conditioned hotels, good restaurants, swimming pools, and a swank country-club casino. But just a mile beyond the neon lights stretches the primeval wilderness with weird sun-baked rock formations, termite hills 20 feet high, giant goanna lizards, and roving wild camels—the Salvador Dali landscape of Dreamtime.

It is largely because of this fascinating contrast that the Alice has become a major tourist attraction. That and the vicinity of another great natural wonder: **Ayers Rock.** This is the landmark of the territory and one of the most stunning marvels on earth. Ayers Rock is actually the summit of a buried mountain, towering **1,143** feet above the desert, the largest monolith on the globe. Measuring 5½ miles around at the base, the sheer size of this monster rising from the flat earth takes your breath away. It is honeycombed with caves and gusts of wind playing through them create macabre "spirit voices." It changes colors—from deep scarlet to molten gold and delicate blue—depending on the time of day. You can climb all the way to the summit, providing you have reasonably good lungs, tough shoes, and a lot of determination.

Ayers Rock ranks almost with the Great Barrier Reef as a tourist attraction. In order to accommodate the swelling tide of visitors, the Northern Territory government, together with private developers, has constructed the $160-million **Yulara International Tourist Resort.** A desert oasis of inspiring proportions, Yulara is entirely self-contained, offering swimming pools, a shopping mall, bars, banks, and a spectacular multilevel Information and Display Centre. The resort is located about 4½ driving hours from Alice Springs and some 13 miles from the Rock itself. Yulara has the multistar **Four Seasons** (tel. 089/56-2100) and **Sheraton** (tel. 089/56-2200) luxury hotels, where guests pay around $130 per night, but also the very moderate **Ayers Rock Lodge** (tel. 089/56-2170) offering dormitory-style lodgings at $17.

Five miles southeast of Alice Springs lies the **Camel Farm,** which breeds camels so hardy that they're actually exported to Saudi Arabia. Their main function, however, is to carry visitors on desert excursions. The animals travel in convoys, and are amazingly comfortable to ride, once you get used to their peculiar swaying and their disconcerting habit of rising on their backlegs first. The farm is open to visitors from 9am to 5pm daily. To arrange a camelback excursion, call 089/53-0444.

The best time to visit Alice Springs is from April to October, when days are sunny—often hot—but night temperatures drop steeply, even below the freezing point.

GETTING THERE

The closest big city to the Alice is Adelaide, 820 miles to the south. Flying time from there is nearly two hours and the trip costs $289. By bus it's an overnight 16-hour haul costing $135. You can also go by train—an enthralling wilderness journey, but not for those on a limited time schedule. Trains run twice a week and take 24 hours.

9. The Northern Territory

This, then, is the "Great Australian Loneliness," the "Last Frontier," the "Never Never," a region twice the size of Texas with about 100,000 inhabitants, of whom 22,000 are Aborigines—a land of almost unimaginable emptiness, with parts as mysterious as the valleys of the moon. The landscape has a wild, surrealistic grandeur—gigantic meteor boulders, white ghost gums reflected in lagoons of incredibly clear blue water, rust-brown deserts, rice grass that closes over a horseman's head, dark rock chasms, and immense pale-green mangrove swamps . . . all this is the Territory.

The road running north from Alice Springs to the capital of Darwin is officially named the Stuart Highway. But Territorians don't call it that. For them it's "the Track," the 954-mile-long sinew of civilization that opened up their land—as far as it *has* been opened. Along that sun-scorched bitumen ribbon moves all the road traffic of the Territory, including the flow of tourists lured by the wildlife, the sight of nomadic hunting tribes, and the thrill of catching safely comfortable glimpses of adventureland.

The Territory promises action, regardless of whether you go armed with gun, fishing rod, or camera. Dingoes howl near the campfires at night, buffaloes eye you warily, flocks of emus race through the mulga, huge pythons slither over rocks, kangaroos—from little dwarf hoppers to "big red" six-footers—race by in fantastic leaps. Rivers and bays harbor catfish, sharks, and crocodiles, and the air teems with swarms of parakeets, ducks, geese, and lonely majestic eagles.

At the northern end of the Track lies **Darwin,** capital and largest town of the Territory. Darwin is a phoenix among cities—in its brief history it has risen twice from almost total destruction: the first time after Japanese bombers flattened it during World War II, the second time after Cyclone Tracy repeated the job at Christmas 1974.

Today this tropical port on the Timor Sea stands as a model of town planning, a thriving city of 62,000, with tree-lined streets, shady parks, and cool, ultramodern public buildings. It houses a dozen air-conditioned hotels, a wonderful botanical garden, a Chinese temple, several excellent restaurants, and the **Diamond Beach Hotel Casino** (tel. 089/81-7755). This gambling palace, set in acres of tropical gardens, also contains a top-ranking cabaret featuring big-name performers, two luxurious restaurants, and a round-the-clock coffee shop.

Darwin is the base for a range of organized safari tours through the creeks, lagoons, and nature parks stretching east and south of the city. Joining a safari is both more comfortable and considerably safer than heading out on your own. The time involved in these wilderness jaunts ranges from one morning to four days and nights.

The greatest experience is a trip to **Kakadu National Park,** the most wildly exotic of Australia's nature reserves. The park embraces

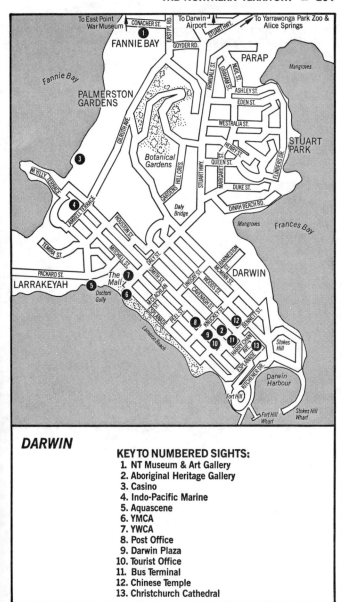

DARWIN

KEY TO NUMBERED SIGHTS:
1. NT Museum & Art Gallery
2. Aboriginal Heritage Gallery
3. Casino
4. Indo-Pacific Marine
5. Aquascene
6. YMCA
7. YWCA
8. Post Office
9. Darwin Plaza
10. Tourist Office
11. Bus Terminal
12. Chinese Temple
13. Christchurch Cathedral

12,000 square miles of jungle greenery, roaring waterfalls, and fabulous rock formations. Kakadu lies 138 miles east of Darwin, and the safaris include boat cruises exploring the South Alligator River (where there are *no* alligators, only crocodiles).

For tour bookings and information, contact the **Northern Territory Government Tourist Bureau,** 31 Smith St. Mall, Darwin, N.T. 5794 (tel. 089/81-6611).

METRIC CONVERSIONS

Australia "went metric" some 15 or so years ago. Most of the older people can reckon comfortably by the pound as well as the kilo, but most of the younger generation can't. The following conversions will guide you (and them):

LENGTH

1 millimeter = 0.04 inches (*or* less than ¹⁄₁₆ inch)
1 centimeter = 0.39 inches (*or* just under ½ inch)
1 meter   = 1.09 yards (*or* about 39 inches)
1 kilometer = 0.62 mile (*or* about ⅔ mile)

To convert kilometers to miles, take the number of kilometers and multiply by .62 (for example, 25km × .62 = 15.5 miles).

To convert miles to kilometers, take the number of miles and multiply by 1.61 (for example, 50 miles × 1.61 = 80.5 km).

CAPACITY

1 liter = 33.92 ounces
        = 1.06 quarts
        = 0.26 gallons

To convert liters to gallons, take the number of liters and multiply by .26 (for example, 50 l × .26 = 13 gal).

To convert gallons to liters, take the number of gallons and multiply by 3.79 (for example, 10 gal × 3.79 = 37.9 l).

WEIGHT

1 gram   = 0.04 ounce (*or* about a paperclip's weight)
1 kilogram = 2.2 pounds

To convert kilograms to pounds, take the number of kilos and multiply by 2.2 (for example, 75kg × 2.2 = 165 lbs).

To convert pounds to kilograms, take the number of pounds and multiply by .45 (for example, 90 lb × .45 = 40.5kg).

AREA

1 hectare (100m² = 2.47 acres

To convert hectares to acres, take the number of hectares and multiply by 2.47 (for example, 20ha × 2.47 = 49.4 acres).

To convert acres to hectares, take the number of acres and multiply by .41 (for example, 40 acres × .41 = 16.4 ha).

TEMPERATURE

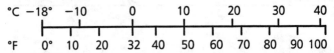

To convert degrees C to degrees F, multiply degrees C by 9, divide by 5, then add 32 (for example 9/5 × 20°C + 32 = 68°F).

To convert deees F to degrees C, subtract 32 from degrees F, then multiply by 5, and divide by 9 (for example, 85°F − 32 × 5/9 = 29°C).

CLOTHING-SIZE CONVERSIONS

If you're going to do some shopping for clothing, know that the sizes you'll find on the tags are very different from what you're used to. The following will get you started:

WOMEN'S DRESSES

Australian	10	12	14	16	18	20	22
American	8	10	12	14	16	18	20

MEN'S SUITS AND SWEATERS

Australian	92	97	101	107	112	117	122
American	36	38	40	42	44	46	48

For shirts, shoes, and hats, the best procedure is to get yourself measured in the shop.

INDEX

GENERAL INFORMATION

SIGHTS AND ATTRACTIONS

Sydney & Environs

Excursion Areas

ACCOMMODATIONS

S y d n e y   &   E n v i r o n s

Key to Abbreviations: *A* = Apartments; *B* = Budget; *D* = Deluxe; *M* = Moderately priced

Excursions from Sydney

RESTAURANTS

Sydney

Key To Abbreviations: B = Budget; D = Deluxe; M = Moderate

THEATER RESTAURANTS

NOW, SAVE MONEY ON ALL
YOUR TRAVELS!
Join Frommer's™ Dollarwise® Travel Club

Saving money while traveling is never a simple matter, which is why the **Dollarwise Travel Club** was formed 31 years ago. Developed in response to requests from Frommer's Travel Guide readers, the Club provides cost-cutting travel strategies, up-to-date travel information, and a sense of community for value-conscious travelers from all over the world.

In keeping with the money-saving concept, the annual membership fee is low—$18 for U.S. residents or $20 for residents of Canada, Mexico, and other countries—and is immediately exceeded by the value of your benefits, which include:

1. Any TWO books listed on the following pages.
2. Plus any ONE Frommer's City Guide.
3. A subscription to our quarterly newspaper, *The Dollarwise Traveler*.
4. A membership card that entitles you to purchase through the Club all Frommer's publications for 33% to 50% off their retail price.

The eight-page *Dollarwise Traveler* tells you about the latest developments in good-value travel worldwide and includes the following columns: **Hospitality Exchange** (for those offering and seeking hospitality in cities all over the world); **Share-a-Trip** (for those looking for travel companions to share costs); and **Readers Ask . . . Readers Reply** (for those with travel questions that other members can answer).

Aside from the Frommer's Guides and the Gault Millau Guides, you can also choose from our Special Editions. These include such titles as *California with Kids* (a compendium of the best of California's accommodations, restaurants, and sightseeing attractions appropriate for those traveling with toddlers through teens); *Candy Apple: New York with Kids* (a spirited guide to the Big Apple by a savvy New York grandmother that's perfect for both visitors and residents); *Caribbean Hideaways* (the 100 most romantic places to stay in the Islands, all rated on ambience, food, sports opportunities, and price); *Honeymoon Destinations* (a guide to planning and choosing just the right destination from hundreds of possibilities in the U.S., Mexico, and the Caribbean); *Marilyn Wood's Wonderful Weekends* (a selection of the best mini-vacations within a 200-mile radius of New York City, including descriptions of country inns and other accommodations, restaurants, picnic spots, sights, and activities); and *Paris Rendez-Vous* (a delightful guide to the best places to meet in Paris whether for power breakfasts or dancing till dawn).

To join this Club, simply send the appropriate membership fee with your name and address to: Frommer's Dollarwise Travel Club, 15 Columbus Circle, New York, NY 10023. Remember to specify which single city guide and which two other guides you wish to receive in your initial package of member's benefits. Or tear out the next page, check off your choices, and send the page to us with your membership fee.

FROMMER BOOKS
PRENTICE HALL PRESS
15 COLUMBUS CIRCLE
NEW YORK, NY 10023
212/373-8125

Date_____

Friends:

Please send me the books checked below.

FROMMER'S™ GUIDES

(Guides to sightseeing and tourist accommodations and facilities from budget to deluxe, with emphasis on the medium-priced.)

☐ Alaska.................$14.95	☐ Germany.....................$14.95
☐ Australia...............$14.95	☐ Italy $14.95
☐ Austria & Hungary $14.95	☐ Japan & Hong Kong...........$14.95
☐ Belgium, Holland & Lux-	☐ Mid-Atlantic States..........$14.95
embourg $14.95	☐ New England $14.95
☐ Bermuda & The Bahamas ...$14.95	☐ New York State...............$14.95
☐ Brazil $14.95	☐ Northwest....................$14.95
☐ Canada................$14.95	☐ Portugal, Madeira & the Azores......$14.95
☐ Caribbean..............$14.95	☐ Skiing Europe.................$14.95
☐ Cruises (incl. Alaska, Carib, Mex, Ha-	☐ South Pacific.................$14.95
waii, Panama, Canada & US). .$14.95	☐ Southeast Asia................$14.95
☐ California & Las Vegas......$14.95	☐ Southern Atlantic States $14.95
☐ Egypt.................$14.95	☐ Southwest...................$14.95
☐ England & Scotland.......$14.95	☐ Switzerland & Liechtenstein........$14.95
☐ Florida $14.95	☐ USA $15.95
☐ France................$14.95	

FROMMER'S $-A-DAY® GUIDES

(In-depth guides to sightseeing and low-cost tourist accommodations and facilities.)

☐ Europe on $40 a Day.......$15.95	☐ New York on $60 a Day $13.95
☐ Australia on $40 a Day $13.95	☐ New Zealand on $45 a Day..........$13.95
☐ Eastern Europe on $25 a Day .$13.95	☐ Scandinavia on $60 a Day..........$13.95
☐ England on $50 a Day $13.95	☐ Scotland & Wales on $40 a Day.......$13.95
☐ Greece on $35 a Day $13.95	☐ South America on $35 a Day..........$13.95
☐ Hawaii on $60 a Day $13.95	☐ Spain & Morocco on $40 a Day $13.95
☐ India on $25 a Day $12.95	☐ Turkey on $30 a Day $13.95
☐ Ireland on $35 a Day $13.95	☐ Washington, D.C. & Historic Va. on
☐ Israel on $40 a Day $13.95	$40 a Day $13.95
☐ Mexico on $35 a Day......$13.95	

FROMMER'S TOURING GUIDES

(Color illustrated guides that include walking tours, cultural and historic sites, and other vital travel information.)

☐ Amsterdam............$10.95	☐ New York....................$10.95
☐ Australia...............$9.95	☐ Paris.......................$8.95
☐ Brazil $10.95	☐ Rome $10.95
☐ Egypt $8.95	☐ Scotland $9.95
☐ Florence $8.95	☐ Thailand $9.95
☐ Hong Kong $10.95	☐ Turkey......................$10.95
☐ London................$8.95	☐ Venice......................$8.95

TURN PAGE FOR ADDITONAL BOOKS AND ORDER FORM

0690

FROMMER'S CITY GUIDES

(Pocket-size guides to sightseeing and tourist accommodations and facilities in all price ranges.)

☐ Amsterdam/Holland. $8.95	☐ Montréal/Québec City $8.95
☐ Athens $8.95	☐ New Orleans $8.95
☐ Atlanta. $8.95	☐ New York. $8.95
☐ Atlantic City/Cape May . . .$8.95	☐ Orlando. $8.95
☐ Barcelona $7.95	☐ Paris $8.95
☐ Belgium $7.95	☐ Philadelphia. $8.95
☐ Boston $8.95	☐ Rio $8.95
☐ Cancún/Cozumel/Yucatán . .$8.95	☐ Rome $8.95
☐ Chicago $8.95	☐ Salt Lake City $8.95
☐ Denver/Boulder/Colorado	☐ San Diego $8.95
Springs. $7.95	☐ San Francisco $8.95
☐ Dublin/Ireland. $8.95	☐ Santa Fe/Taos/Albuquerque $8.95
☐ Hawaii $8.95	☐ Seattle/Portland. $7.95
☐ Hong Kong $7.95	☐ Sydney $8.95
☐ Las Vegas $8.95	☐ Tampa/St. Petersburg $8.95
☐ Lisbon/Madrid/Costa del Sol. .$8.95	☐ Tokyo $7.95
☐ London. $8.95	☐ Toronto. $8.95
☐ Los Angeles. $8.95	☐ Vancouver/Victoria. $7.95
☐ Mexico City/Acapulco $8.95	☐ Washington, D.C.. . . . .$8.95
☐ Minneapolis/St. Paul. $8.95	

SPECIAL EDITIONS

☐ Beat the High Cost of Travel . . .$6.95	☐ Motorist's Phrase Book (Fr/Ger/Sp). . . .$4.95
☐ Bed & Breakfast—N. America $11.95	☐ Paris Rendez-Vous $10.95
☐ California with Kids $14.95	☐ Swap and Go (Home Exchanging) $10.95
☐ Caribbean Hideaways $14.95	☐ The Candy Apple (NY with Kids) $12.95
☐ Manhattan's Outdoor	☐ Travel Diary and Record Book $5.95
Sculpture. $15.95	

☐ Honeymoon Destinations (US, Mex & Carib) $14.95
☐ Where to Stay USA (From $3 to $30 a night) $10.95
☐ Marilyn Wood's Wonderful Weekends (CT, DE, MA, NH, NJ, NY, PA, RI, VT) $11.95
☐ The New World of Travel (Annual sourcebook by Arthur Frommer for savvy travelers) . .$16.95

GAULT MILLAU

(The only guides that distinguish the truly superlative from the merely overrated.)

☐ The Best of Chicago $15.95	☐ The Best of Los Angeles. $16.95
☐ The Best of France. $16.95	☐ The Best of New England $15.95
☐ The Best of Hong Kong $16.95	☐ The Best of New York. $16.95
☐ The Best of Italy $16.95	☐ The Best of Paris $16.95
☐ The Best of London. $16.95	☐ The Best of San Francisco $16.95
☐ The Best of Washington, D.C. $16.95	

ORDER NOW!

In U.S. include $2 shipping UPS for 1st book; $1 ea. add'l book. Outside U.S. $3 and $1, respectively.
Allow four to six weeks for delivery in U.S., longer outside U.S.

Enclosed is my check or money order for $_____

NAME_____

ADDRESS_____

CITY_____ STATE_____ ZIP____

0690